U.S. Foreign Policy and
the USSR, China, and India

ECONOMIC REFORM in THREE GIANTS

Richard E. Feinberg, John Echeverri-Gent,
Friedemann Müller, and contributors:

Rensselaer W. Lee III
Richard P. Suttmeier
Elena B. Arefieva

Series editors:
Valeriana Kallab
Richard E. Feinberg

Transaction Books
New Brunswick (USA) and Oxford (UK)

ISBN: 0-88738-316-5 (cloth)
ISBN: 0-88738-820-5 (paper)
Printed in the United States of America

Library of Congress **Cataloging-in-Publication Data**

Feinberg, Richard E.
  Economic Reforn in Three Giants: US Foreign Policy and the USSR, China, and India.

  (U.S.-Third World Policy Perspectives: No. 14)
  1. Soviet Union—Economic policy. 2. China—Economic policy. 3. India—Economic policy. 4. United States—foreign economic relations—Soviet Union. 5. Soviet Union—foreign economic relations. 6. United States—foreign economic relations.
I. Echeverri-Gent, John. II. Müller, Friedemann. III. Title. IV. Series.

HC336.26.F45 1990   338.9—dc20   90-10739
ISBN: 0-88738-316-5   (cloth)
ISBN: 0-88738-820-5   (paper)

The views expressed in this volume are those of the authors and do not necessarily represent those of the Overseas Development Council as an organization or of its individual officers or Board, Council, Program Advisory Committee, and staff members.

ECONOMIC REFORM in THREE GIANTS

Acknowledgments

Series Editors:
Richard E. Feinberg
Valeriana Kallab

Guest Editors:
John Echeverri-Gent
Friedemann Müller

The Overseas Development Council gratefully acknowledges the support of the Pew Charitable Trusts for the U.S.-Third World Policy Perspectives series, of which this volume is part; the support of the John D. and Catherine T. MacArthur Foundation for ODC's MacArthur Scholars in Residence; and the support of The Ford Foundation, The Rockefeller Foundation, and The William and Flora Hewlett Foundation for the Council's overall program.

On behalf of the Council and the contributing authors, the editors wish to express thanks for valuable comments to John P. Lewis and to members of the ODC Program Advisory Committee and others who participated in the work-shops at which early drafts of the chapters were discussed. Stuart K. Tucker's comments on the Statistical Annexes were also greatly appreciated.

Special thanks are also due to Danielle M. Currier, ODC Assistant Editor, and to Melissa Vaughn for their contributions to the editorial and production phases of this volume; and to Joycelyn V. Critchlow for processing the manuscript.

Contents

Overview

The Giants and the West: From Threat to Opportunity

Richard E. Feinberg, John Echeverri-Gent, and Friedemann Müller

China, India, and the Soviet Union—with 1.1 billion, 800 million, and 280 million people respectively—are by far the three most populous underdeveloped countries on earth.[1] The next nations in line trail distantly behind (the island chain of Indonesia with 170 million, and Brazil with 140 million). Notwithstanding the large differences in history and culture that separate the three "Giants," the size of their populations and the vastness of their lands have stimulated surprisingly similar responses to the changing international environment of the twentieth century. Today, the Giants share a common predicament: How can very large nations with ambitious foreign policies but with underdeveloped, technology-poor economies make headway in a relentlessly demanding, rapidly changing, and ever more intrusive global economy?

This study examines the immense pressures for reform impinging on each of the three Giants. In separate chapters, it also compares and contrasts the political reform processes in each country; considers global trends in technology and the efforts of each Giant to upgrade its technological capacities in order to achieve international competitiveness; and assesses each nation's strivings to remold international relations in Asia in order to create external conditions more supportive of its domestic agenda.

Several key propositions emerge from the policy analysis of this study:

1. Size matters. Evident dissimilarities aside, China, India, and the Soviet Union share important political and economic traits because of their large populations and land mass. The Giants are all economically and culturally heterogeneous and have built multiple administrative layers to cope with their size and diversity. Their economies are turned inward, but their international diplomacy has aspired to global prominence. These common characteristics create advantages as well as disadvantages as the Giants strive to adjust to the new global realities.

2. The central thrust in the reform processes of all three Giants—the decentralization of economic power from central bureaucracies to firms, markets, and provincial officials—is an historically inevitable adaptation to universal features of the development process. India's relatively strong private sector places it furthest along the path of this common trajectory. Unavoidably, the reform course of each nation will suffer detours and even reversals as it struggles to find an efficacious mix between state authority and market mechanisms, and a new balance among alternative forms of property ownership.

Furthermore, the decentralization of political power—toward more pluralistic or democratic norms—will often, but not always, accompany economic decentralization. Economic freedom tends to lay the foundation for political pluralism, although political reform can lag behind economic change.

3. Decentralizing reforms in the Giants are clearly in the interest of the industrial democracies—even if the reforms harbor risks of disorder and reaction. Because the Giants weigh so heavily in international relations, their reform processes could transform global politics.

The Giants are attempting to subordinate their foreign policies to their domestic requirements. At present they are seeking a reduction in international tensions that could bring large peace dividends not only to themselves but to the West. Specifically, the thaw between Washington and Moscow heralds a new era in international relations, in which military confrontation may be replaced by peaceful competition and, in some arenas, by cooperative efforts to resolve common problems. Precisely because of their size and importance, the Giants will be central to the efforts of the international community to address many of the most critical issues of the 1990s, including environmental degradation, the population explosion, and arms proliferation.

The reform processes in the Giants are, of course, under the direct management of their own governments. Nevertheless, it is in the interest and within the power of the United States, Western Europe, and Japan to help propel them forward.

The Essence of Being a Giant

The combined population of the Soviet Union, China, and India accounts for 43 per cent of the world's people (Table 1). Giants also in their geography, these countries are the first, third, and seventh largest countries in the world—together covering almost 27 per cent of the world's land mass.

Table 1. The Giants' GNP (1988 $ billions)

	1988	GNP Average Annual Growth 1975-88 (percentage)	Share of World: GNP 1988	Population 1988 (percentages)
USSR	2,535	2.4	13.6	5.6
China	350	8.5	1.9	21.3
India	271	5.0	1.5	15.9
Three Giants	3,157	3.1[a]	17.0	42.8

[a]Weighted average of national GNPs.

Source: *Handbook of Economic Statistics 1988* (Washington, D.C.: Central Intelligence Agency, Foreign Assistance Center, 1988), pp. 30, 31; *Handbook of Economic Statistics 1989* (Washington, D.C.: Central Intelligence Agency, Foreign Assistance Center, 1989), pp. 12, 30, 31.

The Giants' size has a formative impact on the problems that they confront. It also conditions the strategies available for resolving them. Until now, analysts have paid relatively little attention to the impact of size on a country's political economy; furthermore, most of the analysis of the impact of size on behavior has focused on small rather than giant countries. Below we outline four characteristics shared by the Giants that are crucial to understanding the dynamics of their economic reform.

Heterogeneity

Economically and culturally, large countries tend to be more heterogeneous. Simon Kuznets observed thirty years ago that larger countries tend to have more diversified economic structures[2]; the Soviet

Union, China, and India all enjoy a varied agricultural sector and exploit a broad range of domestic resources through a diversified industrial base. Moreover, cultural diversity has long been associated with geographical size[3]; the Soviet Union and India are veritable mosaics of distinctive ethnic, religious, and linguistic groups. Although China is far more ethnically and linguistically homogeneous than the other Giants, it does contain important minority groups, and stunning regional differences. Each Giant also possesses a vast hinterland whose economic development has lagged behind that of its cities.

This heterogeneity mostly complicates, but in some ways also facilitates, the work of governments. Large countries typically house a wide array of vested interests that can be difficult to reconcile.[4] At the extreme, dissident minorities have recently posed internal threats to each Giant's territorial integrity. In each Giant, systemic reforms inevitably threaten long-standing accommodations among diverse sectoral and regional interests. At the same time, the multiplicity of domestic interests can be advantageous to a reform-minded leadership by reducing its dependence on any single group and increasing its autonomy to negotiate new political coalitions. The social heterogeneity of the Giants places a premium on the vision and tactical skills of leaders who must accommodate a diverse range of interests.

Each of the three Giants has been led during the twentieth century by towering figures—Mahatma Gandhi and Jawaharlal Nehru, Vladimir Lenin and Joseph Stalin, Mao Zedong and Zhao Enlai—whose power rested on new alliances and even new political concepts. The successors of these leaders are now struggling to reform their legacies. However, Nehru's grandson, Rajiv Gandhi, disappointed those who hoped he could breathe new life into India's deteriorating political system, while Deng Xiaoping opted for retrenchment in the spring of 1989 when his nation needed a new social contract. Mikhail Gorbachev is a brilliant tactician; whether he can fashion new alliances, institutions, and mores out of the wreckage of the collapsing Soviet system is yet to be seen.

Multiple Administrative Layers

Administrative layers tend to multiply as country size increases.[5] The requisites of communication and control limit the effective jurisdictional reach of the central government and argue for a devolution of authority. Since the social and economic diversity of countries tends to increase with country size, the governments of larger states frequently create additional administrative agencies based on geographical or functional divisions.

The proliferation of administrative structures in the Giants attenuates communications within the state. Instructions from the top become distorted as they filter down through administrative layers. Conversely, the increase in bureaucratic layers tends to isolate leaders from popular opinion, and the "center" becomes increasingly dependent upon subordinates for information about the grassroots. The consequent decentralization of authority and control over information increases the autonomy of administrative subordinates and often leads to distortions in policy implementation.

Such a proliferation of administrative structures greatly complicates the reform process by increasing the scope of bureaucratic politics. Each agency resists threatening reforms, delaying and distorting directives it is unable to defeat outright. Moreover, in the Giants, placing power in the hands of provincial or local Party officials is not necessarily progressive; in China, for example, as Rensselaer W. Lee underscores in this volume, some provincial bureaucracies use their administrative powers to frustrate market forces with as much gusto as the central planning authority in Beijing. At the same time, these decentralized jurisdictions contain the seeds of a federalist structure that has worked so well for the world's most industrialized Giant, the United States—and arguably not too badly for India. The Soviet Union, in theory also a federation, could soon move in this direction to resolve its "nationalities" problem.

Closed Trade Regimes

The variety of natural resources, the diversification of the economy, and the possibilities for achieving efficient scales of production *within* the domestic economy all positively correlate with country size. The larger the country, the less necessary it is to traverse national borders in order to achieve economic efficiency. Moreover, acting on the suspicion that global markets were capricious and iniquitous, each Giant sought to insulate its economy—through state controlled trade monopolies and non-convertible currencies in the case of the USSR and China, and through extensive licensing and some of the world's highest tariffs in the cases of India and China. It is not surprising, therefore, that the trade dependency ratios (total trade as a percentage of GNP) of the Giants are low (see Table 2).

Leaders of the Giants now admit that this isolation has retarded their economic development, and agree that opening their economies must be a major reform objective. In seeking an entrée into world markets, the Giants' bargaining leverage is enhanced by their size and strategic importance. But reformers face an internal roadblock: Years of protected development have created within each

Table 2. The Giants' Foreign Trade, 1988
(1988 $ billions and percentages)

	Total Trade[a] ($ billions)	Exports as Share of GNP	Total Trade as Share of World Total Trade	Average Annual Growth, 1982–88
USSR	92.9	1.6	1.7	2.0
China	102.9	13.6	1.9	16.7
India	30.5	5.3	0.6	3.4
Three Giants	226.3	3.3	4.1	9.4
World	5,489.3	14.5	100.0	7.7

[a]Exports plus imports. China, India, and World total figures represent an average of IMF figures in *Directory of Trade Statistics Yearbook* and *International Financial Statistics.* USSR figures are based on DOTS statistics and exclude trade with Albania, Bulgaria, Cuba, Czechoslovakia, the German Democratic Republic, Mongolia, and North Korea.

Source: *Directory of Trade Statistics Yearbook 1989* (Washington, D.C.: International Monetary Fund, 1989), pp. 2, 134, 222, 395; *Handbook of Economic Statistics 1989* (Washington, D.C.: Central Intelligence Agency, National Foreign Assessment Center, 1989), pp. 30, 31.

Giant an array of industrial enterprises (in India, both public and private), bureaucrats, and politicians who resist opening up the economy, preferring to perpetuate opportunities for rent-seeking behavior that exist where competition and markets do not. To succeed in opening their economies, reformers in the Giants must overcome these powerful, intertwined interests.

Large Ambitions

The behavior of the three Giants confirms the common sense notion that national ambitions usually increase with the size of a country. Large countries typically aspire to greater military power,[6] and undertake more ambitious programs in science and technology—a relationship borne out by the Giants' large military establishments.[7] Even after demobilizing one million troops since 1985, China ranks first in the world in the number of people under arms, while the Soviet Union and India rank second and fourth respectively. Moreover, the Giants account for three of the world's six countries that have acknowledged exploding nuclear devices.

In science and technology, the Giants' ambitions are illustrated by their research programs. The USSR employs by far more scientists and engineers in research and development (R&D) than any other country. China ranks third—just behind the United States—

while India has one of the largest R&D establishments in the Third World (See chapter 5, Table 1).

Each of the Giants has found that its military and scientific ambitions have incurred serious costs. The large share of government expenditures devoted to the military has diverted funds badly needed for economic development. As a result, scaling back military expenditures is an important objective of the reforms in the Soviet Union and China. The curtailing of defense expenditures in the 1989–90 Indian budget (after years of growth) indicates a similar trend. Moreover, Richard P. Suttmeier argues that the Giants have overemphasized ambitious programs in basic science to the relative neglect of increasing their capacity for commercializing science and technology (S&T); in the process, they have forfeited the advantages inherent in the natural size of their markets for the dissemination of appropriate technologies. The Giants' restrictions on technology imports have also impeded their absorption of new developments from abroad. (India's tapping and adaptation of foreign agricultural innovation to promote the "Green Revolution" is an important exception.) Facilitating the absorption of foreign science and technology is thus a central objective of the reforms in each Giant.

The Rise and Fall of the Centralization Impulse

When the three Giants designed their economic development strategies earlier in this century, the size of their domestic markets tempted them toward "socialism in one country" and "self-reliant" development. The ideological currents of the time reinforced these options, as many nationalists were suspicious of the instabilities and unequal power relations that they felt typified international exchange. Moreover, these Giants—all countries with ancient and proud cultures—wished to keep out the corrosive influence of foreign cultures that inevitably accompanies international commerce.

Socialist ideas proved irresistibly attractive in all three countries because they neatly wedded economic autarky with political nationalism through the transfer of power to the state. Socialists also wished to use the power of the state to promote social equality. In India, this statism was tempered by democratic constitutionalism and the strength of the private sector. But even in India, a dominant state controlled the "commanding heights" of the economy, setting strategic directions, fixing macroeconomic variables, and erecting a sharp divide between the domestic and the international economy. In the political realm of each Giant, a powerful state melded with the dominant political party to affirm central power over distant provinces. This unity of government and party enabled the state to subordinate economics to politics; administrative decisionmaking suppressed market mechanisms in the Soviet Union, in China, and to a considerable degree, in India. Furthermore, in each Giant, the state used its control over economic resources to erect an industrial-military apparatus large enough to glorify the nation-state, help restore national pride following periods of humiliation at the hands of foreigners, protect far-flung borders, and project power against neighboring peoples.

The Decline of Statism

This statism was not without its successes. It dampened ethnic rivalries, imposing unity among populations with tremendous cultural and linguistic diversity. It generated high savings and investment rates, launched impressive industrialization drives, and in the Soviet Union and China, leveled wealth inequalities and improved access to social services.

Historians will debate whether this statist development model was appropriate for the times. What is clear is that it entailed major costs and spawned gross inefficiencies (and in the Soviet Union and China permitted terrible political crimes). It is also clear that, on balance, the value of the statist model declined over time.

As early as the 1960s, many socialists in the Soviet Union and China were aware that central planning suffered from critical weaknesses. It did a poor job of allocating investment capital, failed to stimulate technological change, and was unresponsive to consumer preferences. Increasingly, these failings stood in sharp contrast to dynamic progress underway in the capitalist world, where the speed of technological change and the brilliance of consumer styles increasingly made socialism look bleak and outworn. State socialism, once widely viewed even among Western intellectuals as the progressive path to a prosperous future, now looked stodgily conservative.

For a time, socialist technocrats in Eastern Europe hoped salvation would come through more powerful computers whose input-output matrices would replicate the efficiency of markets. But that technological fix provided illusory, forcing socialist economies to experiment with varying degrees of decentralization—to shift decisionmaking away from central planning agencies to ministries, provinces, and firms. These efforts to find a more efficient mix of bureaucratic control and market mechanisms continue today, and the clear trend is the devolution of more and more power to firms and markets.

The Changing Global Environment and Pressures for Reform

In dialetical fashion, economic successes added to the pressures for reform in each Giant. Economic development increased the diversity and complexity of the three countries' economies, making state management through administrative controls progressively inefficient. In the Soviet Union and India in particular, more education and economic affluence led to a revival of interest in ethnic and religious traditions, reducing tolerance for the central authorities' insensitivity to cultural diversity. Furthermore, the contradictions became more acute between the official ideologies of equality and participation and the baser realities of elite privilege and Party hierarchy. The populace chafed under rigid state controls that stifled popular initiative and creativity even as these traits became essential to promoting economic efficiency and technological development. Meanwhile, autarkic development strategies drove a wedge between the Giants and the spirited pace of global technological innovation, screening out exogenous sources of technological dynamism. This ultimately collided with the strategic ambitions of the Giants, since their influence and power ultimately depend upon the wealth and dynamism of their economies.

The dynamic global environment of the 1970s and 1980s rendered irresistible the many external and internal pressures for reform. Advances in the biological sciences and materials research, and particularly in microelectronics, information processing, and communications—sometimes called the "Third Technological Revolution"—are transforming economic relationships as did the advent of the steam engine in the eighteenth century and electrical power in the nineteeth.[8] These new technologies have internationalized markets and competition, accelerated the pace of technological innovation, recast relations of production, and promoted the globalization of technological change.

Although each Giant has important technological achievements to its credit, most of these are in areas such as nuclear power or ballistic missiles—areas that are amenable to top-down research strategies. Contemporary technological innovation increasingly takes place from the bottom up. It is frequently driven by decentralized units—either teams within large corporations or small start-up firms—and it increasingly requires good communications with end-users.

The military technologies favored by the Giants have matured over the past decades. Innovation in core defense systems such as ships, aircraft, and tracked vehicles increasingly consists of expensive refinements of basic technologies. The requisites for military and civilian technological development have diverged, and the effectiveness of military R&D in driving commercial technological development has declined. At the same time, promoting the technological capabilities of civilian industry has become more important to the Giants' economic and military security. As a consequence, each Giant is under pressure to divert resources from military R&D toward commercial applications in order to keep abreast of global technological frontiers.[9]

The acceleration of technological change, driven in part by new information technologies, creates overwhelming pressures for economic reform. Technological progress was slower when Stalinist economic institutions were established. Once new technologies were purchased, copied, or invented, the major task was to disseminate them rather than to improve them. The shortening of product cycles that characterizes the contemporary global economy means that planners and manufacturers can no longer concentrate on such extensive development if they are to achieve international competitiveness—change and innovation have become essential. But centrally determined physical plans hinder innovation. They contradict the freedom necessary to establish small start-up firms. They also eliminate alternative reviews of proposals for technological innovation. In short, capital markets—frequently shaped by industrial policy—have proven superior to central planning in promoting technological innovation.[10]

Finally, developments in transportation and communications technology have made the international environment relentlessly intrusive. Despite their efforts to maintain cultural and ideological independence, foreign travel, overseas study, and modern media have infused the populations of the Giants with a taste for rock music and blue jeans, the latest in consumer electronics, and other symbols of consumption in advanced industrial economies. The globalization of markets and the intensification of international competition have improved economic efficiency and lifted the standard of living in most countries of the world. The rapid economic progress of Japan and the Asian "Tigers" has dramatically illuminated the economic shortcomings of the Giants.

Notwithstanding their size and relative insulation, growing quantities of information are now broadcast instantaneously both at and from the Giants. The Chinese pro-democracy demonstrations in the spring of 1989, the Armenian earthquake, and the tragedy in Bhopal were transmitted live to living rooms throughout the world. Increasingly, political leaders as well as opposition factions within the Giants use global media links to rally foreign support, and as the international politicking of Mikhail Gorbachev and Rajiv Gandhi illustrates, international support becomes an increasingly valuable asset in domestic politics. Most important, through this freer flow of information and ideas, people and products, citizens in the communist Giants have been exposed to the attractions of democracy.

Obstacles to Reform

The transition from a centralized administrative system to a more market-driven economy is a truly awesome task for any nation. Indeed, no clearly successful model of such a peaceful transition yet exists. Mainstream neoclassical economics specializes in comparative *statics*—not in the dynamics of how to get from here to there. Among the additional difficulties confronting the Soviet Union and China is the absence of a clear vision of the intended outcome: Is the objective "market socialism" (with social property imbedded in market-determined prices), Scandinavian-style "social democracy," or a mixed economy like India's? Or will something totally new and unimagined emerge?

Size and Reform

Giantism presents reformist factions with some negatives as well as positives. Just as the characteristics of bigness stimulated centralization at one moment and later, paradoxically, undermined that very authority, so do these traits now stand in the way of decentralization. The centrifugal tensions of heterogeneity; the mazes of bureaucratic layers; vested interests that resist exposure to international competition; strains of cultural chauvinism and the inertia of military-industrial complexes—all are obstacles to reform intentions. For these reasons, the transition from bureaucratic centralism—however inevitable in light of fundamental historic forces—is likely to be a bumpy and at times probably bloody road.

Yet bigness surely has its virtues: the checks and balances made possible by diversity, the vitality of federalism, the economic stimulus of large domestic markets, the technological infrastructure built in part to service military machines, and the capacity for assertiveness in international affairs. The progress of history will depend, among other factors, on the relative balance of these contradictory characteristics of giantism, and on the capacity of reform leaders to alter the balance in their favor.

Adjustment Experiences in Other Developing Nations

The Giants are not alone in seeking to adapt to global change through the decentralization of economic decisionmaking. While the Giants' population, geographic spread, and high degree of centralization present special problems, other developing countries have also attempted related if less comprehensive reforms in the last decade. Throughout Latin America, Africa, and Asia, as well as Southern and Eastern Europe, old import-substitution industrialization policies are being dismantled in favor of more open and market-oriented strategies. Many nations—Mexico, Costa Rica, Chile, Mauritius, Thailand, Spain, Turkey, Hungary—have made important strides toward streamlining their states and improving the efficiency of their private sectors, but even these countries have encountered severe obstacles, while reform processes in many other nations have stalled altogether. Commonly confronted challenges include: Assembling cadres of technocrats able to design and implement stable macroeconomic policies; building institutional frameworks for well functioning markets in finance and labor; breeding risk-taking entrepreneurs; and overcoming the resistance not only of vested economic interests but also of intellectuals, religious leaders, and politicians, to the heightened inequalities and insecurities implicit in many market-oriented reforms (in part by erecting new social safety nets to replace the old forms of security).[11]

The world has accumulated considerable experience with "structural adjustment" (as these reforms have been dubbed by the World Bank and the International Monetary Fund), even if there is still no consensus on many important matters—such as the optimal sequencing of reforms which seems to depend on the economic configuration and political opportunities of the moment.[12] The Giants can and should learn from the adjustment experiences of other developing countries, even as they necessarily adapt these lessons to their own particular circumstances.

Economic Reform and Political Change

Since the Renaissance, Western European history has witnessed the parallel development of capitalism and democracy. The march of these two systems has not been lockstep, but the parallelism has been sufficient to allow political theorists of such diverse persuasions as Karl Marx and Milton Friedman to posit causal links between free markets and free men.

Decentralized economic systems generate multitudinous units of power that enjoy at least some degree of autonomy from the state. The profits that firms generate can then be invested to create additional units of power—universities, media, trade associations—and to finance independent political parties. These diverse power units have strong vested interests in limiting the power of the state to intervene in markets, reorder property relations, or repress free expression.

Private capitalists—from the France of Louis Napoleon, to the Spain of Francisco Franco, to the Chile of Augusto Pinochet—have been willing to sacrifice democratic norms when social movements seem to threaten their fundamental interests and values. They have used the state to repress antagonistic social forces, trampling on the rights of minorities and sometimes of majorities. But these states of siege have generally been relaxed once the perceived threat dissipates, and the march toward democracy has resumed.

Contemporary developments in some Third World nations affirm that capitalist progress does not necessarily carry full-blown democracy in its arms. Whether for lack of democratic traditions or fear that free trade unions would undermine international competitiveness, governments in South Korea, Taiwan, and Thailand remained authoritarian during the 1960s and 1970s, while their capitalist economies charged ahead. Nevertheless, even in these Asian cases where explosive economic progress has outpaced political renovation, states are responding to growing domestic pressures for broadened political participation.

In the short run, whether transitions to greater economic decentralization foster—or even are consistent with—political freedom will depend very much on the historical context. Throughout Eastern Europe, economic errors are associated in people's minds with the old dictatorships; in dialectical fashion, democratic norms therefore are seen by many to hold the promise of greater prosperity. In China, in contrast, economic reform has become associated in the minds of many Chinese with inflation, corruption, and unemployment—creating some nostalgia for the perceived economic security and political cohesion of the Maoist era. In the Soviet Union, the intelligentsia is displaying its periodic preference for free expression and liberal legal norms, but there is the danger that those workers who enjoyed the security of the Brezhnev era could ally with the Communist Party and ideological conservatives to oppose *perestroika.*

Over the long run, if economic power is decentralized and diverse interest groups proliferate, the social infrastructure for pluralism is then in place, waiting for an opportune moment to break through the surface. One possible intermediate outcome is an Asian-style consultative authoritarianism that is capable of aggregating some pluralistic interests and of generating rapid economic and technological progress. But as these regimes tend to rigidify over time when personalities or coalitions refuse to give way to new generations, each succession crisis becomes an opportunity for democratic forces to assert themselves anew.

Chinese Retrogression

Recent events in China confirm that economic decentralization creates political momentum for greater pluralism, but does not guarantee its triumph. Beyond tactical errors, the setback of the pro-democracy movement there can be attributed to various factors: economic decentralization has not created enough independent power units to outweigh the power of the state; certain undesirable side effects of the reform—inflation, speculation, growing social inequality—generated pressures for restoring state controls; and the Confucian legacy of authoritarianism, reinforced by aspects of Maoist doctrine, equated liberalization with frightening disorder. Nevertheless, Rensselaer W. Lee judges that, in the longer run, economic decentralization and exposure to Western ideas will create new challenges to the Communist Party's monopoly of power; China will not introduce Western-style democracy in the foreseeable future, but renewed movement toward a more open, pluralistic political system seems likely.

Gorbachev's Gamble

In the Soviet Union, President Gorbachev has reversed the sequence and initiated a political opening *prior* to major economic reform. Gorbachev is stimulating a political effervescence to help him oust conservatives and is fomenting public criticism of past economic policies to build support for *perestroika*. Gorbachev also hopes that the energies unleashed by political freedom will spill over into the economic sphere to motivate workers and create risk-taking entrepreneurs.

The Soviet reformers see *glasnost* (openness) as a mechanism for increasing economic efficiency. Firms—whether owned by the state, cooperatives, or individuals—need information for making rational decisions. Nor can technology be efficiently designed and disseminated in an atmosphere clouded by secrecy. A freer flow of information between firms and buyers could improve the allocation of resources and improve product quality. The replacement of the dictatorship of the producer with the sovereignty of the consumer requires information feedback. In fact, information feedback, when combined with competitive market structures, might serve to overcome a syndrome—omnipresent in the Soviet Union, but not unknown in the West (certain airlines, for instance)—whereby firms treat consumers with contempt and the workers are passive or even hostile to the buying public.

But *glasnost* could achieve its economic purposes without bringing society-wide democracy in its wake. The Soviet government could, like many governments in Asia, permit a freer flow of *economic* data while suppressing other categories of information. Political activity could be limited to organizations pursuing economic goals, or to political objectives that coincide with those of the government and are carefully monitored by it. The breadth of *glasnost* is yet to be defined, but a technocratic purpose is one possible outcome.

Now let us turn to the more traditional question: Will *perestroika* lead inexorably to greater political pluralism in the Soviet Union? Certainly, as cooperatives and private ventures gain ground and become independent bases of power, the state apparatus and the Communist Party suffer a relative diminution of their strength. To the extent that *perestroika* also brings with it a devolution of power to the non-Russian republics, the power of the Moscow-centered state will decline. In the short run, however, there could well be a clash between economic reform and political freedom. To the extent that *perestroika* requires austerity and harms powerful vested interests, those adversely affected could use new political freedoms to subvert reforms and resist austerity. Although open discussion could conceivably succeed in building a consensus for reform, it will not be easy to convince losers to endure personal pain for the collective long-term gain. Thus, following many historical examples, authoritarian politics in the Soviet Union could be the bloody handmaiden of freer markets.

Indian Democracy

India initiated its economic reform under quite different political circumstances. In contrast to the other Giants, its political system was not established through revolution, but by an independence movement whose mainstream was guided by principles of accommodation, non-violence, and consensual leadership. Under Jawaharlal Nehru, these traits led to the creation of democratic political institutions that have persisted for the last forty years notwithstanding the country's vast size, social heterogeneity, and economic poverty.

Despite the remarkable record of India's democracy, effective economic reform will also require substantial political change. Over the years, elements in the Congress (I) Party, state bureaucracy, business community, and agricultural elites have colluded to exploit the state's economic intervention for their private benefit.[13] This formidable array of groups therefore has a vested interest in maintaining the status quo. But the corruption emanating from these liasons generated widespread resentment against Rajiv Gandhi and the Congress (I) Party, resulting in their ouster in the November 1989 general elections. The current absence of a strong parliamentary majority will make it difficult to decisively root out these corrupt networks; yet these illicit links must be severed if the legitimacy necessary for implementing economic reforms is to be restored and if India's reformers are to make real progress.

The Impending Transformation of International Relations

The statist models originally adopted by the three Giants antagonized the United States and other Western industrial nations.[14] Despite great differences among them, all three models elevated government over the individual, social ownership over private property, and moral over material incentives. Strategically, statism facilitated the buildup of large military machines targeted against Western interests throughout Europe and Asia. In the perceptions of many in the West, Stalinism was striving to maximize Soviet military capability, Maoism was agitating to undermine U.S. allies throughout Asia, and New Delhi was siding with Moscow against Western interests in South Asia. Although India's brand of Fabian socialism found sympathizers among European social democrats, and even received substantial economic assistance flows, Western strategic circles came to view the India of the Congress Party as essentially a partisan of the Soviet Union and the persistent enemy of the main American ally in the region, Pakistan.

Thus, for ideological and geopolitical reasons, the three Giants were, in varying degrees, considered to be menacing to Western interests. Where Stalin and Mao erected iron and bamboo curtains to keep out foreign influences, the West threw up its own barriers to contain and isolate the antagonistic regimes. India posed less of a military threat but nevertheless proved irritating; its stubborn promotion of non-alignment defied the West's bipolar Cold War vision and ran against efforts to contain Soviet power by surrounding it with anti-communist alliances.

In this hostile world of the Cold War, the West, and in particular the United States, defined its strategic interests primarily in military and power terms: The core of U.S. foreign policy was the NATO alliance; the Pentagon dominated the international affairs budget; and Third World conflicts were perceived as tests of U.S. resolve to resist Soviet expansionism.

Today, fundamental shifts in the ideas and economic policies of the Giants, and in their strategic outlook, make it possible for the West to view them less as threats and more as opportunities. China's dramatically favorable geopolitical shift in the 1970s led to a blossoming of economic exchange in the 1980s. Gorbachev is redesigning Soviet domestic and foreign policies as this book is being printed. India, too, has begun to pare back its military spending and is seeking closer ties with the West.

Elena B. Arefieva of the Moscow Institute of World Economy and International Relations (IMEMO) argues in this volume that the Giants' renewed drive for economic modernization is having a moderating influence on their foreign policies. Their leaders prefer an atmosphere of reduced international tensions that allows them to concentrate their energies and resources on domestic restructuring. New Delhi, Beijing, and, apparently, Moscow have sharply reduced military expenditures in order to channel more resources toward economic development and consumer welfare.

For the West, these historic shifts unveil tremendous possibilities. The improvement of U.S.-Soviet relations has already led to a sharp reduction in global tensions and is catalyzing a redefinition of the agenda of international relations. The Giants' opening to the international economy holds the promise of vast, untapped markets for trade and investment flows. While most of the Giants' 2.2 billion people are too poor to import much today, they and their children could be major customers for Western firms in the twenty-first century.

The Interests of the West

We judge that it is in the interests of the industrial democracies for the Soviet Union, China, and India to advance down the paths of economic decentralization and political pluralism. These are preferences that flow from our own societal structures and that the West has long urged the Giants to emulate. If successful, these reform processes promise major ideological, diplomatic, and economic gains for the West.

The Soviet and Chinese shifts toward decentralization potentially de-polarize contemporary debates over economic policies. Rather than politicize multilateral institutions, Soviet and Chinese entry into global fora could defuse ideology; since their admission would be contingent upon the terms of the existing institutions, the Soviets and Chinese would be signaling their acceptance of the established rules of the game. Moreover, the legitimacy of the international agencies would be enhanced by the presence of the Giants, whose absence has undermined their claims to universality.[15] The advice of these institutions would gain greater legitimacy as well, since they could no longer be accused of being mere tools of "Western capitalism." Within developing countries, the decentralizing tendencies in the Giants would reinforce parallel trends visible in many parts of Latin America, Asia, and Africa, strengthening the hands of pragmatists everywhere.

Historically, India in particular—while certainly inclined to participate in multilateral institutions and programs—has been a leading demandant of trade preferences and concessional transfers for the poorer developing countries. There is a need for a better reconciliation of the perspectives of the West and of the Asian Giants in these areas. While the Bush Administration's singling out of India for possible "Super 301" sanctions under the 1988 Trade Act may have been motivated by irritation at what it saw as that country's resistance to multilateral efforts to liberalize trade flows, the action made Indian concessions more difficult. Greater flexibility on both sides could be more productive.

The Giants' redefinition of their national interests will permit the U.S. to redefine its own interests. The potential exists for economic exchange to join military preparedness at the center of U.S. foreign policy. The National Security Council could pay as much attention to the survival of ecological systems as it has to U.S. ballistic missiles, and could work as hard to stabilize financial markets as nuclear arsenals.

In the past, the spectre of a foreign enemy helped states maintain domestic cohesion behind a common purpose. With the waning of the Cold War, political leaders in the West must find more constructive allegiances to bind their populations. New challenges can be calls for collective international action. The list of problems that affect both the West and the Giants is a long one: the extreme fluctuations of capital and commodity markets, the drug trade and money laundering, arms transfers and nuclear proliferation, international terrorism, infectious diseases, accelerating but unequal science and technology advances, rapid population growth and massive migrations, resource depletion and environmental degradation (the Giants all have unusually high levels of carbon emission in relation to their GNPs[16])—could all be entrées on the menu of items facing future international security managers.

The United States and the Soviet Union may have another sphere of common interests: the political pacification and economic reconstruction of regional zones of conflict in the Third World. From Central America to Indochina, from Southern Africa to Afghanistan, civil conflicts have drawn in the Superpowers, souring international relations and diverting attention and resources from more constructive purposes. The improvement in relations between Washington and Moscow has contributed to peace prospects in several such regions. In the event of political settlements, the industrial democracies could join with the Soviet Union to help spur economic recovery in some of these war-torn areas.[17]

Furthermore, the transformation of the Giants from strategic enemies into trading partners could help the United States resolve its own dangerous, debilitating "twin deficits"; a reduction in defense spending could narrow the U.S. budget deficit, and increased exports to the Giants could help improve the U.S. trade account. Instead of posing national security problems for the United States, the Giants could become part of the solution to the nation's overriding macroeconomic problems—problems that also threaten to hamstring U.S. foreign policy in the 1990s.

In 1988, U.S. import and export trade with the three Giants totaled $23 billion. Under a set of optimistic but not unreasonable assumptions, U.S. trade with the Giants could surge to $86 billion by the year 2000 and reach $230 billion by 2010 (see Table 3). Trade with the Giants would rise from the current 3 per cent of total U.S. trade to 8 per cent. While possibly helping the U.S. trade balance, this trade surge would certainly enhance the efficiency of U.S. firms and diversify their markets, while also benefiting U.S. consumers.

Economic reform in the Giants does, of course, entail risks for the West. More efficient nations become stronger economic competitors; but such competition should improve global welfare, particularly if the Giants are incorporated into multilateral institutions and are induced to play by their rules. There is also the danger that a resurgent Soviet Union could retake the military offensive; but the evidence is strong that the Soviet Union is making significant defense cuts, and arms reduction agreements negotiated today will make it more difficult for any future Soviet government to pursue a destabilizing buildup. In any event, whatever favorable impact *perestroika* may have on Soviet military capability lies well out into the future. By then, a firm Western policy of engagement—one that builds a common agenda, forges strong economic linkages, and negotiates mutually advantageous arms control agreements—could minimize the risk of renewed militarism in Moscow.

Perhaps the greatest risk is that the reform efforts could fail. The collapse of *perestroika* in the Soviet Union could produce an

Table 3. U.S. Trade With the Giants: Projections to 2010 ($ billions)

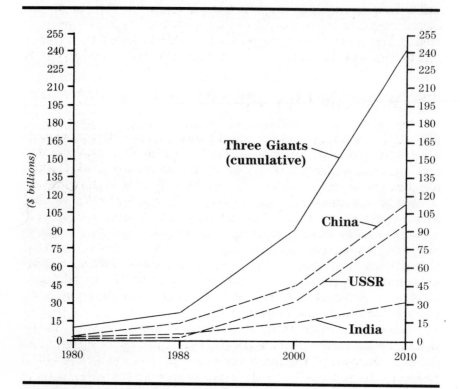

Note: The assumptions underlying the projections are:

(1) U.S.-World trade will continue to grow at an annual average rate of 6.4 per cent through 2010—as it did between 1980 and 1988.

(2) U.S.-Soviet trade will grow at an annual rate of 20 per cent between 1988 and 2000, and 12 per cent between 2000 and 2010. While high, these growth rates begin from a very low base, artificially depressed by official trade restrictions that are expected to be lifted. After the year 2000, trade growth will still be above the projected U.S. world average, but it will be lower than in previous years due to demand saturation in some areas.

(3) U.S.-Chinese trade will grow at an annual average rate of 10 per cent until 2010. This rate is somewhat lower than the 14 per cent annual average achieved between 1980 and 1988 due to a projected moderation in Chinese economic growth and resistance to sustained high import penetration in some sectors.

(4) U.S.-Indian trade will maintain an annual growth rate of 8 per cent (as between 1980 and 1988) until 2010. The Indian reform process is more gradual than that of the Soviet Union or China, and there is no significant reason to anticipate a sharp increase in U.S.-Indian trade growth beyond the 1980–88 rates.

Source: Overseas Development Council projections. Data for 1980 and 1988 from U.S. Bureau of the Census, *Highlights of the U.S. Export and Import Trade, FT 990* (Washington, D.C.: U.S. Bureau of the Census), December 1980 and December 1988.

anti-Western backlash of the sort that followed the Tiananmen Square massacre in China. A descent into disorder could catalyze fierce repression and xenophobic reactions in Moscow. It could also unleash emigration pressures that would make the post-Tiananmen Square requests for asylum pale in comparison. The West thus has a tremendous stake in doing what it can to reduce the risks of failure and to augment the probabilities for successful reform in the Giants.

The West Can Play a Role

The ability of foreign powers to influence events within nations is always limited. This axiom is particularly true with respect to outside influence on large states with strong nationalist traditions and complex and diverse societies. Nevertheless, countries in the throes of change are unusually susceptible to foreign influence because external actors can throw their support behind internal groups or movements. The central importance of markets to economic reform in the Giants renders them particularly open to foreign influence, as their leaders are disposed to learn about the mechanisms of the market from the experience of advanced industrial nations. It is the combination of external and internal forces that can make for winning combinations and victorious reforms.

There is no ready formula for economic reform from a planned to a market economy, or, as in the India case, toward a less regulated mixed economy. But the industrialized capitalist countries do have pieces to the puzzle. They have experience with the institutions of capitalism—financial and labor markets, forms of property ownership, government guidance of firms through indirect instruments, fiscal and monetary policies—that will not arise spontaneously upon the removal of the heavy hand of government but that will have to be created. Moreover, the Bretton Woods institutions can draw on the adjustment experiments of the Third World. The West also has experience with diverse forms of democratic politics; the Chinese may be less impressed with Western norms, but Indian political institutions are in many respects a legacy of British rule and the organizers of the new Supreme Soviet have clearly studied Western parliaments.

External finance can lubricate reform processes. The foreign capital contribution may be small when measured against the recipient's GNP, but, when added to the available discretionary foreign exchange, it can make an appreciable difference in the capacity to import food, consumer electronics, or investment goods. Public and private capital inflows undoubtedly fueled Indian and especially

Chinese growth in the 1980s—just as their sharp reduction after June 1989 will injure the Chinese economy. If the West is not forthcoming, foreign exchange shortages could become a bottleneck to Soviet reform in the 1990s.

The industrial democracies have multiple means whereby they can strengthen the reform processes in the Giants. The many uncertainties underscore the need for clearheaded realism but should not stand in the way of bold action to help steer history in a forward direction:

1. By responding constructively to serious Soviet proposals for arms reduction or the resolution of regional conflicts, the West can enhance the legitimacy of the Soviet leadership while freeing up Soviet resources for *perestroika* (as well as Western resources for civilian use).

2. In all three Giants, reforms have engendered deficits in the fiscal and external accounts that threaten the reform processes themselves (see also Chapter 4, p. 152ff). Experience throughout the Third World demonstrates that foreign assistance, if tied to adjustment programs that promise to close deficits over time, can provide critical support to governments genuinely committed to economic reform. Foreign capital inflows can help stabilize realistic exchange rates, finance imports that sop up monetary overhangs and dampen inflation, spur investment in restructured industries, and provide credit to cooperatives and private firms. Foreign assistance can also allow the government to alleviate political tensions by compensating some of those whose interests are prejudiced by reform.

3. In the case of the Soviet Union, if reforms are accelerated, if sharp cuts are evident in the Soviet military budget, and if *perestroika* is endangered by a foreign exchange constraint, Western governments should be prepared to provide non-concessional trade finance and emergency food shipments. (In the United States, this would mean lifting the Jackson-Vanik amendment to the 1974 Trade Act and the Stevenson amendment to the 1974 Export-Import Bank Act.) Such capital and commodity flows should be contingent upon continued progress toward decentralized decisionmaking in economics and pluralism in politics. These financial flows may impinge upon Western government budgets, but will be much less than the prospective savings in defense expenditures made possible by the fading of the Cold War.

4. By signaling to private investors and lenders that business ventures with the Giants are viewed favorably, by providing appropriate official incentives for private business activity (through bilat-

eral and multilateral export credit and investment guarantee authorities), and by extending development assistance, the West can simultaneously stimulate economic reform and facilitate political change.

5. Participation in the multilateral agencies exposes the Giants to international economic norms while conferring greater legitimacy on their reforms and reformers. India has benefited handsomely from the advice and capital of the World Bank, having received $33 billion in loans since 1949. The Chinese government was quickly admitted to the Bretton Woods institutions in 1980 shortly after it began its economic reforms. The Bush Administration should drop its opposition to contacts between the Soviet Union and the IMF and World Bank, and instead permit confidence-building measures which, if successful, could lead to Soviet membership within three to five years.[19] Similarly, both Soviet and Chinese accession to the General Agreement on Tariffs and Trade (GATT) is desirable over the medium term, provided that their economic reforms proceed and their trade barriers are lowered.[20]

6. The Bretton Woods institutions, for their part, should strive to better understand the sequencing of reforms during the transition to a more market economy—thus better preparing themselves to assist the Giants.[21] Particular attention should be paid to the distributional consequences of reform, and to designing policies to cap the excessive after-tax profit rates that vitiated the moral legitimacy of numerous adjustment programs, including China's, in the 1980s.

7. By establishing programs to foster the transfer and development of civilian science and technology (as outlined in this volume by Richard P. Suttmeier), the West can strengthen the linkages between the global economy and the Giants, as well as between the respective scientific communities. The growing immigrant population of scientists that left the Giants to live in the United States— once considered only a brain drain—can form a bridge between their new and old colleagues. High priority should be given to training programs that bring students to the West and lend Western teachers to the Giants.

8. By fostering people-to-people exchanges, the West can expose the Giants to the spirit of liberal democracy. Western governments can provide moral, logistical, and sometimes financial support for political parties, environmental groups, legal and business associations, and other non-governmental organizations, to form bonds with their counterparts in the Giants—bonds that enrich both parties. Western credit can be channeled to cooperatives, joint

ventures, and other forms of decentralized or non-state owned property.

9. By making clear its sympathy for political pluralism and democracy, the West can inspire reform and at least give pause to those who prefer repression. While being careful to avoid counterproductive measures that delegitimize reformers or leave them exposed to official retaliation, the West can establish contacts and programs that strengthen reform movements.

The extremely complex and stressful reform processes will inevitably suffer setbacks as the case of China dramatically demonstrates. The appropriate Western reaction will have to be determined on a case-by-case basis. But some general guidelines are possible:

- In their *diplomatic rhetoric,* Western leaders should clearly articulate the sentiments of their publics if governments in the Giants step backward and commit flagrant violations of human rights. Judgments of official actions should weigh carefully the dangers that political disorder may pose to the entire reform process; in some circumstances, reformers risk being overthrown by conservatives if they appear to lose control.

- Since *economic ties* over time foster political pluralism, dismantling them can be counterproductive. Moreover, once fractured, business linkages often cannot easily be repaired. While Western governments may wish to suspend official assistance (but with a general prejudice to maintaining those programs which clearly support reform or directly benefit the poor), private exchange should not be interfered with except in the most extreme circumstances.

- *Military ties,* on the other hand, can more readily be curtailed, since Western governments should not directly support bloody instruments of repression.

The country chapters that follow provide more detailed applications of these policy guidelines. For either incentives or sanctions to be effective, however, it is imperative that the industrial democracies coordinate their policies. Specifically, the democracies should establish formal mechanisms to assure coherence among themselves and across issues in relations with the Soviet Union, China, and India. For each Giant, the democracies need formal procedures to weave economic, political, and strategic threads into a tighter cloth. (The existing World Bank or OECD coordination mechanisms, while valuable, are too narrow in their economic concentration to serve this integrative purpose). Only then can the power and wealth of the industrial nations be mobilized behind the reform processes in the three Giants. Only then will the economic and political conditions that should be placed on capital transfers and diplomatic bargains be accompanied with maximum leverage. And only then can the Giants be prevented from diluting Western influence by playing off one industrial democracy against another. The proposed Multilateral Mechanism for Allied Action (or "M2A2") for the Soviet Union might be located in Brussels, at the seat of the European Community; for China in Washington, because Beijing continues to view the U.S. as the centerpiece of its foreign policy; and for India in Tokyo, as Japan will be the chief source of economic support for Asian development.

Reform is a long, indeed never-ending, process. In the spectrum that runs from managed to free-market economies, and from totalitarian to libertarian political systems, the Soviet Union and China may, after several decades of reform, approximate India's current standings. How far India itself will travel is impossible to predict. The one certainty is that all three Giants are *simultaneously* undergoing great changes—and that these changes will shape the world of the twenty-first century.

Notes

Note: The authors wish to thank the following individuals for their helpful comments on earlier drafts of this essay: Nayan Chanda, Harry Harding, Paul H. Kreisberg, Rensselaer Lee III, John P. Lewis, Joan M. Nelson, John Van Oudenaren, John W. Sewell, Andres Solimano, Cynthia Carlisle, Delia Boylan, and Leanne Davis.

[1]Figures are from the World Bank, *World Development Report 1989*, Table 1 (p. 164–65), and Box A.2 (page 232–33).

[2]S. Kuznets, "Economic Growth of Small Nations," in E. A. G. Robinson, ed., *Economic Consequences of the Size of Nations* (New York: St. Martin's Press, 1960), p. 15–18.

[3]Robert A. Dahl and Edward R. Tufte, *Size and Democracy* (Stanford, Calif.: Stanford University Press, 1973), pp. 31–35.

[4]See Boris Blazic-Metzner and Helen Hughes, "Growth Experience of Small Economies," in B. Jalan, ed., *Problems and Policies in Small Economies* (New York: St. Martin's Press, 1981), pp. 85–86.

[5]The observations are developed from Dahl and Tufte, *Size and Democracy*, op. cit., pp. 35–40, 86–88. See also John P. Lewis, "The Political Economy of Giantism: The Case of India," (unpublished paper, Princeton University, 1989), especially pp. 3–6.

[6]One of Dahl and Tufte's most startling findings is that the larger a country's population, the more its per capita expenditures on defense. See Dahl and Tufte, *Size and Democracy*, op. cit., pp. 122–28.

[7]Peter Katzenstein insightfully observes that large industrial states concentrate R&D funds in advanced science-based sectors of the economy characterized by substantial risks, while smaller European states direct R&D to less risky traditional sectors. The smaller states stress the absorption and dissemination of scientific and technological information rather than more ambitious programs. See Peter J. Katzenstein, *Small States in World Markets: Industrial Policy in Europe* (Ithaca, N.Y.: Cornell University Press,

1985), pp. 63–65. This tendency is also characteristic of R&D programs in the United States, see Kenneth Flamm and Thomas L. McNaugher, "Rationalizing Technology Investments," in John D. Steinbruner ed., *Restructuring American Foreign Policy* (Washington, D.C.: The Brookings Institution, 1989), pp. 119–57. The military and technological ambitions are of course related—since security objectives constitute important incentives for the science and technology programs of each country.

[8]For recent discussions of the Third Technological Revolution see John W. Sewell, "The Dual Challenge: Managing the Economic Crisis and Technological Change," in John W. Sewell, Stuart Tucker, and contributors, *Growth, Exports and Jobs in a Changing World Economy* (New Brunswick, N.J.: Transaction Books in cooperation with the Overseas Development Council, 1988); and Daniel Bell, "The Third Technological Revolution," *Dissent* (Spring 1989), pp. 164–76.

[9]These arguments have been made for the United States as well. See Flamm and McNaugher, "Rationalizing Technology Investments," op. cit., pp. 120–21, 145–46.

[10]See, for instance, Marshall Goldman, *Gorbachev's Challenge: Economic Reform in the Age of High Technology* (New York: W. W. Norton, 1987), especially pp. 86–117 and 174–226 for the Soviet and Chinese cases respectively.

[11]For suggestions on how to overcome some of these obstacles, see Joan M. Nelson and contributors, *The Politics of Economic Adjustment: Fragile Coalitions* (New Brunswick, N.J.: Transaction Books in cooperation with the Overseas Development Council, 1989); also, Richard E. Feinberg and Valeriana Kallab, eds., *Adjustment Crisis in the Third World* (New Brunswick, N.J.: Transaction Books in cooperation with the Overseas Development Council, 1984).

[12]See the Comment by Richard E. Feinberg in John Williamson, ed., *Latin American Adjustment: How Much has Happened?* (Washington, D.C.: Institute for International Economics, forthcoming March 1990).

[13]As I. G. Patel, a key architect of India's developmental strategy, observed, "Even those of us who had actively promoted the earlier policies of the 'fifties and early 'sixties have come to realize for quite some time now that we had underestimated the long-term deleterious effects of controls and had not appreciated sufficiently the potential for a self-serving alliance between political leaders and civil servants on the one hand and captains of industry or the large farmers who have sufficient clout both socially and financially on the other." I. G. Patel, "On Taking India into the Twenty-First Century," *Modern Asian Studies*, Vol. 21, No. 2 (1987), p. 215.

[14]The awkward term "West" is used in this chapter to refer to the United States, Western Europe, and Japan. This shorthand convention obviously obscures differences of outlook and interests.

[15]See Richard E. Feinberg, "The Soviet Union and the Bretton Woods Institutions: Risks and Rewards of Membership" Public Policy Paper, Institute for East-West Security Studies (New York, 1989).

[16]*Financial Times*, March 6, 1989, p. 18.

[17]See the forthcoming study by the Overseas Development Council on the international contribution to the reconstruction of zones of regional conflict in the Third World.

[18]Nelson and contributors, *The Politics of Economic Adjustment*, op. cit.

[19]For a fuller description of such measures, see Feinberg, "The Soviet Union and the Bretton Woods Institutions," op. cit.

[20]For a more complete discussion of the steps China should take to gain membership in the GATT, see Nicholas R. Lardy, *Economic Policy Toward China in the Post-Reagan Era* (New York: National Committee on U.S.-China Relations, 1989), China Policy Series, No. 1. On Soviet participation, see *Managing The Transition: Integrating the Socialist Countries into the World Economy* (New York: Institute for East-West Security Studies, 1989), pp. 40–43.

[21]This recommendation also appears in Catherine Gwin, Richard E. Feinberg and contributors, *Pulling Together: The International Monetary Fund in a Multipolar World* (New Brunswick, N.J.: Transaction Books in cooperation with the Overseas Development Council, 1989), p. 26.

Summaries of Chapter Recommendations

Summaries of Chapter Recommendations

1. Economic Reform in the Soviet Union (Friedemann Müller)

Mikhail Gorbachev's *perestroika* has generated a dynamic challenge to the costly structure and perceived stability of the post-World War II order. Changes in Soviet *foreign* policy have proceeded much more rapidly than the efforts to reform the USSR's obsolete command economy. The new foreign policy seems to anticipate the kinds of changes needed to modernize the Soviet economy and society by changing the basic principles underlying past policy: Ideological subordination of Soviet allies is no longer enforced; and military threats and coercion no longer seem to be primary policy instruments for achieving domestic and foreign policy objectives.

The *domestic* process of *perestroika,* on the other hand, has been disjointed and full of contradictions. *Glasnost* created an atmosphere of competing ideas and opinions, a remarkable liberalization in the media, a high degree of intellectual freedom, and notable progress in the construction of a parliamentary system. In contrast, economic modernization and improvements in the supply of consumer goods are not as yet evident. The system of central planning has lost most of its credibility, and the concept of plan fulfillment has come under severe public criticism. But seventy years of a rigid, centrally planned economy have hardly created the preconditions for the risk-taking and cost-saving needed throughout the economy. *Uskorenie,* or economic acceleration—the third concept (in addition to *perestroika* and *glasnost*) designed to promote the Gorbachev reform program—has not yet gathered momentum.

The preconditions for the successful reconstruction of the Soviet economy are:

- A change of mechanisms from central planning to market incentives;
- The education and training of experts (managers and bankers—but also those who can promote a culture of non-profit organizations);
- The modernization of infrastructure—particularly the transportation and communication systems; and
- The availability of private investment to modernize production plants.

The first precondition must be fulfilled by Soviet legislative power and administration alone. All of the others can, however, be supported by the West.

Perestroika's survival is clearly in the interest of the West. It has already lessened international tensions—potentially enabling a reduction in defense expenditures. It has brought an improvement in human rights standards in the Soviet Union and its sphere of influence. It has opened up possibilities of cooperation on urgent global issues such as common approaches to the environmental, drug, and terrorism crises. It may even open the door to the formulation of approaches to Third World development that are not shaped and constrained by the East-West conflict.

Three important ways in which the West can express support for *perestroika* are by:

(1) Helping provide Soviet experts with the training and education capacities needed in a market-type economy.

(2) Extending capital and know-how for the improvement of the Soviet transportation and communication systems;

(3) Encouraging the provision of private investment to modernize the Soviet economy.

It is important that the public funding needed for such an assistance program—insofar as public rather than private funds are called for—be viewed and activated in relation to the long-term defense budget savings that can be expected from the *perestroika* process. The present international situation represents a good chance to reach a burden-sharing agreement within the Western alliance that shifts the major share of the costs to the West Europeans—who also stand to benefit greatly if a change from confrontation to cooperation can be made irreversible.

2. Issues in Chinese Economic Reform (Rensselaer W. Lee III)

In a decade of reform, China has made significant progress toward a more open, market-oriented economic system. Yet the reform movement is now in crisis and may be reversed. Economic decentralization and capitalist progress have produced seemingly intractable problems: high inflation, regional economic separatism, increasing social inequality, and rampant official corruption. The reform process has also sparked demands for a more open and responsive political order. Such demands culminated in the "pro-democracy" movement of April-June 1989, which represented a significant challenge to Communist Party rule.

Beijing has responded to these various pressures by putting the reform movement on hold. The regime's brutal crackdown on pro-democracy activists in June 1989 was followed by the expulsion of the most progressive market reformers from top Party positions. The leadership is now dominated by hardliners who are excessively preoccupied with political control and who favor more central government intervention in the economy as well as preferential development of the state-owned economic sector. Key structural reforms, such as partial privatization of industrial ownership, further decontrol of prices, and bankruptcy for insolvent government enterprises appear to have been postponed indefinitely.

The expansion of trade and investment ties with the West—an important aspect of the economic reforms—is still sought by Beijing. However, China's bureaucratic system in many respects limits the potential for normal commercial interaction with the outside world. The country's commercial policies are protectionist, cumbersome, and exploitative of foreign businessmen. Furthermore, as a result of the June crackdown, China no longer has a reputation for political stability. China's foreign trade growth will slow in 1989, and new foreign investment and international lending will almost certainly decline.

The United States would obviously prefer that China increasingly adopt Western concepts of market economies, implement a fairer trade and investment regime, and introduce basic democratic rights and freedoms. The rulers in Beijing, however, are not now moving in this direction. It is very likely that the reform process will not advance much further without a significant change in the composition of the Chinese leadership.

The United States can do little to influence political development in China. Yet the present situation dictates that the United States reduce its government-to-government ties with the People's Republic. Sino-U.S. military cooperation should be frozen as long as the current regime remains in power. High-level visits and exchanges should be minimized (though some such contacts are necessary to maintain the basic framework of Sino-U.S. relations). At the same time, the Bush Administration should take a tougher public stance against Beijing's repressive policies. The relatively muted Administration response thus far risks discouraging the aspirations of reformist sectors in China and could even encourage Beijing to continue its repressive policies.

U.S. economic policies toward the People's Republic should be geared to U.S. reformist objectives. China's accession to the General Agreement on Tariffs and Trade must await a significant liberalization of China's commercial practices. The United States should not, however, adopt sanctions that would damage the existing network of private Sino-U.S. exchanges, contacts, and commerical ties. Such links have been and will continue to be important catalysts for reform in China. The United States should not, for example, deny China most-favored-nation trade treatment, stop Eximbank programs, widen controls on exports of civilian high technology, or cut imports of textiles from China.

Economic assistance programs that support reform should be encouraged. For instance, international lending to China—suspended in the wake of the June 1989 crackdown—should be resumed, but with a change in emphasis. Instead of propping up inefficient state enterprises, lending policies should encourage changes in the ownership system—for example, more loans should be targeted to the nonstate sector or to enterprises that contain a private shareholding component.

Full normalization of Sino-U.S. ties is impossible under present conditions. U.S. policy should be based on recognition that the strategic significance of "the China card" has greatly diminished in the current international environment. Far-reaching political changes in the USSR and Eastern Europe have changed the face of U.S.-Soviet relations. The Soviets, who are preoccupied with internal reform and actively seeking technology and credits from the West, are hardly likely to want to reestablish a Sino-Soviet alliance hostile to the West. All this suggests that the United States can afford to be significantly bolder in expressing displeasure with events in China and in pressing that country to undertake necessary economic and political reforms.

3. Economic Reform in India: A Long and Winding Road (John Echeverri-Gent)

India, like the Soviet Union and China, is an economy in transition. Its growth is increasingly driven by improvements in efficiency and domestic technological capability rather than by bringing new resources into production. To facilitate this transition, India is gradually reforming its economic institutions and policies. It is also opening up to the global economy so that it may reap the benefits of new technologies and international trade.

Transitional economies such as India pose both opportunities and challenges to the United States. The opportunities stem from their economic opening, their eagerness to acquire new technologies, and their growing capabilities in science and technology. The challenges arise from their increasing reliance on export-led growth and their international competitiveness in certain sectors.

The new priorities that have accompanied India's economic reform have shifted the nature of Indo-American relations. Economic liberalization has created opportunities for expanded Indo-American trade. India is particularly eager to increase its import of items with a high-technology component. Restrictions on foreign investment have gradually eased, and U.S. investment is finding new opportunities.

The relative importance of instruments available to U.S. policy-makers has undergone dramatic change. Though India's immense poverty problem persists, the resource transfer programs that dominated policy in the 1950s and 1960s are no longer seen as viable policy options. The United States can still play an important role in alleviating the plight of India's poor by channeling resources to multilateral development institutions and seeing that India receives a share of funds befitting the scope of its problems. In addition to the humanitarian justification, such support advances U.S. interests in promoting the stability of the world's largest democracy and the dominant power in South Asia.

Exchanges in science and technology have become the centerpiece of Indo-American relations. The Indo-U.S. Sub-Commission on

Science and Technology benefits American science while it improves relations with India. It also enhances the prospects for international cooperation on the growing agenda of global environmental problems. There is scope for expanding Indo-American scientific cooperation and extending it into new areas.

While developmental assistance has been drastically curtailed, USAID has developed some innovative programs that merit continued funding. The Program for the Advancement of Commercial Technology (PACT), for instance, is a low overhead operation that helps to establish joint ventures between Indian and U.S. firms that share interests in developing particular products. Not only do programs such as PACT improve the technological capabilities of Indian firms, they also facilitate the entrance of U.S firms into the Indian market and enable them to accumulate experience about operating in the Third World. The modest funding requirements of such programs are a good investment in the improvement of U.S. export capabilities.

In May 1989, the United States threatened India with sanctions under the Omnibus Trade Act of 1988. It objected to India's restrictions on foreign investment and its government monopoly over the insurance industry. The United States also placed India on a "priority watch list" because of its weak protection of intellectual property rights.

Using the Omnibus Trade Act to advance U.S. interests requires considerable political finesse. While U.S. negotiators must defend legitimate concerns raised within the American political system, they must also take into account India's domestic politics. The United States should not overestimate its leverage and sacrifice the positive aspects of Indo-American relations. In the long term, U.S. interests are best served by building support for its concerns in India. This is best accomplished through constructive dialogue and the encouragement of economic reforms that enhance India's experience with free trade, foreign investment, and the protection of intellectual property.

Establishing mutually beneficial relations with India as well as other transitional economies will be trying at times. These countries have their own agendas and are not about to allow the United States to impose its will upon them. Maintaining good relations will become increasingly important, since transitional economies such as India are bound to become more consequential global actors.

4. The Political Economy of Reform in the Three Giants (John Echeverri-Gent and Friedemann Müller)

The success of economic reform in the Giants hinges not only on expanding the role of markets, but also on forging new institutions and macroeconomic instruments that can effectively regulate the decentralized decisionmaking within markets. In India's mixed economy, many of these mechanisms are already present. China's inability to regulate its markets through such economic levers has meant that reforms have resulted in economic overheating and retrenchment. Avoiding this "China syndrome" is also a central challenge for Soviet policymakers.

Although the Giants' immense size, nationalism, and complexity limits the capacity of foreign countries to influence their internal affairs, their economic reforms tend to produce fiscal strains and current-account deficits. The Soviet Union and China have also felt the need to look to the expertise of advanced industrial countries in establishing economic markets. These factors increase the opportunities for outside influence.

In India, the United States can best promote economic reforms by encouraging the World Bank and the International Monetary Fund to make ample funding and expertise available. The experiences of these institutions in promoting structural adjustment in other developing countries endows them with expertise that is especially relevant to the Indian case.

The contribution of the Bretton Woods institutions to economic reform in India and China has already been considerable. They potentially could also make an important contribution to Soviet reform efforts. The United States should encourage Soviet access to Bank and Fund expertise and should not oppose eventual Soviet membership in both institutions if the USSR is willing to abide by their conditions.

The United States government itself possesses considerable expertise in regulating markets, and U.S. officials have already visited the Soviet Union to provide advice in this area. This interchange should be expanded and institutionalized through a program of official exchanges. The successful operation of markets requires entrepreneurial skills that have been woefully underdeveloped in the Soviet Union. The United States can play a role in strengthening Soviet skills in these areas by sponsoring educational exchanges. Leading U.S. business schools could not only host Soviet students but also make their expertise available in helping the Soviets set up their own programs.

During the 1980s, China benefited from many of the above measures, yet these failed to deter the suppression of the pro-democracy movement in June 1989. How should the United States respond to such reversals in the Giants' reforms? The case of China shows that reforms in the Giants may lead to polarization between hardliners whose material interests and ideological values are threatened by both (a) the advance of reforms, and (b) the forces for democracy promoted by the decline in the legitimacy of the ruling party and the creation of a more pluralist social infrastructure. In such circumstances, the United States will be confronted with the temptation to accommodate hardliners for short-term diplomatic expediency at the expense of democratic forces whose immediate chances for power seem remote. The prospects for democratization will improve, however, if the reforms continue to advance. The long-term interests of the United States are best served by resisting concessions to the hardliners and devising policies to support the democrats.

5. Science and Technology and Reform in the Giants (Richard P. Suttmeier)

Science and technology have figured prominently in the reform thinking of the Giants. With its strengths in science and technology, the United States is in a good position to respond to many of the cardinal issues of reform. Distinct U.S. interests vis-à-vis the individual Giants will dictate separate S&T-related policies toward each in such arenas as export controls, intellectual property protection, trade financing, foreign assistance, access to the U.S. market, and human rights. At the same time, the reforms in the Giants raise a number of *generic* issues associated with the growing importance of S&T in relations among nations.

Reforms in the Giants come at a time of rapid change in the international economy the consequences of which cannot be known. Scientific and technical capabilities are becoming more widely dispersed, with implications for both international trade and international security. The reforms are also coming at a time of heightened concern about global environmental quality. Even without Chernobyl and Bhopal, the scale and intensity of human activity in the Giants make them important factors in global ecological equations.

The United States should seek to establish a thick, comprehensive web of mutually beneficial scientific and technical relations with the Giants. Its design should be both (a) sensitive to the need to buffer the effects of a world of high uncertainty, and (b) consistent with the international collective interest in an open trading system, military stability, and environmental stewardship.

The efficacy of U.S efforts to achieve these goals is not independent of change within the United States itself. A United States whose scientific leadership and capabilities in commercially relevant technological innovation are declining will be a less attractive (and less influential) partner for the Giants than one that has instituted a credible program for the revitalization of its research and development base as well as science education. A creative response to reform in the Giants is thus inseparable from domestic policies to enhance the nation's research and innovation capabilities. Moreover, the Giants, with their large technical communities, contain reservoirs of talent that can be (and indeed already are) useful to the United States. For instance, the future of many science and engineering graduate programs at U.S. universities would be much in doubt were it not for the research assistance provided by large numbers of Chinese and Indian (and other foreign) students.

In addition to augmenting its technical assets, the United States must learn to use them more effectively in a rapidly changing international environment. The establishment of comprehensive technical relations with the Giants will require that international S&T affairs be given a much higher profile—and more powerful organizational resources—in the U.S. policy process. Attention is required in four areas:

(1) There is a need for greater organizational focus on international S&T—to provide a forum for bringing together the disparate commercial, scientific, security, environmental, and human rights issues that must be reconciled if a coherent international S&T strategy is to emerge.

(2) Attention is needed to the staffing of international S&T activities, both in Washington and in U.S. embassies in the Giants' capitals, to ensure that the individuals recruited have technical competence and a good sense for scientific and commercial opportunities.

(3) More flexibility is necessary in the funding of international S&T activities. Criteria for funding—mutual benefit and consistency with the needs of U.S. technical agencies—should be augmented by standards that reflect an understanding that the

building of complex technical relationships requires longer-term investments.

(4) Much greater government-industry cooperation is needed in building a national strategy.

Central to U.S. responses to the Giants is policy in the area of export controls. Pressures to liberalize will mount rapidly, since the fuller integration of the Giants into the world economy will not be possible without facilitated East-West technology flows. In light of the great uncertainties surrounding reform in the Giants, however, it would be prudent to maintain unilateral and multilateral control regimes. Yet liberalization within these regimes is unavoidable. The consideration of decisions to liberalize will be more intelligent if done in a forum that accurately assesses both the risks and the benefits of liberalization comprehensively—taking into account commercial, scientific, and environmental as well as security issues. Decisions to liberalize can also be made in greater confidence once a web of technical relations of the sort outlined in this analysis is in place.

6. The Geopolitical Consequences of Reform (Elena B. Arefieva)

The geopolitical situation in the world, and particularly in Asia, has changed dramatically, presenting the United States with two challenges. It needs to develop a new set of policies that respond to the changed setting of reduced international tensions. It also needs to adjust its policies to take advantage of the opportunities presented by new "geo-economic" realities.

Being basically very different, the Giants vary greatly in the scope and character of the reforms they have introduced (which in turn influence their military and political strategies). The main features of the new geopolitics relate to changes in the Giants' foreign policies. Those changes, in turn, derive not only from the Giants' new external economic interests, but also from the particular social and political aspects of reform within each of them.

The Soviet Union is attempting a comprehensive revision of foreign policy based on the principles of its new political thinking. Although the new geopolitics is less directly connected with economic reform, its irreversibility does depend largely on the internal economic situation, which has become extremely difficult.

The reshaping of China's geopolitics has been motivated by the needs of economic reform to a greater extent than in the USSR. Despite the regression in political reform, the external policy of economic liberalization has not been dismantled—and the seemingly more defense-oriented military posture of the 1980s may be sustained.

India is experiencing a period of uncertainty and political change. Its foreign policy is likely to be shaped by the need to open up the economy, though its domestic political instability may strongly affect its military and geopolitical role.

The most important international effect of the reforms is the shift from military and political confrontation to economic competition and even emphasis on the potential mutual benefits of economic cooperation. Moreover, in the present stage of reform, external economic factors can play a critical role in the irreversibility of the reforms with respect to both economics and internal politics.

The implications of reform in the Giants for the United States are inseparable from the key question of whether or not it perceives their political and economic reforms and the thrust of their present foreign policies to be in its interest. In the author's view, the Giants' reforms merit U.S. support both in terms of *politics*, because the United States would gain in national security, and in terms of *economics*, because it too, would benefit from a general acceleration of the Giants' economic development, the opening up of their economies, and an ultimate increase in their absorptive capacity for U.S. goods and investments. The author argues that the United States should support the new geopolitics and geo-economics of the Giants through reciprocal disarmament measures, political dialogue, and the encouragement of every aspect of economic relations.

The potential forms of support need not be limited to loans, direct private investment, or even the removal of constraints on bilateral trade. It is important to draw the Giants into the world economy through international institutions and to enable the opening up of their economies. That, in turn, could speed up internal political reform in China and the Soviet Union, and it might help stabilize the political situation in India. To reconcile the U.S. national interest with the Giants' progress, it would be reasonable to formulate mutually acceptable "conditionality" through unofficial discussions with the Giants' research and business representatives.

The new circumstances, actions, and potential of the Giants await policy response. Being far from simple, the situation admittedly requires extremely prudent treatment. But the players have to decide whether it is more prudent to step aside or to get involved for the sake of averting a turn for the worse in the area of geopolitics and losses in geo-economics.

ECONOMIC REFORM in THREE GIANTS

Chapter 1

Economic Reform in the Soviet Union

Friedemann Müller

Crisis in the Soviet Economy

During Mikhail Gorbachev's fifth year in power, the Soviet economy has been described as chaotic more often than at any time during the past six decades, and the prospect for the sixth year offers no certainties. On the one hand, the well-known economists Nikolai Shmelev and Vladimir Popov have optimistically called their new book *The Turning Point* and have offered a strategy to revitalize the Soviet economy. On the other hand, going ahead with radical economic reform was still a very controversial subject at a huge, high-level conference held in Moscow in November 1989—leading Leonid Abalkin, Deputy Prime Minister and head of the Soviet Commission of Economic Reform, to warn the assembled economists, government officials, and enterprise managers that unless the sweeping economic reforms needed were adopted soon, Soviet citizens could face further rationing.[1] Will the sixth year of the Gorbachev era bring the turning point or will reform lead to chaos?

Gorbachev is not the first communist leader to begin reform of a centrally planned economy, but he is the first to choose so comprehensive an approach and to recognize the challenge of the "high-tech" age: Participation in rapid technological progress is impossible without the free and fast flow of information. Free information produces competition, and competition produces information. This "feedback" cannot be restricted to the economic sphere. *Glasnost* and democratization became catchwords even before Gorbachev started to talk about "radical economic reform" in 1986. The broad *perestroika* approach to reform—combined with tolerance for pluralistic developments within the Eastern alliance—boosted reform efforts in Eastern European societies (even in the case of Hungary's reforms, the Gorbachev policy was a major impulse). Yet the Soviet domestic economic reform ran into great problems in attempting to overcome stagnation. Within Soviet society, seventy years of a rigid command economy have made it difficult to muster economic behavior and risk taking. In addition, the suppression of conflicts between nationalities has generated deep distrust of any possibility of fair competition within the society.

It was only in 1983, against the background of the failure of previous Soviet efforts to reform the economy in the 1960s and 1970s,[2] that a first comprehensive domestic critique of Soviet society and economy was presented by an established expert. In her famous (though never officially published) "Novosibirsk Report," Tatyana Zaslavskaya, a prominent sociologist, wrote that: "The system of centralized economic management corresponds for the most part to the level of development of the productive forces of the Soviet society in the 1930s."[3]

The Soviet economic system had remained almost identical to that of the Stalin era. Inflexibility seemed to be the system's integral element. In the mid–1980s, even Western analysts thought it highly unlikely that any comprehensive reform would take place in the near future.[4] Today some of them argue that even if Gorbachev's reform approach is more radical than any that could be imagined in the West during the first half of the 1980s, it is not radical enough to provide an environment for a market economy, which is the only way to modernize this backward and inflexible economy.

One of the major problems of the reform process is the interdependence of all reform measures. If they are introduced step by step, they produce contradictions.[5] On the other hand, the lack of education and experience prohibits the introduction of all reform measures at the same time. As Gorbachev's fifth year in office draws to a close, it is far from clear whether his reform efforts will attain the desired results or whether incompetence and resistance will prevail.

The Decline of Economic Performance

Economic Growth

Over the past twenty years, the growth rate of the Soviet economy has been declining steadily—even according to official Soviet statistics. Furthermore, *glasnost* has permitted Soviet economists to express doubts about these statistics. In a February 1987 article in *Novy Mir*, Itsikovich Khanin and Vasili Selyunin challenged the accuracy of Soviet official data, touching off a bitter debate among Soviet experts[6]—with some opponents labeling the authors of the article "dissidents." Yet even the more "mainstream" Institute for World Economics and International Relations (IMEMO) has expressed concern about the highly overestimated long-term growth figures in official statistics.

According to CIA as well as Khanin and Selyunin estimates of growth in the USSR, during the late 1970s and early 1980s, improvement in per capita income (which is at least 1.5 per cent below GNP growth) has been close to zero or even negative. Lending credibility to this assessment, Abel Aganbegyan, one of the chief

Table 1. Economic Growth in the Soviet Union, 1961-1985 (average annual percentages)

	Net Material Product *(Soviet statistics)*	Gross National Product *(CIA estimates)*	Net Material Product *(Khanin/Selyunin estimates)*
1961–65	6.5%	4.8%	4.3%
1966–70	7.8	5.0	4.0
1971–75	5.7	3.1	3.2
1976–80	4.3	2.2	1.0
1981–85	3.6	1.8	0.6
1986–87	3.2	1.9	—

Sources: "Narodnoe Khozyaistvo SSSR za 70 let" (Statistical Yearbook of the USSR for 70 years), Moscow 1987, p. 51; Central Intelligence Agency, *Revisiting Soviet Economic Performance Under Glasnost: Implications for CIA Estimates*, SOV 88–10068, September 1988; Richard E. Ericson, *The Soviet Statistical Debate: Khanin vs. TsSu* (Central Statistical Office of the Soviet Union, Occasional Paper No. 1, Harriman Institute for Advanced Study of the Soviet Union, May 1988); and *CIA Handbook of Economic Statistics*, 1988.

advisors to President Gorbachev, has also argued that official growth figures distort the true condition of the Soviet economy:

> [O]ver the last ten years there has been a growing tendency for hidden price rises which are not reflected in the official statistics. What is more, part of the increase in consumer goods over the past five years has been linked to an excess of imports over exports and so does not result from our own production, and if you take these two adjustments into account, then you can easily see that at a point between 1970 and 1980 our economic development came to a standstill.[7]

Foreign Trade

The emerging crisis in the international competitiveness of the Soviet economy was obscured until the early 1980s by factors related to the high demand for and rising world market prices of Soviet energy exports. Between 1970 and 1980, the Soviet Union's total foreign trade (exports and imports) grew more than fourfold; between 1980 and 1987, however, it grew only 37 per cent; and between 1984 and 1987, it decreased 8 per cent (see Table 2). And while trade with the West (exports and imports) grew more than sixfold between 1970 and 1980 (the annual average growth rate was 21 per cent), it decreased 11 per cent between 1980 and 1987.

Following the first oil crisis in 1973–74, the Soviet Union increasingly became an energy-exporting country—benefiting as a free rider from the price increases of the Organization of Petroleum Exporting Countries (OPEC). While OPEC cut oil production by half (from 11.3 to 5.8 billion barrels per year) between 1973 and 1985 to keep prices high, the Soviet Union increased its production by almost 50 per cent (from 3.1 billion to 4.5 billion barrels per year) and expanded its exports by about 40 per cent.[8] In addition, over the same period, Soviet natural gas exports to the West grew even faster (from 1 billion to 84 billion cubic meters). In 1982 and 1983, energy exports accounted for 78 per cent of total Soviet exports to the West.[9]

The prices of oil and natural gas began to decline in 1982 and collapsed in late 1985 to early 1986, with disastrous effects for the Soviet economy. Between 1984 and 1986, exports to the OECD countries fell by 22 per cent in dollar terms (from $24.4 billion to $19.1 billion). Meanwhile, Soviet total hard-currency arms sales also declined—from $8.2 billion in 1982 to $5.6 billion in 1985.[10] Consequently, planners were forced to choose between cutting vital imports and negotiating increased foreign credits.

Table 2. Soviet Trade, 1970–1988 (billions rubles)

	1970	1972	1975	1980	1983	1984	1985	1986	1987	1988
Total Exports	11.52	12.73	24.03	49.63	67.89	74.39	72.46	68.28	68.14	67.12
Total Imports	10.57	13.31	26.67	44.46	59.59	65.37	69.10	62.59	60.74	65.04
Exports to OECD Countries[a]	2.15	2.44	6.14	15.86	19.65	21.35	18.58	13.11	14.19	14.67
Imports from OECD Countries[a]	2.54	3.44	9.70	15.72	18.72	19.58	19.27	15.85	13.87	16.32
Exports to CMEA Countries[b]	6.26	7.55	13.36	24.34	34.45	38.17	40.05	42.16	40.70	39.05
Imports from CMEA Countries[b]	6.02	7.97	12.88	21.44	30.81	34.62	37.64	37.80	38.86	39.83
Exports to Socialist Countries[c]	7.53	8.29	14.58	26.90	37.71	42.11	44.28	45.63	44.20	42.88
Imports from Socialist Countries[c]	6.88	8.52	13.97	23.65	33.69	38.26	42.21	41.84	42.12	43.37
Exports to Developing Countries[d]	1.84	2.01	3.31	6.87	10.52	10.93	9.60	9.55	9.76	9.56
Imports from Developing Countries[d]	1.15	1.35	3.00	5.09	7.17	7.53	7.62	4.90	4.75	5.35

[a]Member countries of the Organisation for Economic Co-operation and Development (OECD).
[b]Member countries of the Council for Mutual Economic Assistance (CMEA) include Bulgaria, Cuba, Czechoslovakia, Hungary, the German Democratic Republic, Mongolia, Poland, Romania, the USSR, and Vietnam.
[c]All member countries of the CMEA plus China, North Korea, and Yugoslavia.
[d]Developing Countries exclude socialist developing countries (China, Cuba, Mongolia, North Korea, and Vietnam) in Soviet statistics.

Source: *Vneshnyaya Torgovlya SSSR*, Moscow, different volumes.

Soviet trade with the developed market economies has declined as a share of overall Soviet foreign trade since the mid–1970s (falling from 31 per cent in 1975 to 22 per cent in 1987).[11] During this time, there was no growth in Soviet hard-currency exports except in the field of energy. Using constant 1975 prices, between 1974 and 1985, non-energy exports to developed market economies did not grow at all, while exports of machinery and other products of higher technology decreased in real terms.[12] The Soviet Union lost most of its market share in the OECD countries to the East Asian newly industrialized countries (NICs).[13]

The import record was not much better. Those products that could help modernize the Soviet industrial infrastructure and its export sectors lost shares in overall imports. For example, machinery and pipes imports from the West, which accounted for 37 per cent in 1970 and for 42 per cent in 1975, declined to 29 per cent by 1980 and to 26 per cent by 1985. Meanwhile, food and food materials increased their share in Soviet overall imports from 9 per cent to 23 per cent between 1970 and 1975, to 38 per cent in 1980, and back to 30 per cent in 1985.[14]

In the Gorbachev years, there have been some positive aspects to Soviet foreign trade performance (although it is too early to give a reliable explanation of these—or to extrapolate a trend from them). One of these positive signs is that machinery and "investment goods" gained both export and import shares. Exports to the non-socialist countries grew from $3.3 billion in 1985 to about $4.5 billion in 1987, while imports rose from $7 billion to about $8.1 billion. A sharp increase in Soviet arms sales (from $5.5 billion to $8.6 billion) also helped offset the 15–per-cent decline in commodity terms of trade during these two years.[15] Another positive point is that in 1988, after ten years, the declining trend in the Western share in Soviet foreign trade appears to have turned around. While trade with socialist countries is declining, trade with the West shows growth of 7.5 per cent for exports and 23 per cent for imports in 1988 over 1987.[16]

The Soviet Union's debt situation is not serious, as the leadership has followed a cautious credit policy. Gross debt grew from about $25 billion in 1981 to $40 billion in 1987; net debt in 1987 was estimated at $20 billion[17]—an amount equal to less than one year's hard-currency export volume (see Statistical Annexes, Table 17, p. 229). Considering the Soviet Union's massive gold reserves (which could, if only gradually, be converted into hard currency), it is not surprising that banks, especially those in Western Europe, are eager to offer further credits.

The Reform Framework

The Reform Debate

During the first five Gorbachev years, broader recognition has been gained among both Soviet policy analysts and policymakers that "radical" (that is, comprehensive, not partial) changes in the economy are necessary.[18] Higher rates of growth have to be regained—though not through the strategies of the past; the potential for extensive growth based on ever-increasing commitments of capital and labor has been almost exhausted. The investment share in GNP is already extremely high compared with other industrialized countries, and the labor force is not growing faster than 1 per cent per year. Dependence on ever-increasing infusions of capital must be lowered by increasing the efficiency with which capital is converted into output. Measures taken to date within the framework of central planning have failed to solve the problem of misallocation and inefficient utilization of resources.[19]

The ongoing debate in the Soviet Union reveals a wide divergence of views on *how* to achieve an increase in efficiency. Perspectives range from cautious and conservative incrementalism to radical alternatives that challenge the socialist nature of the Soviet system. Gorbachev's approach reflects the widespread recognition that the new reforms cannot be partial, like those of 1965, which were restricted to economic administration.

During the first years of Gorbachev's reform, it became widely accepted that, to be successful, *perestroika* had to be preceded not only by an increased flow of information and frank internal debate, but also by broader participation in the economic process. Directors of companies and institutions were elected by workers along the Yugoslav model, while the market mechanism did not play a major role in reform considerations. Subsequently, the consensus—reflected in the more recent statements of Gorbachev's advisors Abalkin, Zaslavskaya, and Bogomolov—shifted toward emphasizing the market and monetarization.[20] In only a few years, the leadership and intellectual elite have passed through a learning process that has raised the reform discussion to a more sophisticated level. Not all people of influence, however, have taken part in this evolution of views. Resistance from conservative politicians has become more pronounced, as was evident in most speeches at the already-mentioned November 1989 high-level Moscow conference.[21]

Decentralization

Economic reform cannot be sustained without real improvements in productivity, and these can only be achieved through changes in the economic allocation mechanism. A centralized economy compiles information relevant to supply, demand, and technology, and it limits essential decisions to yearly or five-year plans. However, the number of data that can be processed is finite, and information that can be considered firm enough as a basis for planning is also static—it fails to capture the dynamism and interdependency of a constantly changing flow of information. Any central planning process tends to oversimplify, to refuse any diversification, to build few and large units. This denies it the flexibility to maximize efficiency. The inability to react to economic information quickly leads to misallocations of resources—with unused surpluses (idle capacity) or shortages (waiting lines and corruption in the distribution process). Moreover, centralized access to information does not allow individual decisionmakers to take risks and to respond flexibly to changing market conditions.

The first priority is the decentralization of decisionmaking processes, responsibility, and risk taking. This is a precondition for and must be accompanied by the access of decisionmakers to adequate information. These decentralization measures can be taken gradually, allowing Soviet reform planners to introduce limited measures that they can extend later. For example, in 1983, Andropov started with a reform designed to give companies more responsibility in deciding where to buy and how to combine inputs. In January 1984, to create incentives for efficient production, he introduced the principle of self-financing in companies subordinated to five of the industrial ministries. Under Gorbachev, this "experiment" was extended to encompass virtually the entire industrial sector. The significance of this reform remains limited, however, by the difficulty of self-financing efficiency in an environment where prices are totally distorted by subsidies, taxes, and qualitative restrictions. A *partial* decentralization tends to produce contradictions as long as the economic mechanisms are not in place to provide an equilibrium between supply and demand.

Price Reform

Together with decentralization, a mechanism has to be introduced that assures a dynamic equilibrium of supply and demand. There is a basic consensus among Soviet reform-oriented politicians and analysts that a price reform is necessary. Other forms of supply planning in the Soviet Union have led to the misallocation of resources. Even the efforts to simulate a flexible price system using mathematical methods adopted from cost-benefit analysis have failed; they are blamed for the failure of the 1965 reform.

A price reform that abandons centrally planned price fixing and leaves price formation to the market is indispensable if the central problem of shortage is to be solved.[22] Markets assure greater efficiency in the allocation of outputs as well as in the utilization of capital and labor.[23] Capital will flow to where it can produce the highest rates of return. This raises the efficiency of investment, allowing "intensive" growth to take place.[24]

If the Soviet Union introduced a price reform based on these principles, it could achieve levels of efficiency rivaling those of the market economies—perhaps even if state ownership of capital goods were left untouched. Any reform process that does not move in this direction has little chance of achieving a modern technological economy capable of adjusting rapidly and flexibly to changes in product markets, factor markets, and technology.

A price reform introduced into an otherwise planned economy would, however, create extreme disparities. Most of the supply comes from a state monopoly with an extremely low elasticity of supply, which tends to provoke astronomical prices—particularly with as much excess money as is presently in circulation in the Soviet Union. To reduce these disparities to a scale that is tolerable, three additional reforms need to be introduced. First, a monetary policy has to be established; it is necessary to fight inflation by limiting the amount of available money according to the real potential and growth of the economy. If too much money is already in circulation, it should be absorbed by selling state capital (for instance, state apartments, production means, agricultural production equipment). Second, a social policy is needed that guarantees a minimum or decent income to those who are the losers because of subsidy reductions and changes in price relationships. Third, a policy that encourages competition has to be introduced; monopolies must be prevented if competitive pricing is to be induced.

Inconsistencies in the Reform Process

While comprehensive reform is necessary, at least three political and social realities limit the reform of the Soviet economy to a step-by-step approach. First, the execution of comprehensive reform far exceeds Soviet administrative capacities. Second, while some measures are universally accepted, others are the focus of considerable intellectual debate. The reform envisioned by *perestroika* may redefine the very nature of socialism. It is only natural for the establishment of a consensus regarding such measures to be a long and complex process. Third, the Soviet citizenry has developed attitudes inconsistent with those appropriate for an efficient modern economy. The combination of these three factors will slow the pace of reform and force the leadership to pursue a patient and pragmatic course.

A centrally planned economy implies an extremely complex infrastructure. Such an economy claims to integrate all decision-making processes, including those which in market economies are the responsibility of private enterprises or are left to the free market. The change from one system to the other is a delicate operation. For example, if the *perestroika* process incorporates price reform, the establishment of new monetary mechanisms will play an important role; and to understand and manage these mechanisms, new skills have to be cultivated—not only among bankers, but among all decisionmakers. This will take years.

Finally, the population will have to accept that any radical restructuring implies great changes that affect everyday life. Price stability will no longer be assured; periods of inflation will be highly likely. Unemployment in some measure will become a feature of Soviet society. Growing income disparities will have to be accepted. Even more important, the public will have to learn to recognize and exploit the opportunities that radical reform will bring. They will have to act more flexibly and to accept greater risks than those to which they have been accustomed. To mitigate the harmful effects of these changes, a network of measures to prevent extreme social disparities will have to be instituted—not only by the government, but also through the development of a code of non-governmental ethics and social responsibility modified for a new economic culture.

The Reform Schedule

While Gorbachev aspires to effect fundamental change, he has not articulated a specific description of what this change will look like and when it will be implemented. The reform schedule does not follow a master plan codified in Gorbachev's book, *Perestroika*, or any major speech. Even the very next steps in the reform process are dictated by pragmatism.[25] Indeed, Gorbachev's reform process began as the continuation of the reform that Andropov started in July 1983 with a decree that gave all enterprises in two all-union and three republic ministries more autonomy, at the same time making them more accountable for their efficiency and performance by introducing new plan indicators and incentives.[26] Former General Secretary Konstantin Chernenko had implemented this experiment in 1984–85, and Gorbachev extended it and in 1987 placed it in a legal framework. In January 1988, a new "law on socialist enterprise" made enterprises financially responsible for their activities.[27] Enterprises now have to finance their own operating expenses and most investments without recourse to government resources. By the end of 1989, the whole economy had incorporated these administrative reforms.

The "law on individual economic activity," which has been in effect since May 1987, authorizes the existence of *private* enterprises, particularly in the services sector. People working in state enterprises can engage in such activity only on a part-time basis, but other family members, students, and pensioners can participate full-time. Similar regulations were implemented for *cooperative* economic activities in early 1987.[28] These regulations permit the production of consumer goods, services, and minor industrial components on a private-enterprise and cooperative basis. In July 1988, a law on cooperatives extended the legal framework for private activities, allowing the founding of small private businesses in the service and retail trade sector. The dynamic development of the private sector on the basis of this law is remarkable. By April 1989, 3.1 million people—not including those participating on a part-time basis— were working in cooperatives and private individual businesses. The increase was dramatic, as only 0.5 million had been involved a year earlier.[29] As of April 1989, three per cent of the total Soviet labor force was engaged in private business. There was criticism that some of these cooperatives took advantage of quasi-monopolistic relationships to extract unusually high profits. New regulations enacted in January 1989 have sought to reduce such abuses. In the fields of cultural and medical services, these restrictions were not only directed toward quasi-monopolistic structures, but also have discouraged virtually any private investment in these sectors.

Major reform steps have been taken in foreign economic relations. In January 1987, a law was enacted allowing joint ventures with foreign companies on Soviet territory. Although this law was an important ideological breakthrough unimaginable a few years ago, in practice it proved to be too vague and burdened with many bureaucratic obstacles. To counter these problems, an April 1989 amendment to this law allows foreign partners to own up to 99 per cent of a venture and to appoint a non-Soviet citizen as director, and it reduces the duties on equipment imported by joint ventures.[30] In addition, this amendment regulates the establishment of special economic zones like those in the Chinese model; it also introduced a new tariff system starting immediately and acknowledged ruble devaluation as a strategy for reaching convertibility. The first custom-free industrial park is to be located at the Soviet-Finnish border close to Leningrad and leased to Finland.[31] Another special economic zone is to be established in the Soviet Far East—as an invitation to Japan and other East Asian economies to invest there.[32]

To give Soviet companies easier access to foreign trade transactions and to make them more efficient, the Ministry on Foreign Trade and the State Committee for Foreign Economic Relations were merged in 1987 into the Ministry on Foreign Economic Relations. In addition, twenty-two ministries and seventy-seven enterprises received permission to trade with foreign enterprises on their own account.[33] According to the new trade law, all enterprises, associations, and production cooperatives have the right to negotiate trade contracts with foreign partners.

The reality, however, is that, as of May 1989, only two hundred enterprises had access to hard currency reserves giving them the monetary basis to establish direct links with foreign partners.[34] Because of this currency problem, the monetary sector requires certain changes if foreign economic relations are to be improved. Without a realistic price system, it is almost impossible to introduce an exchange rate that leads to efficient trade behavior.[35] In December 1988, the Soviet Union announced plans to devalue the ruble by 50 per cent by January 1, 1990. This plan appears to have been superseded by a 10 to 1 devaluation of the tourist exchange rate only (effective November 1, 1989), which put the exchange rate at 6.26 rubles per dollar, as well as by the first hard-currency auction (November 1989), where bidding Soviet enterprises offered between 13 and 15 rubles per dollar.[36]

Price reform must be the centerpiece of economic restructuring. Two alternative approaches to price correction are possible in the Soviet Union. One is to reduce subsidies, which at present place a tremendous burden on the state budget; this can be done by increasing prices to the level of real costs. The other approach is to bring supply and demand into balance by permitting flexible prices. Published discussion inside the Soviet Union is quite unclear as to which of the two methods the planned reform is to employ. Some Soviet economists and economic advisors appear to feel that market prices are indispensable for an efficient economy but are afraid of their inflationary effects.[37] Asked whether price reform in the Soviet Union might create unrest such as that in Poland, Gorbachev responded:

[T]he major mass of prices is under strict public control. Therefore it is very important to find the facet enabling us to combine the release of the economic mechanism needed with the preservation of the necessary centralized control. I do not think this issue can be solved at one go. The shaping of a new price mechanism will be a process within the framework of economic reform.[38]

The price reform had been scheduled for 1989–90.[39] Due to the poor performance of the economy thus far and the major dispute about the degree of freedom to allow prices, the reform seems to have been postponed indefinitely.[40] At the already-mentioned 1989 major conference, Deputy Prime Minister Leonid Abalkin made an effort to revive the plan of a gradual decontrol of prices starting in 1991.[41] Due to the threatening situation in consumer supply, the resistance against this strategy among Politburo and goverment members was even stronger than a year ago.

Even without price reform, however, a step toward a more monetized economy has been taken in the form of a limited decentralization in the banking sector.[42] Since the beginning of 1988, the state bank holds responsibility for the overall management of the monetary system, but is no longer responsible for the provision of operational credits. A number of credit banks, such as the Bank for Industry and Construction, the Agro-Industry Bank, and the Bank for Housing and Municipal Economy, are in charge of carrying out operational financing. At the same time, the conditions for credit grants have been tightened, so that the volume of credits can be restricted. The plan for 1988 indicated a 10–per-cent reduction in the volume of short-term credits. These are only the first steps toward a tighter monetary policy.

The state budget deficit has grown rather dramatically during the Gorbachev years. According to Western estimates, in 1985 the deficit amounted to 23 billion rubles (2.9 per cent of GNP) and in 1987 it reached 95 billion rubles (11.5 per cent of GNP).[43] According to official Soviet sources, the state budget deficit in 1988 was approximately 100 billion rubles,[44] and at the first Congress of People's Deputies, Prime Minister Nikolai Ryzhkov announced that it would reach 120 billion rubles in 1989 if no additional preventive measures were taken.[45] This massive deficit makes any monetary control measure superfluous.

Social welfare policy and the problem of poverty have been a touchy issue. If the Soviet Union is to follow through with reforms such as major subsidy reductions and the introduction of market prices, this will create inequalities, pressing the formulation of a social policy to deal with the problems of economic insecurity.

At the first Congress of People's Deputies, the topic of poverty was put on the agenda. Gorbachev expressed concern about "more than 40 million people with low incomes."[46] Boris Yeltsin, the unofficial opposition leader in the Congress, demanded that a law be passed on poverty. Prime Minister Ryzhkov reacted by releasing— for the first time—figures on poverty and planned social measures. The subsequent actions were not, however, very dramatic; Ryzhkov's new policy was more or less reduced to an improvement in pensions. While it was important that the Congress showed readiness to introduce social welfare reforms into the *perestroika* process, the measures discussed did not reflect any consistent and comprehensive concept of a social policy. At the same time, it should not be overlooked that the reform discussion within the leadership, in the parliamentary bodies, among experts, and in the media is part of a learning process that is an indispensable precondition for modernization within the economy. This discussion process offers an opportunity (one that was not present in China) for building a more solid foundation for the reformed economy.

Critical Sectors: Agriculture, Informatics, and Military Industry

Three sectors—agriculture, informatics, and military industry— are critical to the reform process. Agricultural reform would lead to immediate improvements in food supply and would gain popular support for restructuring faster than any other reform measure. Information technology is the field in which Western superiority is most manifest; the application of advanced information technology is virtually a synonym for the intensive growth that the Soviet economy so strongly needs. The priority given to military expenditures of course greatly limits the resources available for the reform of the economic system, making a reduction in defense spending a major issue for Gorbachev's *perestroika* program.

Agriculture

In recent decades, assuring adequate food supplies has become one of the country's most urgent problems. Although the Soviet Union allocates 33 per cent of its total investment and 30 per cent of its labor force to agriculture, it has not attained self-sufficiency in agricultural production.[47] In comparison, the United States, which devotes less than 5 per cent of its resources to agriculture, exports large quantities of food.[48] The Soviet Union, once an agrarian state, is becoming ever more dependent on imports of agricultural products. Moreover, imports have not closed the gap between supply and demand. Subsidized prices assure that demand will outstrip supply while guaranteeing a high proportion of waste: approximately 20 per cent of Soviet agricultural production is lost due to inefficient transportation and storage systems. The quantities wasted far exceed the level of agricultural imports.[49]

The reasons for the failure of Soviet agriculture are complex. One important element is the lack of incentives in a sector organized into huge state- or collective-farm enterprises. State (or quasi-state) ownership, however, is not solely responsible for agriculture's poor performance. In other socialist countries, there appears to be no significant relationship between the involvement of the private sector and the efficiency of agriculture. In Poland, for instance, the share of the private sector is very high (80 per cent), but efficiency is low.[50] Private units that are too small show poor performance results in Poland; so do excessively large state enterprises in the Soviet Union. East Germany and Czechoslovakia have much more efficient agricultural sectors with almost exclusively public ownership. In the Soviet Union, major barriers to success in this sector include the eradication of almost any personal initiative, the lack of incentives, poor infrastructure (especially the transportation system), and the neglect of the food processing industry. Moreover, the agricultural sector has suffered due to the relative priority given to heavy industry and to the overemphasis of gross output results in the case of agriculture itself.

Many Western analysts consider Gorbachev's decision to defer agricultural reform a grave error—all the more so since he is an expert in this field. He graduated as an agronomist in 1967 and was Secretary for Agriculture on the Central Committee from 1978 until he took office as General Secretary in 1985. As early as 1981, Gorbachev was identified on several occasions as supporting and praising private initiative in the agricultural sector.[51] As Party leader, however, he hesitated until 1988 to give priority to reform in agriculture. In a speech to the Central Committee in July 1988, following the 19th Party Conference, he elaborated his ideas and linked analysis with concrete proposals, particularly regarding leasing land to farmers.[52] These measures have gained considerable support among reform-minded intellectuals.[53] Bureaucratic and ideological resistance, however, turned out to be anticipated by Gorbachev more correctly than by well-intentioned Western analysts. This might explain the ranking of agriculture behind industrial reform despite the reverse successful model in China.

The struggle over agricultural reform within the Soviet leadership may be more severe than over any other aspect of *perestroika*. The October 1988 appointment of Egor Ligachev as the member within the Politburo responsible for agriculture may indicate the strength of the conservatives in this area of reform. After several rejections of draft programs, the Central Committee plenum in March 1989 approved a resolution that reflected continuing division and lack of compromise. The resolution pledged "to reinstate peasants as masters of the land" by allowing the leasing of land and other dramatic new arrangements. Yet the changes were hedged in by crucial qualifications. The decision to grant leases, for example, was left up to the collective and state farms, which are hardly likely to exercise it liberally. While all farms were promised more scope for decisionmaking on what to grow and how to dispose of the produce, it was made clear that this would not become possible during a "transition" period of two to three years. Moreover, postponement of the "Law on Leasing" meant that the legal environment would not be conducive to taking advantage of the promised radically new forms of tenure.[54] Thus the debate over agricultural reform continues. The influential Academician Vladimir Tikhonov, who for a long time favored land leasing, now argues for private land ownership.[55]

The issue of Soviet agriculture has an important foreign trade aspect as well. While the Soviet Union is the world's largest grain importer, the United States is the largest exporter. Gorbachev aspires to Soviet agricultural self-sufficiency by the mid–1990s. Yet on November 28, 1988, the Soviet Union signed a 27–month extension to the 1983 five–year grain agreement with the United States. According to this agreement, the Soviet Union is committed to buying 9.9 million tons of grain and soybeans annually from the United States. Shortages have been exacerbated by a bad 1988 harvest in the Soviet Union, and imports are expected to exceed 20 million tons annually during the next few years.

Informatics Technology

Technological change in the West represents an ideological and economic challenge to the Soviet Union. During the 1960s, it was still widely believed in the Soviet Union that faster information processing could make a highly centralized system relatively more efficient. This view continued to be popular until the end of the Brezhnev era. Even after five years of *glasnost* and partial decentralization, the system still works mainly on the basis of a vertical flow of information toward the center, where it is processed to supplement centralized planning.

Although the Soviet Union has made major efforts to close the technology gap with the West—especially in the field of computer production—there are no signs that it is approaching Western production levels either qualitatively or quantitatively. The Soviet economy produced 16,000 computer systems and 16,000 personal computers in 1986, compared with 2.2 million systems and 2.1 million microcomputers sold in the United States during 1984.[56] The main Soviet-produced system (Rhyad) is comparable to the IBM 360/370 series of the 1960s and 1970s. The Soviet Union plans to put the Elbrus–3 supercomputer into production only in 1991, whereas mass production of Western supercomputers started a couple of years ago.

The Soviet educational level in this field, on the other hand, is impressive: In 1985 alone, 56,000 engineers graduated with degrees in "electronic technology and informatics." Their level of theoretical expertise seems to be quite high, even though the lack of available computers greatly limits practical experience.

Soviet computers are concentrated in strategic sectors. The military, telecommunications, central planning, and non-industrial science sectors are believed to claim approximately two-thirds of the overall stock.[57] All other sectors of civilian industry and services seem to be poorly equipped.

Several other factors add to the Soviet Union's chronic informatics sector problems. There is a lack of communication between producers and consumers. Producers receive less feedback from users than is necessary to react and adjust to consumer needs. Equipment supply and servicing are inadequate, and there is also a shortage of software programmers and personnel trained in applying computer technology to practical uses. These shortcomings—in addition to limited availability—result in the inefficient application of existing computer capacity.

Gorbachev himself is well aware of the need to accelerate computer production, and he realizes the potential of computers for helping to spur intensive growth of the economy. Shortly after becoming General Secretary, he reported at a Central Committee conference: "Microelectronics, computer technology, instrument making, and the entire informatics industry are the catalyst of progress. They require accelerated development."[58] His "strategy for scientific and technological progress" encompasses an impressive number of measures. It does not, however, indicate a policy of decentralized production or the introduction of market prices. Yet decentralization is necessary to give the producer a chance to make his production decisions responsive to a differentiated and changing consumer market. This includes the provision of specialized software and training. Competition is necessary to adjust supply as quickly as possible to new technological options and to changing demand conditions. These steps are painful for a system that for seven decades relied on an information monopoly at the center and considered planned stability a virtue.

Military Industry

Although decades of debate have failed to establish just how large the defense-industrial sector's share of scare resources actually is, official Soviet statements agree in principle that the losses for the civilian economy are remarkably high. At the first Congress of People's Deputies in May 1989, Gorbachev presented a figure of 77.3 billion rubles as the 1989 defense budget—at the same time announcing a 14-per-cent cut for 1990–91.[59] This would represent less than 10 per cent of Soviet GNP. CIA/DIA estimates suggest that 15–17 per cent of Soviet GNP is devoted to the defense sector.[60] Others, including Andrew Marshall, consider the assumptions of the CIA/DIA estimate on military expenditures too narrow and the GNP estimates too high, leading them to estimate military expenditures at as much as 20–30 per cent of GNP.[61] While the annual growth rate of military expenditures decreased from 4 per cent during the early 1970s to 2 per cent in the late 1970s and 1980s,[62] the decrease in economic growth was even stronger (Table 1). Therefore the share of military expenditures in GNP was slightly higher in the 1980s than in the 1970s.

The defense economy is not totally separate from the civilian. In addition to its dependence on raw and basic materials, semifinished products, and equipment—all provided by the civilian sector—the defense economy's main production plants are organized under the same ministerial system as the rest of the economy. Machine manufacture and metalworking are divided among twenty ministries, of which nine are identified as military-oriented.[63] There is, however, some overlap in production activities. Not everything manufactured by these nine ministries, which account for 56 per cent of the output of all twenty ministries, is military equipment—and a portion of the output of the civilian ministries is used by the defense establishment.

Although the organizational structure of the military sector is similar to that of the overall economy, some special characteristics of the military economy may make it more efficient than the civilian. George Weickhardt emphasizes the following six points:

- The defense sector has a priority claim on labor and material resources;
- It pays higher salaries and provides better benefits;
- It faces competition in the form of an arms race with the West;
- There is competition among the military equipment design bureaus;
- Due to the provision of sufficient capacity, there is more continuity in design, development, and production than in the civilian sector; and
- The customer—the military service—acts as a monopsonist, placing it in a much stronger position to dictate its demands.[64]

Apart from the presence of competition in the military economy, there is no structural element in this list that is transferable to the economy as a whole. This may be of special disappointment to Gorbachev, but it also may explain why efforts to organize civilian industry in the same manner as the military have had only limited results.[65]

The relative efficiency of the military economy does not mean that it is efficient by Western standards. Inability to absorb and diffuse modern technology, especially information technology, is striking—even in the military sector.[66] This leads to a backwardness in key manufacturing technologies and to a simplicity of weapons design that makes Soviet equipment usable under almost any conditions but on the whole less sophisticated in comparison with Western equipment.[67] Richard Kaufman, one of the leading experts on the Soviet defense economy, concludes: "It will be difficult for the Soviets to prevent the technology gap from widening."[68]

U.S.–Soviet Economic Relations and U.S. Policy Options

Due to the isolationist nature of the centralized Soviet economy, foreign economic relations are not highly developed. This is particularly so in the case of trade with Western industrialized countries. The Soviet economy—the second largest in the world in GNP terms—accounts for only 1.7 per cent of the world's foreign trade. In comparison, the United States accounts for 14 per cent of total world trade, while Japan accounts for 8 per cent and West Germany for 10 per cent.[69] U.S. trade with the Soviet Union remains remarkably small—even compared to the low level of Soviet economic contact with other Western nations.

U.S.-Soviet economic relations have never constituted a significant portion of either superpower's total international economic activity—although at the end of the first détente period in 1975 they were more substantial than now (Table 3). Further damage to U.S.-Soviet trade—due to reactions to the Soviet invasion of Afghanistan—still has not been fully reversed. In 1988, the total level of U.S. exports to the Soviet Union reached $2.8 billion—almost twice as much as in 1987, but only three-quarters of the 1979 level (Table 4). U.S. imports from the USSR in 1988 were $0.65 billion, or less than a quarter of U.S. exports to the USSR—and also only about three-quarters of the 1979 import level. In 1988, the Soviet Union accounted for 0.4 per cent of total U.S. foreign trade (exports and imports), while the United States accounted for 0.9 per cent of Soviet trade.

The accompanying tables highlight major differences between U.S.-Soviet trade and the USSR's trade with other industrial countries. The products listed in Table 5 account for 81 per cent of U.S. exports to the Soviet Union, and for 57 per cent of U.S. imports from the USSR. The Soviet Union's Western European trade partners together export fourteen times more to the USSR than does the United States. Moreover, U.S. exports to the Soviet Union are pri-

Table 3. Respective Shares of U.S. and Soviet Trade (percentages)

	1970	1975	1980	1985	1987	1988
Soviet Share in U.S. Trade	0.2	1.0	0.6	0.4	0.3	0.4
U.S. Share in Soviet Trade	0.7	3.2	1.6	1.9	0.9	1.6
U.S. Share in Soviet Trade with the West[a]	3.4	10.1	4.8	7.1	4.3	6.8

[a]Member countries of the Organisation for Economic Co-operation and Development (OECD).

Source: *Vneshnyaya Torgovlya SSSR,* various volumes; and OECD *Statistics of Foreign Trade,* Series A, various volumes.

Table 4. U.S.-Soviet Trade, 1975–1988
($ billions)

	1979	1980	1983	1984	1985	1986	1987	1988
U.S. Exports	3.6	1.5	2.0	3.3	2.4	1.2	1.5	2.8
(of which Agriculture)	(2.9)	(1.0)	(1.5)	(2.8)	(1.8)	(0.60)	(0.90)	(1.4)
U.S. Imports	0.87	0.48	0.37	0.60	0.44	0.60	0.61	0.65
Trade Balance	2.7	1.0	1.6	2.7	2.0	0.60	1.0	2.1

Source: U.S. Department of Commerce and Bureau of the Census.

marily agricultural products and other raw materials. In 1987, raw materials (most of them agricultural produce) accounted for 66 per cent of U.S. exports to the Soviet Union (see Statistical Annexes, Table 9, p. 222). Manufactures represented only 15 per cent, and chemicals 18 per cent, of U.S. exports. In contrast, 68 per cent of Western European exports consisted of manufactured goods and an additional 17 per cent of chemicals. To some extent, this disparity is explained by advantages in geography and long-standing historical ties. But the primary constraints restricting U.S.-Soviet trade are deliberate U.S. policy choices.

The Jackson-Vanik Amendment of 1974 prevented the superpowers from enacting their October 1972 Agreement on Trade Relations, which would have granted most-favored-nation trade status to the USSR. Jackson-Vanik tied this trade agreement to a formal commitment by the Soviets to freedom of emigration.[70] In addition, the Stevenson Amendment of 1974 limits Soviet access to government-backed credits. A further constraint was placed on U.S.-Soviet trade relations when President Carter introduced an oil-drilling equipment embargo in response to human rights violations in 1978, and a grain embargo after the Afghanistan invasion in 1980. President Reagan lifted the grain embargo in 1981, but added additional sanctions limiting the export of equipment needed for the natural gas pipeline project of the early 1980s.[71] The measures affecting the gas pipeline agreement were eventually withdrawn at the Williamsburg Summit in 1983.

The Western allies have agreed for forty years not to transfer equipment and technology of military importance to the Soviet

Table 5. Major Commodities in U.S.-Soviet Trade, 1987 ($ millions)

U.S. Exports	$US millions	U.S. Imports	$US millions
Wheat	389	Anhydrous ammonia	69
Corn	381	Light fuel oils	56
Organic fertilizer	229	Rhodium	49
Soybean cake/meal	58	Palladium	30
Pressure-sensitive tape	56	Aluminum waste	26
Soybeans	43	Sable fur skins	19
Physical analytical equipment	39	Fuel oils (less 25 api)	17

Source: "U.S. Foreign Trade Statistics," prepared by USSR Division, U.S. Department of Commerce.

Union. Much more recently, an arrangement for common embargo measures in "high-tech" fields was established in 1980—following the Afghanistan invasion. This embargo was not lifted until the NATO Summit in May 1989. In addition, important differences have long characterized U.S. and Western European economic and political policies toward the USSR, as is clear from the sixteen-year history of the Conference on Security and Cooperation in Europe (CSCE). During the negotiations in Helsinki and Geneva (1973–75) as well as at the follow-up conferences between 1977 and 1989 (in Belgrade, Madrid, and Vienna), the Western Europeans have tended to give relatively greater weight to East-West cooperation than to accusing the Soviet Union of violations of the Helsinki Agreement as an effective means of decreasing East-West tensions.

In recent years, the Soviet Union has liberalized its emigration policy, freed most political prisoners, and taken some steps toward democratization and legal security for its citizens. The Vienna agreement of January 1989, signed within the framework of the CSCE, committed the USSR to far-reaching improvements in human rights. This progress merits some positive response from the United States concerning trade and economic cooperation. The waiver or repeal of Jackson-Vanik and the enactment of the 1972 (or a revised) trade agreement would be a positive first step toward improving the atmosphere surrounding U.S.-Soviet trade. The current stage of Soviet economic reform might permit a dramatic trade expansion—but one starting from an extremely low level. The main Soviet exports, oil and natural gas, are not of interest to the United States. Yet in a world trading system there is no need to balance U.S.-Soviet *bilateral* trade. If U.S. exports competed more intensively with Western European and Japanese companies that offer manufactured goods to the USSR, the bilateral U.S. trade surplus with the Soviet Union would increase further, thus contributing to the reduction of the overall U.S. trade deficit.

Although U.S.-Soviet trade has its limitations now, the United States could pursue collaborative ventures in high-tech services as well as cooperation in science and technology. The Soviets are very eager to attract U.S. capital and assistance in all fields of science and technology. It appears that this is the area in which the U.S.-Soviet relationship can prosper.

The U.S. comparative advantage in scientific cooperation and the new Soviet approach to attracting foreign capital gives the United States a favorable position in those fields in which expanded Soviet cooperation with the West is likely. Yet as of the end of 1988, the United States had only a 5.2 per cent share in $US joint venture investments within the Soviet Union. This placed the United States in ninth position—behind West Germany, Italy, Yugoslavia, France, Finland, Austria, Switzerland, and Japan (in that order).[72]

The United States should, as President Bush pointed out at the Malta Summit meeting, contribute to integrating the Soviet Union into the international economy, encouraging its participation as a less hostile and more competitive partner. The United States should also exercise its own comparative advantage in high-tech services by founding joint ventures in growth sectors such as technical education, operational analysis, and management consulting.[73] Western Europe and Japan are already moving into this area. The constraints imposed on the United States by its twin deficits and the strong interest already shown by Western Europe in promoting Soviet reform make coordination with other NATO countries extremely important. Most-favored-nation trade status and access to credits should be granted to the Soviet Union by all Western countries, and the denial of technology transfer should be limited to technology that is of military significance according to a narrow definition.

The window of opportunity to transform the Soviet economy might close again if no major coordinated Western effort is made to help stabilize the process of *perestroika*. The common denominator of a harmonized approach should be acknowledgment that *perestroika* is also in the Western interest and that improvements in productivity and consumer goods supply in the Soviet economy are a necessary precondition for the survival of *perestroika*. Furthermore, the USSR's access to and implementation of a higher technological standard is in the interest of a global environmental policy. Therefore the gradual integration of the Soviet economy into the world economy merits priority over ideological reservations. The first step to such integration should be the normalization of the relationship between the Soviet Union and the Western alliance as a whole.

Notes

Note: The author would like to thank Jonathan Lipow and Gregory Chen for their research assistance and careful help in improving the presentation of this chapter.

[1]Radio Liberty, *Report on the USSR*, Vol. 1, No. 47 (November 24, 1989), pp. 28–29. A draft program calling for the introduction of private property, free markets, and a sharply reduced governmental role in the economy was the main subject of discussion at the conference, attended by some 1,300 participants.

[2]Keith Bush, "An Appraisal of the Soviet Economic Reform, Soviet Economic Performance: 1966–67," Study Papers submitted to the Joint Economic Committee, U.S. Congress, Washington, D.C., 1968, pp. 129–44; and Philip Hanson, "Success Indicators Revisited: The July 1979 Soviet Decree on Planning and Management," *Soviet Studies* (January 1983), pp. 1–13.

[3]Tatyana Zaslavskaya (Professor of sociology at the Novosibirsk branch of the Soviet Academy of Sciences), "The Novosibirsk Report," English translation, *Survey* (London), Vol. 28, No. 1 (Spring 1984), p. 90.

[4]For example, in a 1984 article analyzing the alternatives of economic reforms in the Soviet Union a year before Gorbachev came to power, Ed A. Hewett wrote: "It is highly improbable that the Soviet leadership will begin seriously to contemplate radical reforms before the end of this decade. So many vested interests in the party and the goverment would be affected by such reforms, and so much political and economic uncertainty associated with them, that they will be undertaken only if there appears to be no other alternative." Ed A. Hewett, "Economic Reform in the Soviet Union," *The Brookings Review* (Spring 1984), p. 11.

[5]See also Hewett, op. cit., p. 11. Hewett writes: "Radical reforms . . . assume that only by revamping all parts of the system simultaneously will it be possible to deal effectively with performance problems." Similarly, Leonid Abalkin, one of the leading economic advisors to Gorbachev and Deputy Prime Minister since June 1989, wrote in an article in the Party theoretical journal, *Kommunist*: "Economic reforms that are specially intended to bring about radical improvements in the economy cannot be achieved without simultaneous and corresponding changes in the political system and in the social and intellectual sphere." See (English translation of article) Leonid Abalkin, "Relying on the Lessons of the Past," *Problems of Economics* (June 1988), p. 9.

[6]As described by Richard E. Ericson in his excellent inside view *The Soviet Statistical Debate: Khanin vs. TsSu* [Central Statistical Office of the Soviet Union], Occasional Paper No. 1, Harriman Institute for Advanced Study of the Soviet Union, February 1988, revised May 1988.

[7]Abel Aganbegyan, "The Economics of Perestroika," *International Affairs*, Vol. 64, No. 2 (Spring 1988), p. 177.

[8]*Petroleum Economist*, Vol. 53, No. 6 (June 1987), p. 252.

[9]See *Vneshnyaya Torgovlya SSSR za 1983 goda,* Moscow, 1984.

[10]*PlanEcon Report,* Vol. IV, Nos. 30–31 (August 5, 1988), p. 16.

[11]These are the official Soviet trade figures. Using an adjusted exchange rate, the importance of trade with the West would increase. "The increased dependence of the Soviet economy on trade with non-socialist countries could thus be labeled as Gorbachev's quiet or hidden revolution," *PlanEcon Report,* Vol. 5, Nos. 13–14 (April 7, 1989), p. 34.

[12]Philip Hanson, "Soviet Foreign Trade Policies in the 1980s," *Berichte des Bundesinstituts fuer ostwissenschaftliche und internationale Studien,* No. 41, 1986, p. 66.

[13]In 1976, the Soviet Union had a share of 6 per cent in the OECD countries machinery imports from non-OECD countries. This share declined to 1 per cent in 1987. During the same time period, the share of the non-OECD Far Eastern countries expanded from 43 per cent to 68 per cent. In 1975, 16 per cent of the OECD countries' imports of road vehicles came from the Soviet Union. This share declined to 5 per cent in 1987. Over the same period, the non-OECD Far Eastern countries' share grew from 8 per cent to 42 per cent OECD, *Statistics of Foreign Trade,* Series C.

[14]Ibid., p. 60.

[15]*PlanEcon Report,* Vol. IV, Nos. 30–31 (August 5, 1988), pp. 14, 18.

[16]Ibid., *PlanEcon Report,* Vol. V, Nos. 13–14 (April 7, 1989), p. 5. According to Soviet statistics, growth of exports to OECD countries grew by 3.4 per cent and imports by 18 per cent. Ministry for Foreign Economic Relations, *Vneshnie ekonomicheskie cviazi SSSR v 1988 g,* Moscow, 1989.

[17]These figures are drawn from different estimates (OECD, ECE, and The Vienna Institute) that exclude the debts of the Moscow-based Council of Mutual Economic Assistance (CMEA or Comecon) banks. See Jan Stankovsky, "East-West Trade 1987–89: Slight Improvement in Sight," *Forschungsberichte* (The Vienna Institute for Comparative Economic Studies), No. 150 (October 1988), Table 37.

[18]See, for instance, Nikolai Shmelyev and Vladimir Popov, *The Turning Point: Revitalizing the Soviet Economy* (New York: Doubleday Books, 1989), Chapter 8.

[19]In a fascinating two-volume theoretical work written in the late 1970s, the Hungarian economist Janos Kornai describes "shortage," not only in consumer goods but also in investment goods, as a built-in phenomenon in socialist economies. His ideas have had a major influence on the reform discussion in the Soviet Union. See Janos Kornai, *Economics of Shortage* (New York: North Holland Publishing Company, 1980).

[20]In his May 30, 1989 speech to the first Peoples' Deputies Congress, Gorbachev praised the market as the most efficient and democratic mechanism. *Pravda,* May 31, 1989. (See also note 23 below).

[21]Radio Liberty, *Report on the USSR,* Vol. 1, No. 47 (November 24, 1989), pp. 28–29.

[22]There is a basic consensus among Soviet reform-oriented politicians and analysts that a price reform is necessary. Gorbachev pointed out in his speech to the Central Committee on June 25, 1987 (and has repeated later in different versions): "A radical reform of the pricing system is a most important part of the economic overhaul. Without it a complete transition to the new mechanism is impossible." Others, including Abel Aganbegyan have discussed the problem more extensively. See Aganbegyan, "The Economics of Perestroika," op. cit., p. 184.

[23]This was acknowleged by Gorbachev when he said in his major speech at the first Congress of People's Deputies on May 30, 1989: "The market is, of course, not omnipotent. Mankind has not yet, however, created an economic mechanism that is more efficient and more democratic." *Pravda,* May 31, 1989.

[24]"Intensive growth" means growth that is not the result of higher input but of productivity gains within the production process.

[25]Mikhail Gorbachev, *Perestroika* (New York: Harper & Row, 1987). A chronology of "major decrees and associated policy measures" up to July 1987 is given by Ed A. Hewett, *Reforming the Soviet Economy* (Washington, D.C.: The Brookings Institution, 1988), pp. 360–64.

[26]Ibid., pp. 260–73.

[27]Released on June 30, 1987 and published in *Pravda* on July 1, 1987.

[28]Hewett, *Reforming the Soviet Economy,* op. cit., p. 341.

[29]*PlanEcon Report,* Vol. V, No. 17 (April 28, 1988), pp. 6–7.

[30]*Journal of Commerce,* April 7, 1989.

[31]*Financial Times,* November 29, 1988, p. A7.

[32]*Wall Street Journal,* December 12, 1988, p. A9.

[33]In 1988, this privilege was applied to 55 ministries and departments and more than 160 associations, enterprises, and organizations (*Moscow News,* No. 2, 1988, p. 7), and in 1989 it was extended to all economic entities.

[34]*Novoe Vremya,* No. 19, 1989, p. 16; quoted by Radio Liberty, *Report on the USSR,* Vol. 1, No. 24 (June 16, 1989).

[35]Steven Rosefielde recommends the introduction of a partially convertible ruble even before a major price reform. It would allow Soviet companies to bid for foreign currencies in competition with other domestic bidders. This might have an educational effect inside the Soviet Union. Many doubt, however, that this will allow approximation of an optimal monetary flow. See Steven Rosefielde, *U.S.-Soviet Relations: An Agenda for the Future, Part 4: A (Partially) Convertible Ruble* (Washington, D.C.: The Johns Hopkins University, Foreign Policy Institute, School of Advanced International Studies, November 1988).

[36]Radio Liberty, *Report on the USSR*, Vol. 1, No. 46 (November 17, 1989), p. 29.

[37]See, for instance, Leonid Abalkin, "Restructuring the Management of the Economy," *Problems of Economics*, August 1988, p. 19 (translated from *Voprosy Economiki*, No. 12, 1987); and Abel Aganbegyan, *The Economic Challenge of Perestroika* (Bloomington and Indianapolis: Indiana University Press, 1988), pp. 125–39.

[38]*Moscow News*, Supplement to No. 22 (3322), May 29, 1988, p. 3.

[39]"[T]he concept of a reform of price formation has been worked out, the methods are being discussed, and the reform is scheduled to be in place in 1989 and 1990." Abel Aganbegyan, "Basic Directions of Perestroyka," *Soviet Economy*, Vol. 3, No. 4 (1987), p. 282.

[40]Professor Leonid Abalkin, head of the Institute of Economics at the Academy of Sciences, stated in December 1988 that price reform had been indefinitely delayed and that it would not currently be a good idea because of the faltering state of the economy. *The Financial Times*, December 2, 1988, p. 1.

[41]Radio Liberty, *Report on the USSR*, Vol. 1, No. 47, November 24, 1989, pp. 28–29.

[42]Gertraud Seidenstecher, "Zum Stand der Finanzund Kreditreform im Rahmen der Perestrojka," *Berichte des Bundesinstituts fuer ostwissenschaftliche und internationale Studien*, No. 33, 1988.

[43]*PlanEcon Report*, Vol. IV, No. 32–33 (August 19, 1988), p. 16.

[44]*Literaturnaya Gazeta*, No. 4, January 25, 1989, p. 11.

[45]Radio Liberty, *Report on the USSR*, Vol. 1, No. 26 (June 30, 1989), p. 8.

[46]Aaron Trehub, "The Congress of People's Deputies on Poverty," Radio Liberty, *Report on the USSR*, Vol. 1, No. 24 (June 16, 1989), pp. 5–8.

[47]According to Academician Vladimir Tikhonov, "[m]ore than $22 billion of equipment, including some of it imported, already lies around unused." *The Wall Street Journal*, December 2, 1988, p. A12.

[48]Flynn and Severin, op. cit., p. 65.

[49]Judith Flynn and Barbara Severin, "Soviet Agricultural Transport: Bottlenecks to Continue," *Gorbachev's Economic Plans*, Vol. 2, Study Papers submitted to the Joint Economic Committee, U.S. Congress, Washington, D.C., November 23, 1987, pp. 62–78. See also Padma Desai, *The Soviet Economy: Problems and Prospects* (Oxford: Basil Blackwell, 1987), p. 187.

[50]Nancy J. Cochrane, "The Private Sector in East European Agriculture," *Problems of Communism*, Vol. 37, No. 2 (March/April 1988), pp. 47–53.

[51]Penelope Doolittle and Margaret Hughes, "Gorbachev's Agricultural Policy: Building on the Brezhnev Food Program," *Gorbachev's Economic Plans*, Vol. 2, Study Papers submitted to the Joint Economic Committee, U.S. Congress, Washington, D.C., November 23, 1987, p. 42.

[52]"Just look at what is being done by people working under family contracts and lease arrangements. Using the same and sometimes even worse facilities, they show incomparably better results. . . . Man should be offered to give free rein to his talent as a manager. . . . Lease-based relations allow fuller use of the possibilities of socialist property principle . . . the leases, it appears, should be of a long-term nature and granted for a period, say, of 25–30 and even 50 years." Mikhail Gorbachev, Report to a Plenary Meeting of the CPSU Central Committee on July 29, 1988, *Moscow News*, Supplement to No. 33, 1988, p. 3.

[53]See, for example, the article of Academician Vladimir Tikhonov of the All-Union V.I. Lenin Academy of Agricultural Science: "Time for Land Reform," *Moscow News*, No. 32, 1988, p. 10.

[54]Erik Whitlock, "Soviet Agriculture After the March Plenum," Radio Liberty, *Report on the USSR*, Vol. 1, No. 17 (April 28, 1989), pp. 5–7.

[55]"State ownership of land must be abolished so that the Soviets must grant land to those who can cultivate it." Vladimir Tikhonov, "Landownership," *Moscow News*, No. 26, July 2–9, 1989, p. 12.

[56]See Judith A. Thornton, *U.S.-Soviet Relations—An Agenda for the Future, A New Export Regime for Information Technologies*, FPI Policy Briefs (Washington, D.C.: The John Hopkins University, Foreign Policy Institute, School of Advanced International Studies, November 1988).

[57]Thornton, *U.S.-Soviet Relations*, op. cit., pp. 8–9.

[58]Richard W. Judy, op. cit., p. 165, quoting *Pravda,* June 12, 1989, p. 2.

[59]*Pravda,* May 31, 1989.

[60]"Gorbachev's Economic Program: Problems Emerge," Report by the Central Intelligence Agency and the Defense Intelligence Agency presented to the Subcommittee on National Security Economics of the Joint Economic Committee, U.S. Congress, Washington, D.C., April 13, 1988, p. 2.

[61]Andrew W. Marshall, "Defense Industry and the Economy, Commentary," *Gorbachev's Economic Plans,* Vol. 1, Study Papers submitted to the Joint Economic Committee, U.S. Congress, Washington, D.C., November 23, 1987, pp. 481–84.

[62]Richard F. Kaufman, "Economic Reform and the Soviet Military," *The Washington Quarterly* (Summer 1988), p. 202.

[63]Norbert D. Michaud, Stephen O. Maddalena, and Michael J. Barry, "Defense Industry and the Economy: Commentary," *Gorbachev's Economic Plans,* Vol. 1, Study Papers submitted to the Joint Economic Committee, U.S. Congress, Washington, D.C., November 23, 1987, pp. 485–90.

[64]George G. Weickhardt, "The Soviet Military-Industrial Complex and Economic Reform," *Soviet Economy,* No. 2, pp. 195–96.

[65]Ibid., p. 205.

[66]Lee D. Badgett, *Defeated by a Maze: The Soviet Economy and its Defense-Industrial Sector,* The RAND Corporation, N–2644–NA, October 1988, p. 37.

[67]Kaufman, "Economic Reform and the Soviet Military," op. cit., p. 205.

[68]Ibid., p. 206.

[69]Figures for 1988 from IMF *International Financial Statistics,* Vol. 42, No. 1, 1989; and *PlanEcon Report,* Vol. V, Nos. 13–14 (April 7, 1989).

[70]Vladimir N. Pregelj, "U.S. Trade Relations with the Soviet Union Since World War II: A Chronology," CRS Report for Congress, April 15, 1989.

[71]For a more detailed analysis of U.S. restrictions in trade and cooperation with the Soviet Union, see Hertha Heiss, "U.S.-Soviet Trade Trends," *Gorbachev's Economic Plans,* Vol. 2, Study Papers submitted to the Joint Economic Committee, U.S. Congress, Washington, D.C., November 23, 1989, pp. 467–72.

[72]*PlanEcon Report,* Vol. V, Nos. 10–12 (March 24, 1989), p. 15.

[73]The four top sectors/industrial branches of joint ventures with Western participation are: business services, engineering services, machine building, and computers. See *PlanEcon Report,* Vol. V, Nos. 10–12 (March 24, 1989), p. 15.

Chapter 2

Issues in Chinese Economic Reform

Rensselaer W. Lee III

Introduction

In December 1978, roughly two years after the death of Mao Zedong, the leaders of the People's Republic of China (PRC) initiated an ambitious program of economic "adjustment and reform." Two major objectives characterized the reform program. The first goal was to decentralize—to shift to lower levels—responsibility for most economic decisions. In industry, this meant transfering economic and financial authority to local governments and (more importantly) to enterprises, as well as expanding the role of the marketplace in allocating industrial output. In agriculture, decentralization meant dismantling the people's communes, restoring household agriculture, and giving peasants some choice in the crops they could produce. The second and related objective of Chinese reforms was to expand economic and technological cooperation with the West, including, of course, Japan. The opening to the West was seen as critical to building a modern industrial base; it resulted in a sharp expansion of Sino-Western trade and a large flow of foreign technology and capital into China.

A decade of reform has produced important structural changes in China. Enterprises have more financial authority than they did under Mao. A wide range of goods and services is allocated by market forces rather than by government fiat. A dynamic non-state industrial sector has emerged that accounts for more than 40 per cent of industrial output. Networks of private financial institutions have arisen to support this sector. Such changes have clearly benefited China—by accelerating economic growth, especially in agriculture and light industry; by improving urban and rural living standards dramatically; and by reducing the long-standing income gap between urban and rural areas.

However, China is still far from being a market economy. Prices of many products are still controlled. Many industrial enterprises are in effect appendages of central ministries or local industrial bureaus. In 1988, the government spent about $12 billion on subsidies to inefficient state enterprises. Competition (especially in the heavy industrial sector) is weakly developed. Inter-ministry and inter-regional rivalries preclude the development of a unified national market. At the same time, the reform program has spawned a number of economic and political problems: high inflation rates, regional economic separatism, increasing social inequality, and extensive corruption within the Party and government elites.

The net effect of these problems has been to slow the pace of reform. Since the fall of 1988, the leadership has responded to them, especially to inflation, by tightening central control over the economy. Both the reforms and the austerity measures engendered widespread dissatisfaction that found an outlet in the pro-democracy movement of April-June 1989. The brutal suppression of this movement by troops of the People's Liberation Army presaged a further slowdown in the pace of reform. Beijing's policies as of the fall of 1989 emphasized strengthening central planning, giving priority to the state-owned economic sector, and "putting down the counterrevolutionary rebellion."

China's opening to the West has been less controversial politically than the domestic reforms—the Chinese leadership broadly recognizes the country's need for foreign capital and technology. However, China's bureaucratic system in many ways limits the potential for normal commercial relations with the outside world. Furthermore, China's current political instability—epitomized by the Tiananmen Square massacre—has damaged China's foreign economic relations. China's foreign trade will grow much more slowly this year than last, and new foreign investment and international lending will probably decline.

The reform movement in China raises important questions for U.S. policy. In general, the United States would prefer that China increasingly adopt Western concepts of market economics, legal rights, and democratic pluralism. The current Chinese leadership, for its part—although formally still committed to economic reform—seemingly is unwilling to push for key structural changes, especially in the price system and the socialist ownership system. Politically, the leadership apparently wants to turn back the clock—to reintroduce authoritarian communist patterns. A change in the top Chinese leadership might well stimulate economic reform. The United States cannot, however, directly influence political developments in China. For the time being, the most appropriate strategy for the United States is to (1) scale back government-to-government contacts with the present regime, and (2) maintain the existing network of private U.S.-China contacts, exchanges, and economic ties that clearly have provided—and will continue to provide—the impetus for economic and political reform in China.

Ingredients of Reform

Rationale

China's economic policies after 1978 marked a significant departure from the Maoist development model that had guided the Chinese economy for much of the post–1949 period. Under Mao, economic decisionmaking had been overbureaucratized; virtually all key economic decisions—those on output, prices, product mix, and investment, for example—had been made outside the enterprise by central or local government authorities. The decisions of government bureaucrats often failed to reflect the production conditions at the factory or farm level. Production units in industry and agriculture thus had little incentive to improve performance.

By the late 1970s, the Maoist model had ceased to serve China's economic needs in crucial respects. For example, an ever-increasing percentage of resources was being mobilized to obtain an ever-declining payoff in terms of economic output. From the mid–1950s to the late 1970s, investment (accumulation) as a share of national income had increased from 24.2 per cent to 33.3 per cent; yet the rate of growth of national income had declined from 8.9 per cent to 6.0 per cent.[1] Development of heavy industry had been overemphasized. Much of China's capital stock had become obsolete. Total factor productivity (of labor and capital combined) in state enterprises had stagnated since the late 1950s. Serious imbalances and shortages had developed in the economy, and the huge investments required to maintain growth had precluded significant improvements in living standards.[2]

Moreover, under the old model, China's pattern of growth for much of the Maoist period was essentially autarkic. Maoist self-reliance policies discouraged the expansion of trade ties with Western countries, ruled out foreign investment and foreign loans, and made little attempt to integrate China into the world economy. During periods of hyper-nationalism such as the Great Leap Forward (1958–60) and the Cultural Revolution (1966–76), the study of Western science and technology was officially discouraged. Engineers and scientists were told to rely instead on the "wisdom and creativity" of the Chinese masses.

Maoist doctrine provided a unifying focus for Chinese development and thus served an important historical function. However, the "extensive" model of growth of the pre-reform era—increasing rates of investment combined with decreasing rates of return—could not be sustained indefinitely. Furthermore, China was simply too far behind the West economically, scientifically, and technologically to close its doors to foreign influence. As one writer in the early post-Maoist period acidly remarked, "Does patriotism mean that while Westerners take the train, Chinese must stick to the donkey, or that Westerners can use electronic computers but Chinese must make do with the abacus?"[3]

Trends in Domestic Reform

The economic reforms that evolved between 1978 and 1988 were designed to correct the imbalances and pathologies of the Maoist era, and, in general, to make the economy function more successfully. Changes were introduced piecemeal and were modified continually to cope with unforeseen problems. Moreover, no national consensus emerged on the goals of reform. Chinese leaders agreed on the need to abandon what State Council Premier Li Peng called the "old economic mode marked by overcentralized, excessive, and rigid control." They disagreed, however, on crucial issues such as price reform, the role of labor and capital markets, the privatization of state controlled industry, and the division of economic authority between the center and the regions.

Yet a reform consensus of sorts did take shape in China during the 1980s and did push the country some distance in the direction of a market economy. First, Beijing granted state enterprises greater financial autonomy, allowing them to retain a much larger share of their profits—45 per cent in the mid–1980s compared with 4 per cent in 1978.[4] Furthermore, enterprises were given some discretion in using retained earnings. They could spend them on capital construction, new equipment, or bonuses and guest houses for their workers. As a consequence of the reforms, the state's direct role in financing investment greatly diminished. In 1978, the state budget accounted for 66 per cent of fixed investment in the state sector; by

1985, that share had shrunk to 26 per cent, with most investment funds coming from enterprise profits and bank loans.[5]

Second, the reforms reduced mandatory planning in allocating products. The state sets prices and output targets for fewer products today than it did in the pre-reform period, introducing considerable flexibility in the pricing system. Above-plan industrial output (such as "surplus" coal and steel) and cash crops (such as vegetables and fruits and most consumer goods) can be sold at market prices or at prices that float within specified limits. Prices of planned output either are fixed by the state—China's State Planning Commission, for example, decides the output levels and prices of twenty industrial raw materials—or are negotiated between factory managers and the bureaucracy. China is very far from having a completely free market economy, but prices and costs are no longer determined entirely by government fiat.

Third, the reforms produced the rapid growth of non-state (that is, private or collective) enterprises. The share of the non-state sector in industrial output has increased markedly—from 14 per cent in 1979 to more than 40 per cent in 1988.[6] In the eastern coastal provinces, for example Jiangsu and Guangdong, the share is well above 50 per cent. Private, usually family-owned enterprises apparently constitute the most dynamic sector of Chinese industry. Such enterprises accounted for 1.9 per cent of the gross output value of industry in 1985, 3.6 per cent in 1987, and an estimated 5 per cent in 1988.[7] (However, the retrenchment instituted by Beijing in late 1988 seems likely to slow the growth of the private sector.) The emerging non-state sector in China in many cases is supported by extra-bank financing. Companies borrow from trust and investment companies, farmers' cooperatives, and companies based in Hong Kong—or they raise money by issuing bonds or selling shares of stock. As of late 1988, roughly 6,000 Chinese enterprises, mostly in the non-state sector, had sold shares, and a few issues are publicly traded in small stock markets in Shanghai, Shenyang, and Tianjin.[8]

Fourth, the reforms have begun to change China's labor system—the so-called "Iron Rice Bowl" that has guaranteed workers life-long employment and cradle-to-grave social welfare. This system has retarded the development of a market economy. For instance, government departments allocate most industrial labor, and the mobility of labor among enterprises is severely restricted. Workers in state enterprises receive an impressive array of entitlements, such as housing allowances, injury-disability and retirement insurance, medical care, and bonuses (usually distributed regardless of performance). Such entitlements burden the enterprise financially and sap efficiency. Featherbedding is rampant, and although factory managers theoretically have the right to fire workers, there is tremendous social and political pressure to retain factory workers in their jobs permanently. This is because China has no comprehensive social welfare system outside the workplace.

The labor system, however, is changing—if slowly. For example, regulations passed in September 1986 stipulate that most new workers will be hired and fired under a competitive contract system. There is discussion of establishing unemployment insurance and a pension system. The chance for enterprises to recruit labor independently has improved; there are even employment agencies in some cities, and jobs sometimes are advertised in local newspapers. These initiatives are still in an embryonic stage, however; for instance, managers are under considerable pressure to renew contracts, and some of the so-called temporary worker-enterprise contracts expire after ten or more years.

Fifth, the reforms are beginning to chip away at the very bedrock of the socialist system of state ownership and control of industry. A bankruptcy law put into effect in November 1988 is intended to "promote the independent operation" of state enterprises. In theory, the threat of bankruptcy makes the enterprise responsible for its own profits and losses; in practice, however, the government probably will not allow most of the enterprises that it now subsidizes to go out of business. Many prominent reformers advocate the partial privatization of state enterprises, transforming enterprises into joint-stock companies. (Shareholders would include government organizations, banks, other enterprises, workers, and the public at large, and would be represented by boards of directors.) Advocates of a shareholding system say it would foster the "separation of government and enterprises" and in general would rationalize economic decisionmaking. However, the regime has indicated that the selling of shares in state enterprises would be limited to a few "pilot experiments." (One example is the Golden Cup Auto Corporation in Shenyang, which in July 1988 issued stock that could be freely traded.) Whether or how rapidly the shareholding system develops doubtless will depend on the overall fate of economic reform.[9]

Finally, the reforms have radically changed the agricultural system. The communes, Mao's radical experiment of 1958, were functionally abolished and control over agricultural land was transfered to individual peasant households. Although land is still collectively owned, peasants can rent it on contract for periods of at least fifteen years. Since 1985, when the state stopped mandatory purchases of agricultural products, peasants in theory have been free to decide what crops to grow and whether to sell their crops to the government or on the open market. Informal pressure from village bosses (and ultimately from the state) hedge these freedoms to some extent, but direct government intervention in agricultural production is largely a thing of the past.[10]

Evaluating the Domestic Reforms

The Benefits

The reforms have produced clear economic benefits for China. Statistics in Table 1 suggest that the reforms accelerated the growth of agriculture and light industry more rapidly than that of heavy industry. State ownership is more pronounced in the heavy industrial sector, which probably accounts for the relative absence of dynamism in that sector.

Table 1. Percentage Changes in Economic Growth: Pre-Reform and Reform

	Pre-Reform		Reform
	1952-78	1970-78	1979-87
Gross value of industrial and agricultural output	595%	80%	198%
Agriculture	203	37	175
Industry	1,111	100	195
Light industry	711	87	225
Heavy industry	1,844	111	172

Source: State Statistical Bureau, *Statistical Yearbook of China 1988*, p. 34.

Furthermore, the reforms have raised living standards. Peasant income more than tripled between 1978 and 1987, and the income of urban residents more than doubled. The corresponding rural-urban income gap narrowed from about 4.6 to 1 to about 3.1 to 1. Rural per capita expenditures on consumer goods, services, and recreation increased more rapidly between 1978 and 1987 than they did over the much longer period from 1952 to 1978. Nationally, savings deposits per capita rose from 2.19 billion renminbi (RMB) in 1978 to 28.64 billion RMB in 1987; the number of television sets per 100 people increased from 0.3 to 10.7; the number of bicycles per hundred people rose from 7.7 to 27.1; and pork consumption per capita increased from 2.7 kilograms to 14.54 kilograms. In sum, the reforms produced revolutionary changes in the livelihoods of the Chinese people, especially in the countryside.[11]

The Side Effects of Reform

A number of problems have accompanied China's transition from a planned to a quasi-market economy: unprecedentedly high inflation rates, increasing regional self-assertion (vis-à-vis the central government and other regions), growing social and regional inequality, and extensive corruption in Party and government organs. These problems, which are discussed below in more detail, are side effects of reform—but they also reflect the incompleteness of the reform process.

Inflation. Inflation in China has assumed politically unacceptable proportions. In 1988, the official inflation rate was 18.5 per cent—compared to 7.3 per cent in 1987, 4.3 per cent for 1979–1988, and 1.2 per cent (on average) in the pre-reform era (1951–1978).[12] In China's cities, the rate reportedly approached 30 per cent. Inevitably, there were rumblings of discontent. Said a worker in a Shanghai metal factory, "I wish we could go back to Mao's day. At that time, we had no inflation and we were guaranteed a certain living standard. Now I can hardly afford to feed my family."[13] Such sentiments undoubtedly prompted some workers' groups to display posters of Mao Zedong during the April-June pro-democracy demonstrations in Beijing.

What precipitated such high rates of inflation? A proximate cause was the leadership's decision in mid–1988 to eliminate price controls on certain products, such as pork, eggs, sugar, and vegetables. More fundamental inflationary factors were, however, at work. One of these was uneven growth in the economy. In 1988, for example, the manufacturing sector grew by 23 per cent, and investment in fixed assets (including capital construction) grew by 18.5 per cent. In comparison, the production of industrial raw materials increased by 10.8 per cent and energy production by a mere 4.8 per cent, while cotton production declined by 1.1 per cent. Such imbalances put tremendous upward pressure on the prices of energy and raw materials. Moreover, lagging grain production—per capita output dropped 11 per cent between 1984 and 1988—directly or indirectly contributed to inflation. (Low official grain prices drove peasants to cultivate more profitable crops, such as citrus fruit, peanuts, and sugar cane.) In addition, personal income grew much faster than national output: In 1988, income from wages and other sources rose 26.5 per cent, 5.8

per cent more than the income from national industries and 23.3 per cent more than agricultural income.[14]

A second source of inflationary pressure was deficit spending by central and local governments. In 1988, China's budget deficit was estimated by the Central Intelligence Agency (CIA) at about $9.5 billion or approximately 2.5 per cent of GNP. The deficit is growing rapidly; according to the CIA estimate, it increased by 400 per cent from 1985 to 1988.[15] Helping to create the deficit were huge price subsidies (more than $2 billion in 1988) and massive outlays for capital construction projects. Subsidies to inefficient state-run factories rose to $12 billion in 1988—18 per cent more than in 1987.[16] Government spending apparently far exceeded tax revenues, which fell as a percentage of national income from about 32 per cent in 1979 to 19 per cent in 1988. The state financed its deficit by expanding the money supply by 47 per cent in 1988 and by an average of 36 per cent from 1984 to 1988.[17]

In September 1988, in an attempt to confront severe inflation and an economy that Politburo hardliners perceived to be careening out of control, the Chinese regime initiated a campaign to "rectify the economic order." The retrenchment, apparently spearheaded by State Council Premier Li Peng, seemed comprehensive enough. Beijing decreed a near-moratorium on price decontrol for at least two years. Indeed Beijing reimposed price controls on steel, copper, aluminum, and other production materials. The leadership also announced plans to cut state investment spending by 20 per cent in 1989.[18] Between September 1988 and March 1989, at least 18,000 construction projects were cancelled or suspended, eliminating possibly millions of construction jobs. Bank branches nationwide were ordered to rein in credit and to raise interest rates on loans. Particularly affected were small-scale manufacturing ventures, which were deemed "inefficient" users of energy and raw materials, and "nonproductive" construction projects such as hotels and guesthouses. An estimated 17,000 companies, most in the private or collective sector, closed down in late 1988 and early 1989. From the end of 1988 to the end of June 1989, the number of small private businesses (those employing less than eight workers) declined 15 per cent, and employment in such enterprises dropped 16 per cent.[19] Some foreign ventures that needed local financing to pay bills and to purchase supplies were hurt by the credit squeeze. In the countryside, the government began paying the peasants for grain with IOUs instead of cash, further reducing the incentives for peasants to grow grain.

In general, the cure seemed worse than the disease. In April-June 1989, inflation was still running at an annual rate of 23.9 per cent and in the first six months of 1989, the rate was 25.5 per cent.

At the same time, the government's actions had both reduced economic activity and increased unemployment. Such *economic* pressures helped to generate the massive popular challenge to the regime's authority—the pro-democracy movement of April-June 1989. Beijing's austerity policies now seem to be producing "stagflation." During 1989, industrial growth slowed much faster than inflation. Growth for the January-October 1989 period was 7.7 per cent (compared to 20.7 per cent for all of 1988), but inflation remained above 20 per cent. As of November 1989, the State Planning Commission was projecting an inflation rate of 20 per cent for the year (compared to 18.5 per cent for 1988).[20]

Regionalism. Regionalism is predominantly a legacy of China's experience in local self-sufficiency. Under Mao Zedong, provincial and even sub-provincial units (prefectures) were encouraged to build "small, comprehensive industrial systems." Consequently, most provinces and hundreds of prefectures are engaged in a wide range of economic activities. For example, fertilizer, steel products, cloth, and food grains are produced in all of Jiangsu's fourteen prefectures.[21] The reforms tended to increase provincial control over industry, investment, and tax revenues. (Today, for example, the central government commands about 45 per cent of national tax revenues, compared with about 60 per cent in the 1970s.)[22] Moreover, the economic planning function in China has largely devolved from the center to the regions. Provinces manage their own foreign trade plans, trading corporations, and foreign exchange revenues. Private financial networks are well developed in certain regions such as Guangdong, Fujian, and Jiangsu.

This dispersal of economic and financial authority has enabled provinces to challenge central authority. For example, despite the austerity program that has been under way since September 1988, Guangdong's spending in regionally controlled investment projects rose by 58 per cent in January and February 1989, compared with such spending in the same period in 1988. Regional investment also increased in 10 other provinces, although not as dramatically. As of the fall of 1989, Beijing planned to recentralize economic control by creating several regional bureaus that would serve as "an administrative tier" between the provinces and the central government and would "enable the Politburo and the State Council to ensure that their orders are carried out throughout China."[23] Adding another layer of bureaucracy will not in itself, however, do much to rein in the provinces.

Regional challenges to the central government's authority are probably good for reform, as they promote diversity and dynamism in the economic system. Less favorable to reform, however, is the growth of trade wars among regions and localities. Schooled in the idea of self-sufficiency, provincial officials associate economic success with increased forward integration: Regions that produce cotton and silk want to create textiles; tobacco-producing regions want to manufacture cigarettes; wool-producing regions want to operate spinning mills; non-ferrous metal-producing regions want to manufacture automobile parts. Intense inter-provincial competition bids up the prices of scarce raw materials. Provinces have established customs barriers both to protect local industries and to prevent the outflow of scarce raw materials. For example, in 1988, Sichuan's provincial government barred shipments of silk to consumers outside the province. Entrepreneurs from Guangdong managed to circumvent the prohibition, however, by "paying high commissions and even using military vehicles to transport the silk through Sichuan's checkpoints."[24]

Inequality and Corruption. Although life in China by all indications improved over the past decade, the economic reforms also exacerbated social divisions. They narrowed income differences between the cities and the countryside, but they also worsened the income inequalities among regions, creating a new class of rich peasants in the countryside (the so-called "10,000-yuan households") and producing a system of privilege, favoritism, and corruption in the cities. The abandonment of egalitarianism by the regime was intentional; the Dengist maxim, "To get rich is glorious," replaced the Maoist ideal, "Serve the people."[25] The social effects of the reforms have aroused widespread resentment and—as the pro-democracy movement showed—demands for a change in leadership.

Regionally, the important division is between the coastal and the interior provinces—that is, between east China and west China. Generally speaking, the eastern coastal provinces have been favored in Beijing's development strategy—they have had more control over tax revenues and foreign exchange and more general economic decisionmaking authority than the interior provinces. In effect, Beijing has opted to capitalize on the coastal regions' advantages: their relatively modern industrial base, their greater supply of skilled labor, and their physical accesibility to the outside world. (Zhao Ziyang's "coastal development" strategy announced in January 1988 constituted a formal acknowledgment of these advantages). The coastal provinces have also absorbed the vast majority of the overseas investment funds flowing to China. For example, nine coastal provinces accounted for 83 per cent of the foreign direct investment in China from 1983 through 1987. (Guangdong alone absorbed 42 per cent of the investment.)[26] Also, coastal provinces have provided more than 70 per cent of China's exports in recent years.[27] Not suprisingly, Beijing's policies have produced a much faster rate of growth in the eastern provinces (dramatically demonstrated by the figures in Table 2). The strategy also could provoke a political backlash in the form of demands by the disadvantaged interior provinces for a reassertion of central control.[28]

During the reforms, income inequalities have also increased within both urban and rural areas. In the countryside, this trend has been associated with the delegation of agricultural decisionmaking to individual households. In urban areas, the expansion of the non-state sector has created a new class of successful managers and entrepreneurs. The reforms have made Chinese society more money-conscious and have opened new illegitimate avenues to wealth and power. Abuse of public office is rife. For example, officials frequently accept money or gifts in return for issuing business licenses, for arranging state loans to favored enterprises, or simply for allowing enterprises to operate. The bureaucracy has also capitalized on an anomaly of the reforms: the disparity between government and free-market prices for the same commodity. For instance, a speculator can buy a ton of steel at the state price of $240 and resell it on the market for between $485 and $540.[29] Many departments, bureaus, sections, and offices or ministries have established "corporations" to trade illegally in sought-after commodities. Some factories have halted production, finding it more profitable to resell their state-priced allocation of raw materials to the highest bidder. Such activities have created a class of instant millionaires in China. According to a March 1989 article in Beijing's *Jing Ji Xue Zhou Bao (Economic Studies Weekly),* as many as one million Party and government officials may be guilty of profiteering.[30]

Extensive official corruption has been perhaps the most serious negative by-product of the reforms. As Zhao Ziyang noted in October 1988, "We cannot allow corruption to spread unchecked; otherwise we will be unable to establish a new order and system or continue reform."[31] Zhao's words were in some sense prophetic; corruption was probably the single most important rallying point for the pro-democracy movement. Public opinion polls taken in 1988 and early 1989 showed that official corruption was consistently ranked as the number one political issue. As one student protester at Beijing University said, "Corruption is everywhere. That is why we need democracy—to make people in power responsible for their actions." Another student leader said, "Our goals are first, democracy, and next an end to official profiteering."[32]

Table 2. The Growing Economic Gap Between Policy-Favored, High-Performance Eastern Coastal China[a] and Western China[b] (100 million yuan)

	1981	1985	1986	1987
Total industrial and agricultural output value	2,561.60	4,359.99	5,390.75	6,785.99
Total volume of retail sales	591.61	1,106.45	1,282.70	1,558.20
Total industrial output value	2,188.90	3,486.03	4,711.21	5,955.03
Total agricultural output value *(yuan)*	372.70	873.96	679.54	757.72
Rural areas, per capita net income	72.07	170.67	259.62	331.62

[a]Eastern coastal China includes the ten provinces and municipalities of Hebei, Shangdong, Tianjin, Liaonning, Jiangsu, Shanghai, Zhejiang, Fujian, Guangdong, and Beijing.
[b]Western China includes the eleven provinces and autonomous regions of Shaanxi, Tibet, Gansu, Qinghai, Ningxia, Sichuan, Guangxi, Guizhou, Yunnan, Xinjiang, and Inner Mongolia.

Source: Yang Jisheng "East-West Dialogue in China—The Strategy of Unbalanced Economic Development in the Mainland in Perspective," *Liaowang Overseas Edition* (Hong Kong), February 27, 1989, pp. 5–7.

The Reform Movement in Crisis

The inflation, corruption, and inequality generated by the reforms have produced new social and political tensions in China. These tensions exploded in April-June 1989, when students, workers, and other groups mounted a direct political challenge to the leadership. The pro-democracy movement included diverse and even contradictory elements. Most protesters were apparently motivated by democratic ideals, but some displayed a nostalgic longing for the pre-reform era. As one Beijing factory worker (carrying a Mao poster during the demonstrations) remarked, "Mao was a real leader, a lot better than the current lot. In fact, I oppose reform."[33]

China's leaders themselves are probably divided over whether to proceed further with the economic reforms or to turn back the clock. As of November 1989, it is difficult to predict the future direction of the reform movement. A number of key reform initiatives of recent years—the decontrol of prices, the introduction of more competitive markets for labor and capital, and the preferential development of the coastal regions—were clearly associated with Party leader Zhao Ziyang, who has been ousted from his position of leadership. The most likely prospect is a slower pace of reform, if not an actual retreat from the open-market principles that were introduced earlier in the decade.

The Opening to the West

Major Trends

The expansion of China's economic and technological ties with the West in the past decade has been dramatic. Foreign trade increased from $20.5 billion in 1978 to $102.8 billion in 1988, and the ratio of exports to GNP rose from 5–6 per cent to 12–13 per cent.[34] In 1978, China was not essentially a borrower nation, but by mid–1989, its medium and long-term foreign debt stood at $40–45 billion. China has joined the World Bank, the International Monetary Fund, and the Asian Development Bank, and is seeking membership in the General Agreement on Tariffs and Trade (GATT). Exchanges with foreign countries (which constitute an important vehicle for science and technology transfer) have flourished under the reforms. By 1988, for instance, some 40,000 Chinese students and scholars were studying in the United States—the largest contingent of any country sending students to the U.S.

China has actively sought investment from abroad. From 1980 to 1988, the number of foreign-funded enterprises (measured in terms of contract signings) increased from less than 100 to almost 16,000, and the paid-in value of foreign investment in China rose from $210 million to $11.5 billion. (The contract value was an estimated $25 billion by 1988.)[35] All provinces, including Tibet, are open to foreign investment. Such investment encompasses a variety of ownership forms, such as equity joint ventures, contractual joint ventures, and wholly owned foreign enterprises. Foreigners can invest in most sectors of the economy, although most foreign funds probably have flowed into hotel and tourism ventures and into the extractive industries (primarily oil prospecting and coal mining).[36] In addition, Chinese investment funds have moved abroad—and not just to Hong Kong. By the end of 1987, China reportedly had made direct investments totaling $353 million in some sixty-seven countries.[37]

China's opening to the West has been closely related to the general decentralization characterizing the reforms. In the pre-reform period, virtually all of China's foreign trade was monopolized by a handful of state corporations (FTCs) under the Ministry of Foreign Trade (renamed the Ministry of Foreign Economic Relations and

Trade in 1982 and commonly known as MOFERT). By the mid–1980s, 1,500–2,000 economic units in China were authorized to sign trade contracts directly with foreign firms. The new units were primarily comprised of specialized import and export corporations established by ministries, provinces, and municipalities, as well as a few large enterprises. By 1989, there reputedly were about 5,000 such entities, but the regime plans to reduce the number of authorized traders as part of a general drive to reassert central control over the foreign trade regime.

Furthermore, authority over foreign investment was transfered downward and diffused geographically. In 1979, China designated four areas in southeast China—Shenzhen, Shantou, Zhuhai in Guangdong, and Xiamen in Fujian—as special economic zones (SEZs). Within these areas, special incentives were offered to foreign businesses, primarily in the form of preferential tax rates, easier market entry and exit procedures, and streamlined approval procedures for investment projects. In 1984, Beijing extended elements of the SEZ regime to fourteen coastal cities and Hainan Island; and in 1985, the State Council established three "development triangles"—the Pearl River delta, the Yangtze River delta, and the Southern Fujian delta—as priority investment and development areas.[38] In 1988, Beijing made Hainan Island both a province and an SEZ and also designated the Liaodong and Shandong peninsulas as two new "coastal open areas." The entire area targeted by this coastal development strategy was estimated to be 320,000 square kilometers, encompassing a population of 200 million people.[39]

By the late 1980s, all of China, even Tibet, was officially open to outside investment. Each province or authorized city offered its own peculiar mix of investment incentives, such as tax holidays or waivers, reduced land use fees, quick approval of investment projects, and rapid depreciation rates. Still, the coastal provinces and cities wield substantially more authority over investment than the interior provinces—as of early 1989, nine provinces and five cities in east China as well as the SEZs were officially empowered to approve projects valued at as much as $30 million without involving central authorities. Interior provinces and a few interior cities could approve projects valued at as much as $10 million. In the wake of the June crackdown, though, provincial approval ceilings may have been lowered for certain kinds of investments, such as hotels and consumer goods enterprises.

China's opening to the West also has been accompanied by changes in the institutional framework for foreign investment. Since the 1979 Joint Venture Law was enacted, literally hundreds of regulations have been promulgated, governing almost every aspect of investment: contract approval procedures, management, labor, foreign exchange controls, taxation, technology transfer, patents and trademarks, and relations with the bureaucracy. As Jerome Cohen has noted, the body of laws is sufficiently large that "it is no longer necessary to reinvent the wheel each time subjects come up in negotiations."[40]

In general, Beijing takes an instrumental view of China's ties with the West. As Li Peng once said about reforms, "We want your technology, but we don't want your democracy."[41] This mindset is similar to that of reformers in late nineteenth-century China, who hoped to import Western techniques while insulating the imperial system from Western values and thus preserving it. That attempt of course failed completely. Today, China's increased interactions with the West have helped to generate powerful pressures for political change, including demands that the regime respect basic human rights and introduce democratic freedoms.

Chinese Economic Reform and Western Economic Interests

Limits of the Chinese Market. Beijing's open door policy produced high expectations in the West about the prospect for profitable ties with China. Because of its enormous population, China was viewed as a huge untapped market for Western goods. Western businessmen cited population-product ratios to explain investment decisions; an American Motor Corporation executive, for example, justified his company's Beijing Jeep venture with the argument that there are 1,100 Chinese per car compared to less than three people per car in the United States and Western Europe.[42] Such calculations were, however, somewhat misplaced. Population is not an unimportant determinant of market size, but it affects a country's buying power through intervening variables, such as wealth, export earnings, and government trade and investment policies. The real market (in contrast to the theoretical market) for Western goods in China is relatively modest.

By international standards, China is extremely poor: Its annual income per capita was estimated at $320 in 1988, which is somewhat more than India's ($290)—but less that one tenth that of Taiwan ($4,325), less than one twenty-fifth that of the Soviet Union ($8,750), and about one sixtieth the cost of a jeep produced by the American Motor Company's Beijing Jeep venture ($19,000).[43] In early 1989, China had more foreign-exchange holdings than India ($17 billion compared to $4 billion), but far less than Taiwan ($76 billion). In 1988, China's exported goods amounted to $57 million—or slightly less than Taiwan's $59 million—despite the fact that Taiwan's population is only 2 per cent that of the PRC. To be sure, the economic dimensions of the Chinese market have expanded considerably in the past decade; however, the fantasy market of Western expectation seems unlikely to materialize for many years— perhaps for several decades.

Furthermore, access to the China market, such as it is, is restricted by a system of import licenses (issued by central or provincial governments) and protective tariffs, quotas, and outright bans. The system is designed to conserve foreign exchange and to protect domestic producers. (According to a 1987 World Bank study, the average tariff on manufactured goods coming into China is 91.2 per cent—one of the highest tariffs in the world.)[44] At the same time, China encourages imports of advanced technology and of materials for processing and assembling for export. Consequently, there is some incentive to establish manufacturing facilities in the country. Unfortunately, certain features of China's bureaucratic system pose daunting problems for overseas investors, and the economic record of foreign ventures in China is generally poor. According to China's State Economic Commission, only one-third of the estimated 4,000 joint ventures operating in China as of November 1987 were earning profits in foreign exchange—that is, money that could be remitted abroad. One-third were losing money, and one-third were profitable in terms of non-convertible Chinese currency.[45]

Perhaps the most serious drawback to investing in China is the system of foreign exchange controls. China's currency—the renminbi (RMB), or yuan—is not freely convertible at the official rate of exchange. Consequently, foreign enterprises seldom can earn hard currency from domestic sales, which makes it difficult to repatriate profits or to import essential components. The convertibility problem has, however, eased somewhat in recent years. Since late 1986, foreign investors have been able to exchange some of their RMB earnings through a government network of Foreign Exchange Adjustment Centers. (In 1988, approximately twenty of these centers were operating in China.) The difficulty is that companies take a tremendous financial beating by making such exchanges. The official rate of exchange in 3.72 yuan to the dollar, but at the swap centers, it ranges between 6 and 7 yuan to the dollar. The foreign exchange issue thus continues to be a major irritant in relations between China and the foreign business community.

Another structural problem is the legal framework of the Chinese business environment. As noted earlier, new investment regulations have proliferated enormously in the past several years. However, the legal framework is still inadequate in important respects. One major problem is that China has no copyright law. Consequently, piracy of intellectual property—computer software and other protected and trademarked items—is rife. Piracy of computer software by Chinese engineers reportedly costs U.S. companies between $100 million and $400 million each year.[46] Furthermore, the Chinese do not have a particularly good record of honoring contracts. During periods of retrenchment or organizational reform, major contracts have been cancelled outright. Some Chinese leaders display an almost callous attitude toward contracts. As the governor of Fujian noted in late 1988: "With regard to Sino-foreign joint ventures on which contracts have been signed, we must honor the contracts—with the exception of a few."[47] Moreover, the Chinese consistently try to renegotiate the terms of contracts once they are signed. Usually they want foreign companies to transfer additional technology, to lower their prices, or to provide increased training for Chinese staff (in joint ventures). A signed contract simply does not have the legal or cultural significance in China that it has in the West.

A third problem faced by foreign businesses in China is the absence of a unified national market. In part because of the reforms, markets are increasingly partitioned, both bureaucratically and regionally. The result is restricted business opportunities. For instance, one joint venture was excluded from bidding on state projects controlled by the Ministry of Machine Building; the venture's product line apparently competed with one of the Ministry's own factories. The Heinz baby food joint venture in Guangdong makes 80–90 per cent of its sales within the province; sales outside the province are sporadic and in odd lots. A U.S. joint venture in Tianjin wanted to buy electronic equipment from suppliers in Fujian, but could not get the Tianjin authorities to make the appropriate contacts.[48] The trade wars between provinces in the past year no doubt have intensified the marketing problems confronting Western joint ventures.

Yet another problem for investors, specifically Western investors, reflects the *political* underpinnings of China's opening to the West. Part of the rationale for China's new policy has been giving substance to the PRC's "one China, two systems" policy—that is, facilitating the absorption of Hong Kong, Macao, and (eventually) Taiwan into mainland China. Accordingly, China's investment policies contain some special signals for Chinese compatriots abroad. In the SEZs, for example, Chinese from Taiwan receive tax holidays and exemptions that are more generous than those granted to other foreign investors. The city of Guangzhou grants special tax benefits for all overseas Chinese investors. Fujian gives overseas Chinese a 50–per-cent reduction on land-use fees. Shanxi offers overseas Chinese the right to apply for preferential treatment. Hainan sets aside a special export processing zone for Taiwan Chinese investors.[49] Such official ethnocentrism does not strengthen the appeal of China to the Western investor; indeed, it seems almost gratuitous, given the ability of overseas Chinese businessmen to exploit ethnic and linguistic ties as well as family contacts in establishing enterprises in China.

Finally, the country's bureaucratic system represents a formidable barrier to commercial success in China. The decentralizing thrust of the reforms has made the situation worse. Substantial uncertainty surrounds who is in charge and who is authorized to make what decisions. Economic authority has been transfered downward, but provincial governments rather than enterprises are the main beneficiaries of this change. State-owned enterprises, although they enjoy much more autonomy than they did under Mao, still are not independent decisionmaking units—they cannot manage commercial relations with the outside world on their own.

China's huge bureaucracy (24 million officials or more), which traditionally performed the market's role, still wields enormous economic power. Yet this bureaucracy is increasingly fragmented. The reforms have aggravated center-region, inter-region, and inter-ministry coordination problems. The centrifugal tendencies of the reforms have diminished China's ability to approve and to implement very large investment projects.[50] Some foreign companies have found this out the hard way. For instance, it took Occidental Petroleum 8 years (1979 to 1987) to negotiate a $650–million joint venture to mine coal at Antaibao in Shanxi province. As of late 1988, the mine reportedly was producing at only one-half of capacity and could not meet delivery obligations to its customers. A huge gas field was discovered by ARCO off the coast of Hainan in 1983 (the offshore field would increase China's internal gas supply by an estimated 20 per cent), but it will not go into production until 1993, if then. ARCO may not be able to recover the $230 million that it has invested in the project. Both the ARCO and Occidental projects might have fared better under a more centralized economic system than China has displayed under the reforms.

Understandably, most foreign investors have opted to think small: The smaller the investment, the fewer the interactions with the bureaucracy. For example, the average contract value of the 5,890 foreign-funded enterprises approved in 1988 was only $883,000. For the entire 1979–1988 period, the figure was only $1.57 million.[51] Many of these ventures, and perhaps most of those that actually turn a profit, are not contributing significantly to China's technical and industrial modernization. They are small, low-tech operations (such as fish ponds, clothing sweatshops, and the like) that take advantage of China's cheap labor, exploit local contacts, and export most or all of their products. This investment pattern is unlikely to change much unless China either recentralizes its economy or proceeds much farther toward a full-fledged market regime.

Business as Usual? Despite the progress made under the reforms, China's foreign economic ties still lack a strong foundation. The country's real buying power is limited, and the Chinese bureaucracy constitutes a serious obstacle to normal commercial relations with the outside world. Yet foreigners have been attracted to China over the past decade—in part because of the hope of bountiful future benefits (the country's large population continues to capture Western imaginations) and in part because of China's decade-long image as a stable, modernizing, reform-oriented country.

The events of April-June 1989, culminating in the June 3–4 "Saturday Night Massacre" in Tiananmen Square and the subsequent show trials of arrested workers and students have of course damaged China's reputation for *political* stability; and the country's *economic* ties with the West—which, from the Western point of view, are based more on expectations than on current profitability—have suffered as a consequence. (Most foreign firms in China operate either on very thin profit margins or at a loss.) Not surprisingly, the leadership is trying to minimize the damage—to reassure the world that both the economic reforms and the opening to the West will continue. Yet the hope that China can continue business as usual with the West is probably unrealistic. For example, after June 1989, Japan froze $5.7 billion in low-interest loans intended for infrastructure projects (subways, ports, dams, and the like) in China; West Germany suspended a $240–million loan earmarked for a subway in Shanghai; and the United States embargoed sales of $600–700 million of military equipment and technology to China. The United States also used its leverage in the World Bank and the Asian Development Bank to delay consideration of about $1.3 billion in loans from these agencies to China. In addition, the United States suspended the Overseas Private Investment Corporation's insurance coverage of new Chinese projects, and withheld export licenses to launch U.S. satellites on Chinese rockets. The Congress voted in July 1989 to codify these sanctions into law (although both the Senate and the House bills would allow the President to lift the sanctions if he deemed it in the national interest). China's disregard of human rights conceivably could trigger substantial public and stockholder pressure on U.S. companies to restrict their business ties with

China. Investing in China could become almost as unpopular politically as investing in South Africa.

Moreover, the April-June events have damaged China's foreign economic relations, raising doubts about the country's future political stability. The Chinese leadership and Chinese society as a whole are seriously divided over the pace, the timing, and even the goals of reform. Such conflicts could signal a long period of political uncertainty in China—an interregnum characterized by periodic outbreaks of anti-government violence followed by government crackdowns and campaigns against "bourgeois liberalism." The prospect of such instability will doubtless slow the pace of new foreign investment.

In June 1989, many foreign companies withdrew their expatriate staff and cancelled plans to build plants and other facilities in China. Although some foreign companies are returning to China, new foreign investment contracts will almost certainly fall short of the $5.2 billion in new contracts signed last year. Furthermore, export volume could decline as Western importers seek more stable supply sources for toys, calculators, clothing, and other labor-intensive products. Such decisions will further aggravate China's trade deficit—which was already $5.79 billion for the first six months of 1989, representing a fourfold increase over the same period in 1988. Moreover, much of China's expected $2.2 billion in tourist revenues this year will not materialize. Chinese spokesmen are predicting a $1.3-billion decline in tourist revenues in 1989, compared to 1987.[52] Finally, Western commercial banks—sensing that China is a greater political risk—have since June 1989 increased interest rates on conventional loans to the PRC. In November 1989, Moody's Investor Service downgraded China's long-term credit rating (from A3 to Baa1). These actions will make it harder for China to refinance its foreign debt and in general will aggravate an already difficult economic and financial situation.[53]

In sum, the prognosis for China's foreign economic relations is uncertain. The leadership's efforts to repress manifestations of "bourgeois liberalism"—that is, of capitalist or democratic ideas— while maintaining the opening to the West is a sure prescription for continuing political instability. Continuing crackdowns on dissidents, including persecution of student leaders, stepped-up ideological education, and the reinstatement of Maoist reform through labor policies will further undermine China's reformist image. Such measures will make it difficult for the United States and other Western nations to normalize their relations with China. For China, escape from the current debacle lies in political renewal at the top. Deng Xiaoping's resignation as head of the Party's Central Military Commission and his replacement by Party Leader Jiang Zemin is a step in the right direction; however, it will probably take many years for a politically responsive and reform-oriented leadership to emerge. Such a transition undoubtedly will occur eventually, but the timing is anybody's guess.

Conclusions

China's current situation testifies to the dangers of partial reform. The reform movement reduced the state's role in economic planning and its control over financial resources. Reforms introduced free market mechanisms in parts of the economy and unleashed new entrepreneurial energies in those sectors. Yet the reforms have not successfully transformed the pricing system or the system of socialist ownership in industry, and they have failed to introduce a program for political change. A hybrid economic regime has emerged in which the state and the market guide decisions on production, pricing, investment, and capital flows. This regime apparently is unstable and is producing extreme inflationary pressures, massive official corruption, and an increasingly alienated populace.

The persistence of socialist ownership under the incomplete reforms clearly contributes to China's inflationary crisis. The state-owned industrial sector, which still accounts for most of China's industrial output, is more or less insulated from competition; enterprises in this sector have little incentive to cut costs, innovate, or expand productive assets. An estimated one-eighth to one-fifth of Chinese enterprises operate in the red.[54] The state props up inefficient enterprises with budgetary loans and bank credits, creating a network of subsidies that has produced rapid and accelerating upward pressure on prices. The bankruptcy law introduced last year is mainly cosmetic: As of March 1989, not a single state enterprise had been shut down under the new law. Breaking the state's grip on economic life will require stronger measures, such as selling shares of state enterprises to employees, to outside institutions, and to the public at large. However, key leaders such as Premier Li Peng and Party First Secretary Jiang Zemin oppose privatization. In a September 1989 speech celebrating the 40th anniversary of the Chinese revolution, Jiang emphasized that China's development policy does not include "weakening or eliminating the position of public ownership, much less privatizing the economy." Jiang's speech also stressed the need for stronger central planning and for increased Communist Party supervision of the economy. Hence the future of ownership reform in China is uncertain at best.[55]

Widespread official corruption is a second consequence of incomplete reform. The partial price reforms of the past decade have produced multiple prices for the same commodity, encouraging officials who hold "the right to ration" materials in short supply to buy low and sell high. Official speculation has assumed the role of the marketplace, bringing buyers and sellers together in the absence of an effective price-setting mechanism. Unfortunately, price reform, like ownership reform, apparently is not on the leadership's agenda. The ongoing "rectification" campaign is designed to curb "social demand" by cooling the overheated economy and slowing inflation. Artificially low official prices for key materials such as steel, oil, and grain perpetuate shortages, however, and China's emerging class of official profiteers ensures that much of the available output circulates at market prices anyway. Consequently, the current price system guarantees a worst case scenario for China: the prevalence of both inflation and corruption.

The incompleteness of the economic reforms is also apparent in China's economic relations with Western countries. China opted to open its doors to foreign trade and investment, and there is little doubt that Western capital, technology, and loans can contribute significantly to China's development. Yet China's bureaucratic system still inhibits normal commercial relations with the outside world. The country's trade policies are protectionist and cumbersome. The conditions governing foreign investment in China can only be described as exploitative of foreign investors. The reforms fragmented the economic control structure, but they did not excise the government from economic life. The result has been to increase bureaucratic confusion and to discourage foreign investors from taking large risks.

In short, China's current foreign trade and investment policies limit the potential for China's integration into the world economic system. (Of course, China's relatively low per capita income also constitutes an important limitation.) Up to now, China's reputation for political and social stability and its modernizing image have attracted foreign businesses that otherwise might have rejected Chinese ventures. However, the Tiananmen Square massacre and the subsequent purges of pro-reform elements in the leadership raise questions both about China's stability and about the future of its economic reforms. In light of these events, it cannot be assumed that China's economic ties with the West will expand. Indeed, they will probably contract, at least temporarily. Trade growth will slow to single digits this year. For the first three quarters, it was 4.7 per cent over the same period last year; this compares to a 24 per cent increase from 1987 to 1988. Data for January-September 1989 suggest that commitments of new foreign investment will fall below the 1988 level of $5.2 billion.[56] (In the July-September period, the value of new investment contracts dropped 23 per cent over the same period the year before.) There are troubling signs that the leadership is beginning to interfere more directly in the operations of foreign joint ventures in China; for example, the access of some Sino-foreign ventures to local markets has been blocked and price controls have been instituted on some joint ventures' products. One joint venture was told by Chinese authorities in October 1989 that its annual profit would be limited in the future to 3 per cent of gross earnings. Such measures will inevitably dampen the enthusiasm of Western companies for investing in the PRC.[57]

China's reform movement is also incomplete because it has not embraced a program for *political* change. The suppression of the pro-democracy movement epitomized the Chinese leadership's strategy of pursuing economic reform while maintaining tight political control. Such a dichotomy, however, will be difficult to sustain in the long term. The stated philosophical basis of China's political order— Marxist-Leninist-Maoist thought, the socialist path of development, and the monopoly of power by the Communist Party—seems incongruous in a society that already functions partly on capitalist principles. To be sure, free market systems can coexist with authoritarian political regimes; countries such as Thailand, Indonesia, South Korea, and Taiwan point to this conclusion. Yet even in these countries, (which never have been as rigidly controlled as China), the trend seems to be toward greater political pluralism and openness.

In China, the new prosperity and new social tensions engendered by economic reform will seek expression in the political system; there will be demands for wider political participation and also for political renovation at the top. The Chinese leadership can respond to these pressures in various ways: by ignoring and repressing dissent, by reshuffling the ruling bodies, by introducing real democratic freedoms, and (to reduce the incongruity between market economics and communist politics) by freezing or rolling back the economic reform program itself. As of late 1989, the Chinese leadership seems to have opted for a combination of repression, cosmetic leadership change (e.g., Deng Xiaoping's resignation), and recentralization of economic control.

Yet the pressures for political change may prove too strong to hold back. China's decision to open its doors to the West has created a multitude of new channels for introducing Western democratic ideas—"evil influences," as Deng Xiaoping calls them. China has sent tens of thousands of its brightest young people to study in the West. Nearly 2,800 foreign business offices reportedly operate in

China.[58] The flow of "evil influences" into China is being facilitated by China's own telecommunications revolution: the rapid introduction of information receptors such as telephones, televisions, radios, computers, and facsimile machines. (Such influences, of course, are now being introduced from Eastern Europe as well, where entire ruling groups are resigning and non-communist governments are being formed.) At this point, returning China to a policy of isolation would be a wrenchingly difficult task. The leadership nevertheless seems to be moving in this direction—banning Western books, expelling Western news correspondents, jamming Western radio broadcasts, setting up surveillance cameras on Beijing's streets (to monitor contacts of Chinese citizens with foreigners), and limiting the number of Chinese students allowed to study in the West.[59]

China currently faces a clouded future. Much will have to be done to regain the momentum of the reforms and to rebuild relationships with Western nations. The government should loosen its hold on the economy, further decontrolling prices, reforming the system of socialist ownership, and allowing insolvent state enterprises to go bankrupt. Foreign economic policies should be further liberalized; the current system imposes too many disincentives on foreign traders and investors and undoubtedly detracts from China's ability to acquire needed Western capital and technology. Finally, China's rigidly authoritarian political system, which is simply out of step with the modernizing process in China and with world political trends, must be reformed. Unless basic civil guarantees are introduced and institutionalized methods for expressing dissent developed, China can only look forward to continuing political unrest—to a cycle of demonstrations, crackdowns, purges, widening dissent, and further repression. Unfortunately for China, the current leaders seemingly lack the vision or (by now) the moral authority to take the essential *positive* steps.

What are the implications of the recent violent repression and economic "rectification" in the PRC for U.S. policy? The United States has both an economic and a political interest in the success of China's reforms in both spheres. A China that is prosperous, politically stable, and closely integrated into the international economic order would contribute significantly to peace and security in the Asia-Pacific region. The failure of reform, on the other hand, could exacerbate political conflict in Asia, foster a partial return to autarkic development policies, and lead to the resurrection of Beijing's revolutionary and ideological objectives abroad.

The U.S. economic stake in China is still extremely small: In 1987, China absorbed less than 1.5 per cent of U.S. exports and accounted for less than one-tenth of 1 per cent of U.S. overseas assets.[60] Successful reform in China, including the modernization of the foreign trade and investment system, could alter this picture considerably. Expanding prosperity and economic freedom would make the Chinese economy more congruent with the economies of Western nations, thus creating the preconditions for a far greater expansion of trade and investment opportunities in the PRC.

The United States also holds an interest in political modernization in China. This interest is based partly on the U.S. commitment to basic human rights and freedoms. The Tiananmen Square massacre has of course brought human rights issues to the forefront of the U.S.-China relationship. U.S. concerns, however, are also pragmatic and econmically oriented. The current political order in China does not augur well for modernizing the economic mechanism (witness the leadership's position on price reform and ownership reform). Moreover, the inability of the system to accommodate and to channel dissent is a harbinger of continuing political instability, which naturally will damage both the domestic economic reforms and China's relationship with the outside world.

Despite the strength of U.S. interests in the success of reform in the PRC, however, the U.S. capacity to influence developments in a country the size and character of China is obviously limited. Whether the reform process succeeds or fails economically and politically will largely reflect *domestic* factors such as leadership struggles, regional alignments, and the general state of the economy. The United States must face the likelihood that the present leadership will not push China very far down the road to economic or political reform. Indeed, a strong, modernizing coalition may not emerge in China for years. This suggests that the basic U.S. approach to the PRC should be to reduce government-to-government ties while simultaneously maintaining as much as possible of the existing network of private contacts, exchanges, and economic relations. The purpose of such an approach would be to indicate disapproval of the present regime (and encourage the process of leadership reform) while maintaining links that have served and will continue to serve as important catalysts for reform in China. Such a policy will be difficult to sustain with respect to the private sector. Former U.S. Ambassador to China Winston Lord notes that: "Based on both practical and moral grounds, thousands of individual decisions each week are wiping out trade deals, investment, and scientific plans. In the cultural and academic areas. . . . lots of promising projects are dying or placed in cold storage."[61] Such decisions are hardly surprising given China's current situation and the U.S. response to it; however, the United States should not deliberately rupture the network of *private* commercial and cultural dealings that has been painstakingly nurtured over the past decade.

On the other hand, some cooling of Sino-U.S. *official* ties seems inevitable and even desirable. The Bush administration could, for example, take a tougher stance in criticizing China's repressive political policies. The PRC has compiled a long record of persecuting both pro-democracy activists and minority groups seeking greater religious or cultural autonomy (witness the brutal suppression of minority aspirations in Tibet). The Bush administration's official reaction to Tiananmen Square and its aftermath was remarkably restrained—"pathetically weak," in the words of one Republican Senator.[62] For more than a decade, in fact, successive U.S. administrations have been extraordinarily tolerant of human rights abuses in China. At the same time, the United States has vigorously criticized instances of political oppression in the Soviet Union. (Ironically, at this writing, the United States still denies most-favored-nation trade treatment to the Soviet Union—despite the fact that that country, in contrast to China, has introduced a very significant measure of political reform.) The United States should scrap this double standard; it should get over its long-standing reluctance to criticize China. The current policy of restraint risks discouraging the aspirations of reformers in China for a freer, more democratic, and more open society.

Other U.S. policies must be carefully fine-tuned in the current situation. The sanctions imposed by the Bush administration in the wake of the June crackdown, the suspension of military sales, the cessation of high-level government visits, and pressures on the World Bank and the Asian Development Bank to postpone new loans to China were all appropriate ways of signaling U.S. displeasure with China's oppressive regime. Military cooperation should be frozen and cabinet-level government contacts kept to a minimum as long as the current repressive leadership remains in power. China's accession to the GATT and proposals for bilateral assistance programs for China also should be placed on indefinite hold. (Chinese commercial practices will have to improve significantly before China can be allowed entry into the GATT.) At the same time, the United States should not take steps that would seriously damage the Chinese economy or injure China's trade and investment ties with U.S. businesses—for example, steps such as denying China most-favored-nation trade status, expanding controls on exports of civilian high technology, or cutting Chinese textile imports. Such sanctions would trigger widespread anti-U.S. resentment in China, and would also interfere with the progress of reform. Similarly, international lending to China should probably be resumed, but with some change in emphasis. New loans should not be used to prop up inefficient state enterprises (this would run counter to the objectives of reform); rather, they should be tied to changes in the ownership system—(i.e., recipient enterprises should include a private shareholding component) or should be earmarked for infrastructure projects such as railways, power plants, and telecommunications networks.

There are of course risks in offending the current Chinese leadership. These risks are defined by the strategic importance that the United States attaches to its ties with the PRC. The United States perceives China as a counterweight to Soviet ambitions in Asia and also maintains certain intelligence ties with China. The importance of the "China card," is, however, greatly diminished in the current international environment. The U.S.-Soviet strategic dialogue has entered a less confrontational phase, and far-reaching political changes in the Soviet Union raise hopes for a more peaceful East-West relationship. In addition, the Soviet Union, which is preoccupied with internal reform and is actively seeking technology and credits from the West, probably would not welcome a return to the Sino-Soviet alliance of the 1950s. Consequently, other aspects of the U.S.-China relationship no longer must be held hostage to the strategic aspect; in other words, the United States can afford to be significantly bolder in expressing displeasure with events in China and in pressing that country to undertake necessary economic and political reforms.

Notes

[1]Robert Dernberger and Richard Eckhaus, *Financing Asian Development 2* (Lanham, Md.: University Press of America, 1988), pp. 16–18.
[2]For a good discussion of the background of reform, see A. Doak Barnett, "Ten Years After Mao," *Foreign Affairs* (Fall 1986), pp. 40–41.See also The World Bank, *China: Finance and Investment* (Washington, D.C.: The World Bank, 1988), pp. 1–5.
[3]"Learn and Make Use of Advanced Foreign Experience," *People's Daily,* November 3, 1978. Quoted in Rensselaer Lee, "Political Absorption of Western Technology: The Soviet and Chinese Cases," *Studies in Comparative Communism* (Spring-Summer 1982), p. 28; and Foreign Broadcast Information Service (FBIS), *Daily Report,* November 6, 1978, p. E8.
[4]Shahid Javed Burki, "The World Bank in China," Unpublished paper, May 30, 1989, p. 7 (The government imposes a 55–per-cent tax on the gross profits of enterprises); and Harry Harding, *China's Second Revolution: Reform After Mao* (Washington, D.C.: The Brookings Institution, 1987), p. 115.
[5]Dernberger and Eckhaus, op. cit., p. 43; and William Byrd and Gene Tidrick, "Factor Allocation and Enterprise Innovation," in Gene Tidrick and Chen Jiyuan, eds., *China's Industrial Reform* (New York: The World Bank, Oxford University Press, 1989), p. 84. The term "fixed investment" refers to investment in capital construction and technical innovation.
[6]Burki, "The World Bank in China," op. cit., p. 6; and "China Begins a Long March," *Business Week,* June 5, 1989, p. 38. *Business Week* estimates the non-state sector to be 44 per cent of the national economy.
[7]Nicholas Kristof, "State's Share of Business Falls in China," *The New York Times,* March 20, 1989, p. D4; and State Statistical Bureau, *Statistical Yearbook of China 1988* (Hong Kong: International Center for Science and Technology Ltd., 1989), p. 268

[8]"Long March to Free Markets," *The Economist,* November 19, 1988, p. 76.

[9]On shareholding, see, for example, Mei Yunan, "Preconditions for Implementing the Shareholding System in State Enterprises," *Jingji Guanli* (Beijing), No. 2, 1989, pp. 28–31; and "Privatizing China," *The Economist,* February 11, 1989, p. 36. On the regime's current stance, see Adi Ignatius, "Beijing Unveils Tough Measures in Plan for '89," *The Asian Wall Street Journal,* March 22, 1989, p. 1.

[10]On the agricultural reforms, see Harding, "China's Second Revolution," op. cit., pp. 101–8; and Barnett, "Ten Years After Mao," op. cit., pp. 56–57.

[11]State Statistical Bureau, op. cit., pp. 709, 715.

[12]State Statistical Bureau, op. cit., pp. 191; and "The Communiqué on the Statistics of 1988 Economic and Social Development Issued by the State Statistics Bureau of the PRC, 28 February 1984," *Renmin Ribao* (Beijing), March 1, 1989, p. 2.

[13]Adi Ignatius, "Beijing Faced with Economic Crisis, Draws Back from Liberalization Drive," *The Wall Street Journal,* September 22, 1988, p. 22.

[14]"The Need for Macro-Economic Regulation," *Beijing Review,* April 10–6, 1989, pp. 21–23; and "The Communiqué on the Statistics of 1988," op. cit., p. 2.

[15]CIA, *The Chinese Economy in 1988 and 1989: Reforms on Hold, Economic Problems Mount* (Washington, D.C.: Office of the Director of Intelligence, August 1989), p. 16.

[16]Xie Zhenjiang, "Price Subsidies: Where Have They Gone?" *Jingji Ribao* (Beijing), February 27, 1989; and Adi Ignatius and Amanda Bennett, "Beijing's Economic Ills Pose New Threat of Social Upheaval," *The Wall Street Journal,* August 3, 1989, p. A8.

[17]Ibid; and *Moody's Foreign Credit Report: The PRC,* September 1988, p. 20.

[18]CIA, "The Chinese Economy in 1988 and 1989," op. cit., p. 3.

[19]Li Peng, "Report on the Work of the Government," *Beijing Domestic Service* (Beijing), 0703 GMT, March 20, 1989; and "Free Market for Free People," *The Economist,* May 27, 1989, p. 89; and Ma Zhipeng, "Small Private Businesses Decline in Number," *China Daily* (Beijing), August 11, 1989, p. 1.

[20]"Factory output shows first decline since 1979," *Kyodo* (Tokyo), 1004 GMT, November 10, 1989; Wu Shishen, "Statistics Bureau Official Views Economic Work," *Xinhua Domestic Service* (Beijing), 0806 GMT, December 3, 1989; and Li Ping, "Initial Success for Economic Rectification and Improvement," *Beijing Review,* November 27–December 3, 1989, pp. 16–18.

[21]The World Bank, *China: Long-Term Development Issues and Options* (Baltimore, Md.: Johns Hopkins University Press, 1985), p. 21.

[22]Xiao Yu, "The Central Financial Situation Is Grave and Worrisome," *Jingji Xue Zhou Bao* (Beijing), May 7, 1989, p. 3; and Dai Yaping, "Hidden Worries About China's Rapid Economic Development," *Zhonguo Xinwen She* (Beijing), 0231 GMT, October 19, 1988.

[23]"Regional CEI Database Published," *Beijing CEI Database,* March 22, 1989, pp. 50–51; and Willy Wo Lop Lam, "State Tightens Central Economic Planning," *South China Morning Post* (Hong Kong), September 28, 1989, pp. 50–51.

[24]Xia Yang and Wang Zhijang, "Initital Study of Local Economic Independence in China," *Liaowang Overseas Edition* (Hong Kong), September 26, 1988, pp. 3–4.

[25]Roderick MacFarquhar, "The End of the Chinese Revolution," *The New York Review of Books,* July 20, 1989, p. 9.

[26]U.S.-China Business Council, *A Guide to China's Trade and Investment Organizations* (Washington, D.C.: The China Business Forum, 1989), p. 24.

[27]CIA, *The Chinese Economy in 1988 and 1989,* op. cit., p 2.

[28]On this point, see David M. Lampton, "Driving Beyond the Headlights: The Politics of Reform in China," in David M. Lampton and Catherine Keyser, eds., *China's Global Presence: Economics, Politics, and Security* (Lanham, Md.: American Enterprise Institute, University Press of America, 1988), p. 11.

[29]Colin MacDougall, "Turnabout Brings Recentralized Controls," *Financial Times* (London), December 14, 1988, p. III.

[30]"Where Will the Double-Track System Land China?" *Jingji Xue Zhou Bao* (Beijing), March 20, 1989, p. 2.

[31]"Zhao Speaks at Forum," *Xinhua Domestic Service* (Beijing), 1735 GMT, October 14, 1988.

[32]"Behind China's Anger," *U.S. News & World Report,* June 5, 1989, p. 20; Michael Dobbs, "A Historic Tumultuous Summit," *The Washington Post National Weekly Edition,* May 22–28, 1989, p. 6; and Pei Minxin, "Democracy or Death in China," *The World and I,* July 1989, pp. 91–92.

[33]Adi Ignatius, "Chinese Communism Faces a Crossroads as the Masses Speak," *The Wall Street Journal,* May 19, 1989, p. A10.

[34]State Statistical Bureau, op. cit., p. 156; and "The Communiqué on the Statistics of 1988," op. cit.

[35]"Foreign Investment Figures Cited," *Xinhua* (Beijing), 1157 GMT, January 23, 1989.

[36]As of 1986, an estimated three-quarters of U.S. investment in China was in these sectors. See National Council for U.S.-China Trade (NCUSCT), *U.S. Joint Ventures in China: A Progress Report* (Washington, D.C.: NCUSCT, 1987), p. 114.

[37]Wang Yuewen, "China's Investment Abroad Grows Steadily," *Liaowang Overseas Edition* (Hong Kong), May 1, 1989, p. 21.

[38]Harding, *China's Second Revolution*, op. cit., p. 167; and Elson Pow and Michael Moser, "Law and Investment in China's Special Investment Areas," in Michael Moser, ed., *Foreign Trade Investment and the Law in the People's Republic of China* (New York: Oxford University Press, 1987), p. 247.

[39]Ji Chongwei, "China's Foreign Trade Strategy," *Beijing Review*, July 31 to August 6, 1989, pp. 25–28.

[40]Jerome Cohen, "Legal Framework for Investment," in Eugene Lawson, ed., *U.S.-China Trade: Problems and Prospects* (New York: Praeger Publishers, 1988), p. 108.

[41]Lampton and Keyser, *China's Global Presence*, op. cit., p. 33.

[42]Susan Goldenberg, *Hands Across the Ocean* (Boston, Mass.: Harvard Business School Press, 1988), p. 95.

[43]Ibid., p. 96.

[44]The World Bank, *India: An Industrializing Economy in Transition*, (Washington, D.C.: The World Bank, 1988), p. 95.

[45]Susan Goldenberg, *Hands Across the Ocean*, op. cit., p. 92.

[46]Daniel Southerland, "U.S. Businesses Urge Trade Sanctions to Stop Piracy of Software in China," *The Washington Post*, April 11, 1989, p. E7.

[47]Adi Ignatius, "China's Effort to Curb Economic Growth Is Likely to Damp Foreign Investment," *The Wall Street Journal*, October 26, 1988, p. A19.

[48]NCUSCT, *U.S. Joint Ventures in China*, op. cit., pp. 156–57.

[49]Ibid., pp. 23–46; and Richard Gillespie and Sharon Ruwert, "Hainan: Facts, Figures, and Fantasies," *U.S. China Business Review*, January-February 1989, p. 28; Pow and Moser, "Law and Investment," op. cit., p. 207.

[50]On this point, see Michel Oksenberg and Kenneth Lieberthal, *Bureaucratic Politics and Chinese Energy Development* (University of Michigan, Center for Chinese Studies, August 1986), p. 389. (Report prepared for the Department of Commerce, International Trade Administration.) The authors conclude that the reforms "have created a situation in which China's ability to approve and construct very 'lumpy' investment projects is diminishing. That is, where very large, long-term projects are concerned, the Chinese system may begin to suffer increasingly from immobilism."

[51]"Foreign Investment Figures Cited," op. cit.

[52]Fred C. Shapiro, "Letter from Beijing," *The New Yorker*, July 3, 1989, p. 67; and Ma Lixin, "Officials Calculate Lost Tourism Earnings," *China Daily*, September 19, 1989, p. 1.

[53]Sheryl Wu Dunn, "China's Credit Rating Downgraded by Moody's," *The New York Times*, November 10, 1989, p. D2.

[54]U.S. Central Intelligence Agency, *China: Economic Performance in 1987 and Outlook for 1988* (Washington, D.C.: Directorate of Intelligence, 1988), p. 4; and Wang Mengkui, "Certain Questions on Curbing Inflation," *Qiushi* (Beijing), October 1, 1988, pp. 12–17.

[55]"Report by Comrade Jiang Zemin, General Secretary of the CPC Central Committee on Behalf of the CPC Central Committee and the State Council," *Beijing Television Services*, 0703 GMT, September 29, 1989.

[56]"Minister Says Trade Develops Steadily," *Xinhua* (Beijing), 1538 GMT, October 28, 1989; "Foreign Investment Increases in January-September Period," *Xinhua* (Beijing), 1515 GMT, October 28, 1989. The *Xinhua* report said $4 billion in new investment had been approved in the first nine months of 1989, but this incorporates a surge in new contracts in the January to June period.

[57]Graeme Browning, "After Tienanmen, Ominous Signs on Road to China," *The Washington Post*, November 5, 1989, pp. H1, H4.

[58]Marc Lerner, "Foreign Businessmen Anticipate Slower Economic Reforms," *The Washington Times*, June 26, 1989, p. A8.

[59]Shapiro, "Letter from Beijing," op. cit., pp. 67–70.

[60]The estimate for investment is based on statistics provided by Jeffrey Lowe of the Bureau of Economic Analysis, Department of Commerce.

[61]Winston Lord, "China's Big Chill," *Foreign Affairs*, Fall 1989, p. 10.

[62]"Small Carrot, Big Stick," *Newsweek*, July 3, 1989, p. 28.

Chapter 3

Economic Reform in India: A Long and Winding Road

John Echeverri-Gent

The course of India's economic reform has been long and winding. It has produced incremental rather than radical advances. Often it has seemed to lack direction and a coherent strategy. India's road to reform is shaped by a political and cultural terrain that makes dramatic new reforms difficult. The continuing resonance of Fabian socialist ideology, the country's democratic political institutions, and its structure of political power have facilitated movement in some directions while impeding advances in others.

This chapter examines India's economic reform with a special focus on the measures taken by the government of Rajiv Gandhi. It begins by discussing the development regime established during the first three decades of India's independence. The chapter then describes the measures taken under Rajiv Gandhi to reform India's economy and examines the limits of those reforms. Finally, it explores the implications of India's economic reform for Indo-U.S. relations.

Economic Development Under the Old Regime

Indian economic development has been characterized by the pursuit of multiple and sometimes contradictory objectives. Economic growth has always been viewed as essential for creating a prosperous society, and India's economic institutions and policies have been designed with the goal of maximizing the efficient use of the country's resources. Yet efforts to promote economic growth have been embedded in a political culture that places a high value on national self-reliance and social equity.

The pursuit of these objectives led to the creation of what is arguably the most regulated economy in the non-communist world. The general guidelines of India's economic strategy are enunciated by the central government's Planning Commission, whose five-year plans establish development priorities, production goals, and guidelines for allocating investment. A large public sector was created to ensure that strategic sectors of the economy remain responsive to state objectives. A comprehensive system of licensing was established to regulate industrial investment and production capacity. Under this regime, a single application to set up an industrial plant had to satisfy as many as eight-six different enactments and control agencies before receiving approval.[1] Trade policy became dominated by pervasive quantitative controls and some of the world's highest tariffs, and foreign investment and technology transfer have been closely regulated to safeguard the country's self-reliance.

How far has India progressed toward its goals of economic growth, self-reliance, and social equity? The country's economic growth performance has been disappointing. India began the 1950s in quite favorable circumstances compared to other Third World nations; it possessed relatively good infrastructure, an ample endowment of natural resources, a large internal market, a good supply of technically skilled labor, an abundance of cheap labor, and a stable political system. Despite these favorable factors, India's rate of growth was relatively low (Table 1). When compared with nine other large and diversified developing economies, India's 3.7 per cent average annual rate of GDP growth from 1965-80 was less than all but one (Table 1). Its 4 per cent average annual rate of industrial growth was particularly laggard compared to the 9.1 per cent average for the nine other countries.

India's economic performance showed modest improvement during the 1980s, while other countries suffered from the debt crisis and declines in oil revenues. Its GNP grew at an average annual rate of 4.6 per cent from 1980 to 1987. This approached the 4.8 per cent average for the other countries listed in Table 1. An important factor in India's improved performance was the increase in its industrial growth rate from 4.0 per cent to 7.2 per cent—considerably above the 5.4 per cent average for the nine other countries. Despite these recent improvements, however, India's growth rate still remains below its aspirations.

Table 1. Comparison of Economic Performance: India and Selected Other Countries ($US and percentages)

| | GNP Per Capita | | Average Annual Growth Rate | | | | | | | |
| | | | Total GDP | | Industry | | Agriculture | | Services | |
	1987	Average Annual Growth, 1965–87	1965–80	1980–87	1965–80	1980–87	1965–80	1980–87	1965–80	1980–87
Argentina	2,390	0.1%	3.5%	−0.3%	3.3%	−0.9%	1.4%	1.6%	4.0%	−0.3%
Brazil	2,020	4.1	9.0	3.3	9.8	2.4	3.8	2.6	10.0	4.1
China (PRC)	290	5.2	6.4	10.4	10.0	13.2	3.0	7.4	7.0	7.6
India	**300**	**1.8**	**3.7**	**4.6**	**4.0**	**7.2**	**2.8**	**0.8**	**4.6**	**6.1**
Indonesia	450	4.5	8.0	3.6	11.9	2.1	4.3	3.0	7.3	5.6
Mexico	1,830	2.5	6.5	0.5	7.6	−0.3	3.2	1.4	6.6	0.8
Pakistan	350	2.5	5.1	6.6	6.4	9.1	3.3	3.4	5.9	7.1
South Korea	2,690	6.4	9.5	8.6	16.5	10.8	3.0	4.4	9.3	7.7
Thailand	850	3.9	7.2	5.6	9.5	5.9	4.6	3.7	7.6	6.4
Turkey	1,210	2.6	6.3	5.2	7.2	6.7	3.2	3.3	7.6	5.0

Source: The World Bank, *World Development Report 1989* (New York: Oxford University Press, 1989), pp. 164–67.

India attained considerable success in achieving self-reliance. It established a diversified industrial base that fulfilled 90 per cent of the domestic demand for manufactures and virtually all of the country's demand for manufactured consumer goods. Merchandise imports accounted for only 8.0 per cent of India's GDP in 1986. This was below the shares of other large Third World countries and considerably less than the 19.4 per cent average for all developing economies.[2] India also attained a level of agricultural production that eliminated the country's reliance on imports. In FY1987–88,[3] India's accumulated foodgrain surplus enabled it to endure the worst drought since independence without resort to emergency imports.

India has received relatively low levels of foreign direct investment (FDI). One study estimated that over the period 1969–82 the annual average of *gross* FDI (i.e., not subtracting repatriations) in India was $2.9 million. In comparison, during 1979–80, *net* FDI (deducting for repatriations) in Brazil was $14 billion. In Mexico, South Korea, and Argentina it was $7 billion, $648 million, and $1.5 billion, respectively. Indian industry relied on the acquisition of foreign technologies less than any other newly industrializing country (NIC). India's total licensing payments as a percentage of manufacturing value added in FY1979–80 was estimated to be 0.7 per cent. The rates for South Korea, Brazil, and Mexico were 1.1, 1.9, and 2.7 per cent respectively.[4]

India's traditionally conservative fiscal policies minimized problems with its external debt through the early 1980s. The ratio of India's total external debt to its GNP was a modest 11.9 per cent in 1980. Its total external debt accounted for a manageable 157 per cent of its exports. A large share of India's debt was accrued on concessional terms. Only 1.9 per cent of its long-term debt was owed to private sources in 1980. The average interest on new commitments for its loans was only 4.7 per cent.[5]

Progress toward achieving social equity has been limited. India still has more people living in poverty than any other country, with the possible exception of China. Estimates of the number of people living below India's poverty line are controversial. The debate is complicated by the fact that there are sharp fluctuations in the number of people living below the poverty line at different points in time. It is generally agreed that from the 1950s through the late 1970s there was no statistically significant trend in the relative incidence of poverty.[6] The government contends that the combination of accelerated economic growth and poverty-alleviation programs has lowered the percentage of the population living below the poverty line from 48.3 per cent in 1978 to 37.1 per cent in 1984. It projects the continuation of this trend so that the poverty level will decline to

25.8 per cent in 1990.[7] Although most economists agree that the incidence of poverty declined from 1978–84, the range of the decline is a matter of dispute. Many contend that government estimates overstate the improvement.

Another body of evidence suggests that India's economic growth has failed to translate into a substantial reduction in the country's poverty. One of the biggest disappointments of India's development regime is the failure of industrial growth to generate enough jobs for the rural poor. Structural change in economic production has not been accompanied by a comparable change in the structure of employment. Although agriculture's share of GDP dropped from 60 per cent in FY1950–51 to 33 per cent in FY1987–88, its share of the labor force decreased only slightly, from 68.1 per cent in 1951 to 66.5 per cent in 1981.[8] As a consequence, Indian agriculture has had to sustain the livelihoods of a rapidly growing population. Per capita net domestic product (NDP) in the agricultural sector has remained stagnant while that outside of agriculture exhibits an annual growth rate of 2.5 per cent.[9] Furthermore, the increase in the number of people dependent on agriculture has placed growing pressure on land. From 1970 to 1980, the number of operational farmholdings increased from 70.5 million to 89.4 million while the area operated increased by only 0.67 million hectares. The percentage of marginal farmers (i.e., those owning less than one hectare) increased from 50.6 to 56.5 per cent.[10] The portion of the rural labor force working as wage laborers rose from 34 per cent in FY1972–73 to 40 per cent in 1983.[11]

Economic Reform Under Rajiv Gandhi

Reform of India's industrial policy can be traced as far back as the mid-1970s. While no political leader has been more closely identified with liberalization than Rajiv Gandhi, most of his reforms reflected an evolution in the thinking of India's policymaking community that began long before his rise to power.[12] Many analysts trace the improvement in India's economic performance since the mid-1970s to the impact of previous reform initiatives.[13] Rajiv Gandhi's identification with reform is in part explained by the fact that his reforms went further and were more systematic than those of his predecessors. He is also distinguished by his fascination with high technology. Rajiv Gandhi enunciated a sweeping rationale for reform, asserting that India had reached a watershed. Deploring the country's high-cost industry with its technological obsolescence and inadequate attention to quality, he declared that India must address its shortcomings through greater efficiency, more competition, and the absorption of new technologies.[14]

The Elements of India's Economic Reform

India's economic reform has had a substantial impact in five areas. Unprecedented emphasis has been given to stepping up investment in infrastructure. The reforms have liberalized the regulation of industry in order to promote greater efficiency, the development of high-tech industries, and the geographical dispersion of investment. The government has taken steps to promote the growth of the country's capital markets. India's economic reform also stresses developing India's technological capabilities by importing new technologies, promoting domestic research and development, and easing restrictions on foreign investment. Finally, the reforms have included measures to increase exports.

Greater Priority for Infrastructure. Since the late 1960s, infrastructural bottlenecks have acted as major constraints on development. Energy demand outpaced supply, leading to crippling power shortages. India's railroads were unable to meet the needs for freight transport. Communications were antiquated and highly inefficient. In recent years, increased emphasis has been placed on investment in infrastructure. In the budget for FY1988–89, expenditures on power, transport, and communications were projected to account for 47.8 per cent of all plan outlays. This represented a substantial increase from their 42.8 per cent share in FY1980–81. India's need to meet its growing demand for energy is an important factor in this reorientation. The energy sector alone accounted for 29.8 per cent of plan outlays in the FY1988–89 budget.[15]

Investment in infrastructure will have to accelerate to meet the country's needs. For example, demand for power is projected to more than double—from 30,200 to 72,711 megawatts—between 1985 and 1995. The government proposes to modernize and expand the country's telecommunications systems: It plans to increase the number of lines from two million in 1985 to 30 million by the year 2000. Port traffic is expected to grow from 145 million tons in FY1987–88 to 320 million tons at the end of the century.[16] Accommodating this increase will necessitate doubling the country's 150 million ton port capacity. Upgrading India's infrastructure to meet future needs will require technological modernization and investments of immense proportions. Recognition of the country's inability to mobilize sufficient capital to meet these needs has led to a series of efforts to attract private resources into sectors such as power generation, telecommunications, road construction, port construction, and air transport—all of which traditionally have been dominated by the public sector. Private investment in infrastructure is likely to play an increasingly important role in helping the government meet the country's infrastructural needs.[17]

Relaxing Industrial Regulation. Economic reforms under Rajiv Gandhi have brought significant relaxation in industrial regulation. While the measures taken have curbed the intrusiveness of the regulatory regime, they reflect a continuing belief in the need for state intervention to guide the economy. The new measures are intended as much to promote structural change in India's industrial base—by encouraging development of backward areas, high-tech industries, and economies of scale—as to alleviate inefficiencies resulting from regulation.

In March 1985, licensing was eliminated in twenty-seven major industries for firms not covered by the Monopolies and Restrictive Trade Practices Act (MRTP) and the Foreign Exchange Regulation Act (FERA). The delicensed industries included electrical equipment and components, machine tools, office equipment, automotive ancillaries, and some essential drugs. In June 1988, the government announced that licensing would be further restricted to twenty-seven specified areas. It raised the ceiling for exemption from licensing from Rs. 50 million to Rs. 150 million ($US 8.8 million)[18] for investments outside of India's twenty-one largest cities and to Rs. 500 million ($US 29.4 million) for projects in backward areas. The share of foreign exchange in total investment that brings a project under licensing was raised from 15 per cent to 30 per cent. The changes are estimated to remove two-thirds of all projects previously subject to licensing. This is likely to expedite the licensing process for the remaining larger projects, which account for 70 per cent of all private sector investment. To make investment in backward areas more attractive, the government is implementing a program to create "growth centers" with infrastructure equal to the best in the country.[19]

Several measures were taken to reduce the rigidity of licensing and to eliminate red tape. "Broad-banding," or extending licences to enable companies to produce a variety of similar products, was granted to firms in thirty-four industrial groups to facilitate diversification of production. The government also lengthened the validity of letters of intent from one to three years.

The government enacted reforms to promote more efficient scales of production. In March 1985, the ceiling for exemptions from excise taxes—the primary fiscal subsidy to small-scale industry—

was raised from Rs. 2.5 million to Rs. 7.5 million ($US 441,118). In addition, tax rates above the new ceiling were slowly graduated for firms with turnover between Rs. 7.5 million and Rs. 15 million ($US 882,353). These changes were intended to reduce the incentives for dynamic small-scale sector firms to split up to avoid losing their excise tax exemptions. The government later agreed to allow a 5 per cent automatic growth in capacity subject to a maximum of 25 per cent over five years for selected industries. It regularized production in excess of licensed capacity in thirty-four core or mass consumption industries, and it allowed up to a 49–per-cent increase in capacity as a result of a firm's modernization of its plant and equipment. In May 1986, the government also abolished maximum limits on plant capacity for the production of sixty-five items, instead requiring minimum capacities for their production. The industries affected included chemicals, electronics, autos, and sugar. Finally, in April 1988, the Indian government announced that it would automatically re-endorse licenses for productive capacity at maximum levels of production achieved during the following two years.[20]

Though most of the reforms were targeted at smaller firms, large companies also benefited from limited relaxation of the MRTP. In March 1985, the government raised the asset threshold for application of MRTP regulations from Rs. 200 million to Rs. 1 billion ($US 58.8 million). On June 30, 1988, the government announced that "dominant undertakings"—that is, those controlling more than 25 per cent of the production capacity in an industry but employing investment of less than Rs. 1 billion—would be exempted from MRTP restrictions. This removed 69 of the approximately 1,732 firms subject to MRTP regulation. Since 1985, MRTP companies in seventy-one industries have been delicensed if they set up production in backward areas.[21]

Deregulation has contributed to accelerated industrial growth. Industrial production increased at a compound annual rate of 7.6 per cent from FY1980–81 to FY1986–87. This compares quite favorably to the 4.2 per cent average achieved during the 1970s and the 6.0 per cent growth rate for the three decades prior to the 1980s.[22] In FY1987–88, industrial production continued to grow at 7.3 per cent despite serious drought—which in the past has slowed industrial as well as agricultural production. Recent estimates show that industrial production increased by 8.8 per cent in FY1988–89.[23]

Promoting the Development of Capital Markets. Policy reforms creating new incentives for equity and debenture issues have helped to make India's capital markets an increasingly substantial source of investment finance. From 1980 to 1988, market capitalization more than tripled—from $7.5 billion to $23.8 billion. The value of equity traded increased from $2.8 billion to $12.2 billion.[24] From 1981 to 1987, the number of companies listed on India's exchanges rose from 2,114 to 6,017. This makes India second to the United States in the total number of companies listed on its exchanges.[25] The total number of investors jumped from one million in 1980 to 16 million in 1989. As a result of these changes, India's private sector, traditionally dependent on public sector finance institutions, now receives 40 per cent of its capital requirements from the country's stock markets.[26]

The Government of India has initiated measures to curb abuses and to promote the continued growth of India's emerging market. In April 1988, it established the Securities and Exchange Board of India (SEBI) to regulate the country's exchanges. In August 1988, it created the Credit Rating and Information Services of India, Ltd. (CRISIL) to rate capital issues. The SEBI is promoting measures to standardize prospectuses, streamline trading procedures, and computerize the operations of India's stock markets.[27] The government is taking steps to set up over-the-counter trading. It is also encouraging the creation of new mutual and venture capital funds.[28] The developments in India's capital markets have already been a source of new dynamism in Indian business. They have facilitated the rise of new entrepreneurs and led to an unprecedented number of corporate acquisitions and mergers.[29]

Measures to Improve Technological Capabilities. Concern for improving India's technological capabilities preceded Rajiv Gandhi's rise to power. In 1984, a government White Paper on Technology Policy and the Report of the Committee on Trade Policies, chaired by Planning Commission member Abid Hussain, each recommended measures to increase imports of modern foreign technologies and to provide greater support for indigenous research and development. Rajiv Gandhi's government stressed the importance of India's technological modernization. In pursuit of this goal, he liberalized imports of capital goods, increased funding for research and development, reformed public sector research institutions, and relaxed restrictions on foreign collaboration.

Policy reforms have facilitated the import of modern technologies in three ways. First, the government liberalized provisions for imports under its Technical Development Fund.[30] Second, quantitative controls on the import of an array of goods have been removed. The import-export policy for 1988–91 added ninety-nine new capital goods to the list of items eligible for import under Open General Licenses (i.e., without quantitative restrictions).[31] Finally, import duties on selected capital goods have been lowered. In 1985, duties were substantially lowered on a range of imports, including power plant, fertilizer equipment, computers, and project goods. The changes were followed by a large increase in capital goods imports, which rose by 98 per cent—from Rs. 31.7 billion in FY1984–85 to Rs. 62.8 billion in FY1987–88—despite selective increases in tariffs in 1988. Their share of India's total imports rose from 27.0 to 34.3 per cent in this period.[32]

Significant measures have been taken to increase government expenditures on science and technology and to improve their efficiency. Expenditures on science, technology, and the environment have increased by 86 per cent from FY1985–86 to FY1988–89.[33] In addition, the government has sponsored special "technology missions" to resolve problems in high-priority sectors. However, the problem with public sector efforts in R&D may stem more from a failure to convert research into technologies suitable for industry than from a lack of funds. The government has initiated measures to deal with the problem. The Council for Science and Industrial Research recently required its thirty-nine laboratories to earn a third of their revenues by selling their research. It has also instructed each lab to concentrate its research on three "thrust areas" to be selected with the advice of potential users who have been made members of their advisory council. The government has also encouraged the formation of small consulting firms by researchers to help bridge the gap between industry and the country's research institutions, and it has founded the Technology Development and Information Company of India to provide venture capital and support to technological entrepreneurs.[34]

In recent years, the encouragement of technology transfers and foreign investment has steadily grown in importance as an element of India's strategy for technological modernization. An important explanation for its increased attractiveness is that foreign firms not only bring new technologies when they locate in India, they also bring a potential to generate export earnings that can finance other technology imports. India's efforts to attract foreign capital have accelerated as its balance of payments has deteriorated and its debt-service ratio has risen.

Efforts to attract foreign investment and technology intensified under Rajiv Gandhi. Since most joint ventures are subject to the MRTP, their regulation was eased with the various measures taken to liberalize the act. In addition, government officials began to interpret the FERA more flexibly. They made more generous use of the exceptions to the act's 40-per-cent limit on foreign equity for areas of high technology and 100-per-cent export-oriented units. Attracting foreign investment became an even higher priority during 1988. In March, the government announced that it would consider granting 100-per-cent export-oriented firms the option of selling up to 25 per cent of their production on the domestic market. Later in the spring, Rajiv Gandhi traveled to Japan and West Germany, where he met with government officials and business leaders to solicit more foreign investment. He promised to set up a "fast track" to expedite the processing of proposals. In the summer of 1988, the government announced two reforms intended to provide new incentives for foreign collaboration in high-tech areas. On July 7, 1988, it relaxed "phased manufacturing programs" (PMPs) requiring foreign collaborations to reduce the import content of their production to a maximum of 10 per cent within five years. The maximum import content of PMPs was raised to 30 per cent, and the timetable for meeting this requirement was changed to an indefinite period subject to government discretion. In August 1988, the government announced that foreign companies could apply for permission to set up projects without an Indian firm as collaborator, and instead meet the FERA's 60–per-cent domestic ownership requirement by selling equity in Indian capital markets.

The government took few initiatives to attract foreign investment in 1989 because the accommodation of foreign capital is usually considered a political liability in election years. Increasing India's openness to foreign direct investment (FDI) also remains controversial within the Indian government. Nevertheless, India's Planning Commission, in an approach paper to the Eighth Plan, has advocated a reappraisal of FERA restrictions on foreign investment. It recommended a major increase in FDI and observed that "the levels of direct foreign investment in industry should at least double without detriment to our overall goals of self-reliance."[35]

The result of these measures has been a significant increase in the number of foreign collaborations and in the volume of foreign investment (see Tables 2 and 3). The annual average of foreign collaborations from 1957 to 1979 was 248. During the first four of Rajiv Gandhi's years in power, the annual average rose to 940. Beginning in 1984, the value of investment proposals that were approved by the Indian government as well as the investment that actually materialized also increased sharply. The rise in 1988 was particularly steep. While these increases are significant developments, it is important to keep them in the proper perspective. The volume of investment in India remains relatively low. From 1981 to 1987, India received $509 million in foreign investments. During the same period, foreign investment in Indonesia was $9.516 billion; in Singapore, $4.162 billion; in Taiwan, $4.159 billion; and in Thailand, $3.876

Table 2. Approvals for Foreign Collaborations and Investment

	Total Collaborations			Financial Collaborations			Investment Approved (Rs. millions)		
	All Countries	U.S.	U.S. as Percentage of all Countries	All Countries	U.S.	U.S. as Percentage of all Countries	All Countries	U.S.	U.S as Percentage of Total Investment Approved
1957–79	5,706	1,175	21%	—	—	—	—	—	—
1980	526	125	24	—	—	—	—	—	—
1981	389	85	22	—	—	—	—	—	—
1982	590	110	19	113	24	21%	628	50	8%
1983	673	135	20	129	32	25	619	139	22
1984	752	147	20	151	37	25	1,130	89	8
1985	1,024	197	19	238	66	28	1,261	399	32
1986	957	189	20	240	71	30	1,070	295	27
1987	853	196	23	242	90	36	1,077	295	27
1988	926	191	21	282	71	25	2,261	971	43
1989[a]	355	82	23	102	19	19	1,989	183	9

[a]January–June 1989 only.

Source: Indian Investment Centre.

Table 3. Foreign and U.S. Investment in India
($ US millions)

	U.S. Investment	Total Foreign Investment
1981	2.8	13.7
1982	5.7	70.6
1983	14.4	48.3
1984	8.7	109.7
1985	33.5	105.8
1986	25.0	91.0
1987	20.0	n.a.
1988	65.0	121.0
Total	175.1	n.a.

Sources: USAID, *Country Development Strategy Statement FY1990*; and U.S. Department of Commerce.

billion.[36] From 1980 to 1988, China received almost $9 billion in foreign investment and had concluded agreements for a total of $25 billion.[37]

Promoting Exports. Recent reforms of India's trade policies have attempted to remove the disadvantages and disincentives that exporters suffer as a result of the Indian regulatory regime. Measures to curtail quantitative controls and reduce tariffs on the import of capital and intermediate goods have been an important element of this strategy. These policies have been designed to benefit an array of "thrust industries" that the government has selected for export promotion. India's trade reform is predicated on a calculated risk that liberalization of imports in the short run will reduce trade deficits in the long run.[38]

India's exporters operate in an environment of pervasive regulation. The reforms have attempted to reduce the regulatory costs they incur when importing capital goods and inputs. To provide greater policy continuity, the government in April 1985 began to issue export-import policy statements outlining its policy framework for three-year periods. It introduced the Export-Import Passbook Scheme, and it reformed the Automatic Licensing Scheme to reduce the administrative costs that exporters incur by complying with complex procedures for importing inputs.

The government has also taken measures to increase the profits of exporters. The benefits from the export promotion programs already in place were enhanced to offset their decline in real value during the first half of the 1980s. One of the most important changes in these programs occurred in 1988 when Replenishment (REP) licenses were extended to benefit virtually all exports.[39] In addition, taxes on profits from exports have been reduced; in the 1985 budget, 50 per cent of export profits were exempted, and the budget announced in spring 1988 exempted all export earnings. The government extended the International Price Reimbursement Scheme for steel to cover all categories of steel and alloys. The 1988–91 export-import policy also set up a program whereby producers exporting more than 25 per cent of their production will receive diesel fuel for captive power generation at world market prices.[40] It also made "indirect exports" (i.e., supplies of raw materials and components to manufacturing exporters) eligible for all benefits extended to exporters. Perhaps the best indication of the priority given to export promotion is the growth of export promotion subsidies. After declining by 2 per cent in real value from FY1980–81 to FY1984–85, they grew by 66 per cent in real terms from FY1984–85 to FY1987–88.[41]

The government's management of the external value of the rupee may well be its most effective means of export promotion. Devaluation has remained a sensitive issue in India ever since the political backlash that followed a major devaluation in 1966. Nevertheless, the government has quietly let the value of the rupee fall against most major currencies. From January 1985 to November 1989, the rupee declined by 34 per cent against the dollar, 144 per cent against the yen, and 133 per cent against the deutsch mark.[42]

The government's measures have produced positive results. The growth of India's exports has surged since 1986: From 1986 to 1988, they increased by 55 per cent in rupee terms and 43 per cent in dollar value. This is an especially impressive performance considering that exports of Bombay High crude oil dropped from 13 per cent of total exports in FY1984–85 to nil in FY1986–87. Labor-intensive manufactures have been an important factor driving the increase. From FY1980–81 (before exports of Bombay High crude began) to FY1987–88, the share of gems and jewelry, textiles and leather and leather manufactures in India's total exports grew from 28.9 per cent to 45.3 per cent. The past two years have also seen substantial increases in engineering goods and basic chemicals. The former grew from Rs. 11.5 billion to Rs. 22.6 billion from FY1986–87 to FY1988–89. Exports of basic chemicals are reported to have jumped by 79 per cent in FY1988–89. The improving competitiveness of Indian exports is reflected in the growing share of India's exports going to the OECD countries. The share has increased from 45 per cent in FY1984–85 to 59 per cent in FY1987–88.[43]

The Limits of India's Economic Reforms

Industrial Regulation. Economic reforms in India have brought substantial changes, but the measures taken until now are only initial steps on what remains a long and difficult journey toward a more flexible and efficient economy. The scope for competition and freedom of maneuver introduced by the reforms is limited. Most industrial deregulation has been directed at India's small and medium-size units, and many measures apply only to firms willing to locate in backward areas. India's 1,663 largest private sector firms are still restricted by the MRTP. In most cases, government approval in one form or another remains necessary for substantial expansion and diversification.

If market competition is to efficiently allocate resources there must be an effective mechanism to weed out the losers. At the same time that economic reforms have augmented competition, India has suffered from the unrelenting growth of "sick" industrial units. These are firms that, after being registered for a minimum of seven years, have accumulated losses equal to the value of their assets. Despite the introduction of measures designed to curb their growth (the creation of the Industrial Reconstruction Bank in 1984 and the 1985 Sick Industrial Companies Act) the number of sick units has risen dramatically—from some 25,000 in December 1980 to nearly 160,000 in June 1987. The outstanding credit tied up with these firms tripled from Rs. 18 billion to Rs. 57 billion. This latter figure equals 9 per cent of India's domestic capital formation in FY1987–88.[44]

Technological Development. India's efforts to upgrade its technological capabilities have been limited by a variety of unresolved problems. Utilization of resources by India's research institutions remains inefficient. Planning and control of the country's research institutions continues to be overcentralized.[45] Projects often waste resources because they are managed by scientists lacking administrative skills.[46] The reforms must overcome the disdain of Indian scientists for collaboration with the private sector. The result is that India's technological development remains constrained not so much by its scientific capabilities as by its inability to convert them into viable technologies.

Most of the reforms have targeted India's public research institutions and neglected the deficiencies of private sector research and development. Private sector R&D remains very low, accounting for only 13 per cent of India's R&D expenditures in FY1985–86.[47] Part of the problem has to do with market structure. In many industries, the small scale of production leaves firms with insufficient resources for significant R&D programs. Industrial licensing has contributed to the fragmentation of capacity. The government's insistence on speedy indigenization and its limits on the duration of agreements compels small firms to focus what R&D they do perform on adaptation to local conditions. While some initiatives have been taken to make venture capital accessible to entrepreneurs, further measures are needed. In industries with large or oligopolistic firms, regulation discourages R&D by limiting the prospects for growth and the introduction of new products. The high costs of domestic production curtail the possibilities for exports, thereby curbing incentives for innovation. Ceilings on royalties and technological fees have reduced the quality and volume of imported technologies. These conditions persist despite the current reforms. New measures designed to encourage private sector R&D are necessary if it is to make a more substantial contribution to India's technological modernization.[48]

Efforts to modernize India's technological base through foreign investment (FDI) face constraints. Domestic industry mounts strong lobbies against any FDI that threatens to increase competition.[49] The reform of regulations governing foreign investment has provided government officials with wide scope for discretion. This creates uncertainty among foreign investors. Having struck a deal with government officials, an investor has no guarantee that a competitor will not be able to follow with an even more advantageous deal.[50]

Trade Policy. India's trade reforms also have limitations. Its programs to compensate exporters for the high costs of inputs have added a new layer of bureaucracy, which increases the administrative costs of conducting trade. Complicated controls have been created to limit leakage of the benefits provided to exporters. The costs of compliance diminish the benefits of the subsidies. At times, administrative problems have meant that exporters have received payments only after lengthy delays.[51] The need for subsidies would be lessened if protective barriers were reduced, but the measures taken in this direction have been very limited. Only some 20 per cent of India's imports are available on OGL,[52] and most of these are still subject to high tariffs.

Liberalization of restrictions on imports has largely failed to introduce competition for domestic producers. With the exception of a limited number of capital goods, most of the items placed on OGL are goods not produced in India. Even within the capital goods sector the lobbying of domestic industry has succeeded in circumscribing the scope of international competition.[53] Restricted competition and continued protection enable many firms to make higher profits in the domestic market than they can through exports. India's large firms in particular continue to have poor export performance despite increased imports and the export obligations imposed by the government.[54]

The limitations of India's reforms have impeded any substantial reduction in the country's trade deficit (Table 4). After the recovery that followed the second oil shock, the deficit jumped to near-record levels in 1985. The situation improved slightly in the following two years, though this was largely due to declining oil prices. In 1988, the deficit returned to its peak level for the decade, prompting the government to take measures to slow import growth.

The deterioration of India's trade deficit is especially troubling in view of the country's diminishing foreign exchange reserves and its growing debt. As of September 1989, India's foreign exchange reserves covered barely six weeks' imports.[55] Since 1984, India's external debt has doubled from $US 31 billion to an estimated $US 60 billion in 1989. During this period, its debt-service ratio grew from 8 per cent to more than 30 per cent.[56] In the past, conservative policymakers have responded to deterioration in the balance of payments by curbing imports. The challenge facing India is to keep its balance of payments manageable without curtailing the imports necessary for the modernization of its technological base.

Fiscal Policy. India has run up sizable budget deficits during the period of economic reform. Although tax revenues have increased (in part because of fiscal reforms under Rajiv Gandhi), they have been insufficient to cover proliferating government expenditures. While gross tax revenues have risen from 11.4 per cent of GNP in FY1984–85 to 12.5 per cent in FY1988–89, government expenditures have increased from 20.2 per cent to 22.8 per cent.[57] As a consequence of these trends, the government of India has run substantial deficits. In FY1987–88, deficit financing amounted to almost 8 per cent of India's GDP.[58] The large deficits are made more troublesome because they are increasingly created by non-plan expenditures that make little contribution to long-term growth. Interest payments have risen from Rs. 59.7 billion in FY1984–85 to a projected Rs. 141.0 billion in FY1988–89—a 61-per-cent increase in real terms. Defense expenditures have grown from Rs. 66.6 billion to 130 billion, or by 33 per cent in real terms. Subsidies grew from Rs. 42.1 billion to Rs 73.2 billion—19 per cent in real terms. From FY1984–85 to FY1988–89, the share of these three categories in total central government expenditures grew from 40.4 to 47 per cent; the increases since FY1984–85 to FY1988–89 amounted to more than the total of all budget deficits during this period.[59]

Although originally set up with the expectation that they would make a net contribution to government finances, public sector enterprises (PSEs) remain another drag on central government

Table 4. India's Foreign Trade, 1980–88[a]
($ billions and percentages)

	1980	1981	1982	1983	1984	1985	1986	1987	1988
Exports	8.51	7.56	9.56	9.46	10.02	9.65	9.99	12.10	14.32
(Percentage change from previous year)		*(−11)*	*(26)*	*(−1)*	*(6)*	*(−4)*	*(4)*	*(21)*	*(18)*
Imports	14.84	14.98	15.34	14.96	16.41	16.79	16.91	18.60	21.74
(Percentage change from previous year)		*(1)*	*(2)*	*(−2)*	*(10)*	*(2)*	*(1)*	*(10)*	*(17)*
Trade Balance	6.33	7.42	5.78	5.50	6.39	7.14	6.92	6.50	7.42
(Percentage change from previous year)		*(17)*	*(−22)*	*(−5)*	*(16)*	*(12)*	*(−3)*	*(−6)*	*(14)*

[a]Data based on averages of *Direction of Trade Statistics (DOTS)* and *International Financial Statistics (IFS)* statistics.

Source: *Direction of Trade Statistics Yearbook 1989* (Washington, D.C.: International Monetary Fund, 1989), p. 222; and *Direction of Trade Statistics Yearbook 1987* (Washington, D.C.: IMF, 1987), p. 224.

expenditures. According to the Seventh Plan, central government PSEs are supposed to provide 66 per cent of their investment from internal resources; in fact, they have provided an average of only 34 per cent during the first three years of the plan. This was accomplished only after substantial increases in administered prices, and most of the amount was concentrated in the ten most profitable central government PSEs. The central government's budget has provided another 45 per cent. In FY1987–88, this accounted for 28 per cent of all central plan outlays and 11 per cent of all central budget expenditures.

The government has recognized the inefficiency of the PSEs for years, and it is considering far-reaching measures to improve the situation. So far, however, the tentative measures that it has taken have had little impact. An important reform has been to oblige PSEs to increase their financing from extra-budgetary resources such as bonds and external commercial borrowings. The share of central PSE investments derived from extra-budgetary resources increased from about 8 per cent to 28 per cent between FY1984–85 and FY1987–88.[60]

In the past few years, both the central government and PSEs increasingly have resorted to borrowing from private savings to cover their expenditures. Continuation of this trend creates the potential for "crowding out" of private sector investment. It would be an unfortunate irony if government borrowing should constrain private investment just as liberalization of India's industrial policy is providing opportunities for greater dynamism.

Limited Impact on Poverty. India's economic reforms have yet to overcome the entrenched barriers that impede the diffusion of the benefits of economic development to the poor. Despite its long-standing commitment to employment generation, India's industrial policies have promoted job security and rising real wages for a limited number of workers in the organized sector at the expense of creating new jobs. Industrial licensing and the subsidization of "sick" industrial units protect sluggish firms and obstruct investment in more dynamic enterprises that would generate more jobs. Restrictions on the retrenchment of workers and the closure of plants discourage organized sector firms from hiring new workers—since they will be stuck with them even if market conditions change. India's labor law greatly complicated industrial relations by recognizing any union able to document the membership of seven or more workers and by allowing competing unions within a single shop. Lengthy delays in settling disputes also raise the costs of labor.[61]

Industrial employment in the organized sector has virtually

stagnated as a consequence of these and other factors. From FY1984–85 to FY1988–89, employment in the organized sector rose only from 24.6 million to 26.0 million.[62] The annual compound rate of growth for this period of 1.5 per cent is considerably below the rate of new entrants into the labor force and continues the steady decline in the growth rate of organized sector employment. Most of the increase in employment has come in the public sector, especially in the category of "community and personal services."[63] Private sector employment grew from 7.3 million to 7.5 million—just 2 per cent— from FY1984–85 to FY1987–88. Employment in the private sector manufacturing declined from 4.5 million in March 1981 to 4.4 million as of March 1988. These trends are especially troublesome given the accelerated growth and investment that have characterized Indian industry during the 1980s.

Growth in industry and services has increased incomes rather than jobs. From FY1960–61 to FY1984–85, the real income of public sector workers more than doubled, and the real income of those in the private organized sector rose by 60 per cent, while real per capita income for the country as a whole rose by just 39 per cent.[64] The subsequent pattern of demand has shaped the course of economic growth. Consumer durables have been the fastest-growing industrial sector in the 1980s, expanding by nearly 15 per cent a year FY1980–81 to FY1986–87.[65] Production of televisions grew at more than 56 per cent a year from 1981 to 1986.[66] Sales of cars have quadrupled over the decade. The contrast between the increasingly affluent lifestyle of the top echelons of India's social structure and the continued suffering of the vast number of people still living in poverty violates the principles of social equity held by many Indians. Over the long-term, critics charge that India's trade and budget deficits, along with the limited scope of its domestic market, will make it difficult to sustain the rates of economic growth experienced during the 1980s.[67]

The Future of India's Economic Reform

The change in government following the November 1989 elections is likely to alter the course of India's economic reforms only in marginal ways. While inflation was an important electoral issue, the relaxation of industrial regulation did not stir much controversy. Under India's new Prime Minister V.P. Singh—the architect of many of the reforms under Rajiv Gandhi, when he served as Finance Minister—trends toward the liberalization of domestic industrial policy and the promotion of domestic capital markets and exports are likely to continue. Fiscal and monetary policy, however, will become more conservative as the new government attempts to reduce inflation. The new government has also pledged to step up its investment in agriculture. The liberalization of imports that took place under Rajiv Gandhi has come under attack from some within the new government. Further restrictions on imports are likely—with a battle already shaping up over whether these should be limited to consumer durables and luxury items or whether they should extend to capital goods. Solicitation of foreign investment will probably be less enthusiastic, but opportunities will continue in areas that augment India's technological capabilities.

Economic Reform and Indo-U.S. Relations

Relations between India and the United States have changed considerably in recent decades. The Indian economy has undergone substantial development since the 1950s, when it looked to the United States for foodgrain imports and advice on rural development. Sophisticated institutions now guide the Indian economy, and India has advanced to the point where it can make a significant contribution to the economic welfare of the United States. Examination of India's economic reforms is useful in understanding the evolution of Indo-U.S. relations. It highlights India's social and economic priorities, and it reveals opportunities for mutual benefit.

Trade

Economic liberalization has created opportunities for expanding Indo-U.S. trade. India, for its part, looks to the world's largest market in its drive to increase its exports. Its exports to the United States have grown considerably during the 1980s; from 1982 to 1988, they increased by 110 per cent (see Table 5). The U.S. share of India's exports has also risen. Already in FY1980–81, the United States accounted for 11.1 per cent of India's exports, making it India's second largest market (after the Soviet Union). By FY1987–88, the United States received 18.5 per cent of India's exports and was India's largest market.[68] Even so, India remains a minor player in the U.S. market. In 1988 its exports accounted for only 0.7 per cent of total U.S. imports.

For the United States, India's economic reforms have created opportunities for exports. If the United States is to successfully manage its status as the world's largest debtor, it will have to make its economy more export-oriented. India's efforts to upgrade its technological base have improved prospects for U.S. exports in an array

Table 5. Indo-U.S. Trade, 1982 to 1988
($ millions)

	1982	1983	1984	1985	1986	1987	1988	1989[a]
Indian exports to United States[b]	1,404	2,334	2,737	2,478	2,465	2,529	2,952	3,378
(Percentage change from previous year)		*(66)*	*(17)*	*(−3)*	*−1)*	*(3)*	*(17)*	*(14)*
U.S. exports to India[b]	1,599	1,827	1,565	1,640	1,529	1,434	2,444	3,026
(Percentage change from previous year)		*(14)*	*(−14)*	*(5)*	*(−7)*	*(−6)*	*(70)*	*(24)*
Total Trade	3,003	4,161	4,302	4,118	3,994	3,963	5,396	6,404
(Percentage change from previous year)		*(38)*	*(3)*	*(−4)*	*(−3)*	*(−1)*	*(34)*	*(19)*
U.S. high-tech exports to India	365	361	324	348	451	572	904	1,066
(Percentage change from previous year)		*(−1)*	*(11)*	*(7)*	*(30)*	*(27)*	*(58)*	*(18)*
High-tech exports, *as a percentage of total U.S. exports*	23%	20%	21%	21%	29%	40%	37%	35%

[a]Estimates based on projections from January-August data.
[b]Indian exports are in c.i.f. values through 1986 and customs values thereafter. U.S. exports are in f.a.s. values.

Source: Official statistics obtained by author from the U.S. Department of Commerce, Washington, D.C.

of capital goods and high-tech industries. Prior to the signing of the Indo-U.S. memorandum of understanding (MOU) on technology in 1985, U.S. policy constrained the possibilities for American firms to take advantage of opportunities in India. Even since the MOU was initiated, U.S. firms have been relatively slow to increase their trade with India. From 1984 to 1987, U.S. exports to India declined by 8 per cent. In 1988, however, led by substantial increases in transport equipment and cereals, U.S. exports to India grew by 70 per cent; and in the first eight months of 1989, they increased 24 per cent over the same period in 1988—despite a large reduction in cereal exports. From 1984 to 1988, high-tech exports rose from 21 per cent to 37 per cent of all U.S. exports to India.

U.S. Investment in India

India's relaxation of its regulation of foreign investment and collaborations has led to a substantial increase in the presence of U.S. business. From 1957 to 1979, the number of U.S. collaboration proposals approved by the Indian government averaged 51 a year (see Table 2); from 1985 to 1988, the annual average was 194. Throughout the 1980s, India had more collaborations with the United States than with any other country. The value of U.S. investment has also grown rapidly. After averaging $9.6 million during the three years prior to Rajiv Gandhi's accession to power, it rose to an annual average of $35.9 million from 1985-88 and peaked at $65 million in 1988. These sums are small in relation to overall U.S. foreign direct investment, but they indicate a growing appreciation of business opportunities within India, especially in the areas of computers, telecommunications, and food processing.

U.S. Development Assistance

U.S. development assistance in India has made significant contributions to India's economic progress. Yet in both the United States and India, circumstances have changed considerably since the program was initiated. Not only has India made remarkable economic progress over the years, but the willingness of the United States to sustain past levels of assistance has declined precipitously. Total economic assistance already has dropped from a peak of $902 million in 1966, when the value of the dollar was more than three times greater than it is now, to $133 million in 1988, and of the latter sum, developmental assistance accounts for only $22 million.[69]

Should aid to India be terminated altogether? Despite the country's economic progress, India's immense poverty problem persists.

Nevertheless, large bilateral resource transfer programs no longer appear politically viable in the United States. In addition, many Indians would find such programs unacceptable. Given the budget constraints confronting the United States and the pressing needs of other regions of the world, the limited resources available to the United States arguably can be more productively employed by their concentration in areas such as Sub-Saharan Africa. The United States should simultaneously use its influence in the World Bank, the Asian Development Bank, and other multilateral institutions to see that India receives a share of funds befitting the scope of its problems. In addition to the humanitarian justification, such support advances American interests in promoting the stability of the world's largest democracy and the dominant power in South Asia.

While it is difficult to justify large-scale developmental assistance, a more limited program focusing on areas of mutual self-interest can contribute to improved relations and the welfare of both countries. India's efforts to advance its science and technology create opportunities for mutually beneficial cooperation. Former Prime Minister Rajiv Gandhi declared that "science and technology is at the heart of the Indo-U.S. relationship."[70]

Over the past decade, the importance of science and technology in Indo-U.S. relations has increased considerably. The Indo-U.S. Sub-Commission on Science and Technology has become a vital element of Indo-U.S. relations. The Sub-Commission includes working groups in seven areas: health, medical, and life sciences; physical and material sciences; earth sciences; atmospheric and marine sciences; energy; environment and ecology; and informatics. These working groups currently preside over more than eighty-seven projects involving the collaboration of Indian and U.S. scientists.

Although promoting Indo-U.S. cooperation is an important objective of this program, the benefits provided to U.S. science alone are sufficient justification. A recent study of Indian science conducted by the U.S. National Science Foundation (NSF) found that Indians are performing world-class research in chemistry, physics, microelectronics, biotechnology, and materials science.[71] The NSF applies virtually the same rigorous scientific standards to its review of Indo-U.S. proposals as it does to domestic project proposals. The projects are a bargain because the costs of doing research in the United States are much higher than in India. The exchanges have also led to substantial purchases of U.S. scientific equipment and to closer interaction among influential scientific opinion leaders.

Indo-U.S. scientific cooperation is likely to bring even greater benefits over the long term. Scientific discovery is increasingly an *international* enterprise. As expertise diffuses throughout the globe, maintaining contact with the scientific communities of other countries has become essential to keeping abreast of new advances. In addition, problems such as global warming, erosion of the ozone layer, and various other concerns are increasingly global in scope. International scientific cooperation is essential to their solution. It accelerates the development of new approaches, and it spreads common understandings that facilitate apportioning the costs that must be borne to maintain a healthy global environment.

Hopes for expanded Indo-American scientific cooperation may have suffered a setback in October 1989, when the State Department was ordered to establish a special review process for all new proposals for scientific cooperation with the potential for generating intellectual property. The review process must carefully balance American concerns for intellectual property rights with the potential benefits of Indo-American scientific cooperation if it is to avoid creating a bureaucratic bottleneck that would deter the development of new projects.

India's efforts to promote the technological capabilities of its private sector present a second area of mutual benefit. In the past few years, the U.S. Agency for International Development (USAID) has developed some innovative programs that benefit U.S. as well as Indian business concerns. The Program for the Advancement of Commercial Technology (PACT) exemplifies the new approach.[72] It helps set up joint ventures between Indian and U.S. firms that share interests in developing particular products. PACT provides a conditional grant to support their pre-manufacturing research and development costs. The joint ventures repay twice the original grant after they begin production. PACT was initiated in the fall of 1986 with a provision of $10 million. As of December 1989, it had approved eighteen projects in areas such as computer software, agriculture, and chemicals. These projects augment the technological capabilities of Indian firms. Since many of them are designed to produce exports to third countries, they increase India's exports as well. PACT provides U.S. firms with opportunities to jointly develop new products and with access to India's lower research costs. It facilitates their entrance into the Indian market, and enables them to accumulate experience about operating in the Third World.

The Omnibus Trade Act and the Future of Indo-U.S. Relations

In May 1989, the United States threatened India with sanctions under the Omnibus Trade Act of 1988. The Office of the U.S. Special Trade Representative (USTR) specified three key issues for negotiation. It identified India's restrictions on foreign direct investment and the government monopoly over the Indian insurance industry. It also placed India on a "priority watch list" because of its weak protection of intellectual property rights.

Using the Omnibus Trade Act to advance U.S. interests requires considerable political finesse. U.S. negotiators must defend legitimate concerns raised within the American political system, but they must also take into account the politics in targeted countries in order to avoid exerting pressures that might lead to counterproductive outcomes. As noted above, India has made modest progress over the last few years in relaxing its restrictions on FDI. The public pressure entailed in the U.S. Trade Representative's demands complicates new reform initiatives since they provide ammunition to the opponents of reform. The USTR's negotiations in the area of life insurance may generate more anti-American resentment than progress since the Indian government is reticent to curtail the monopoly of the Life Insurance Corporation of India—one of the linchpins of India's social welfare system. In the area of intellectual property rights, the weak provisions of India's Patent Act of 1970 are the primary concern. The Act was specifically designed to facilitate the absorption of new technology by weakening patent protection.[73] It denies patent coverage for products and grants protection only to production processes in areas such as pharmaceuticals, semiconductors, and biotechnology. The Patent Act has facilitated the Indian pharmaceutical industry's efforts to undercut U.S. multinationals in the Indian market and rapidly expand into global markets.[74] American pressure must overcome the resistance of the Indian Drug Manufacturers Association—a powerful lobby whose membership has reaped immense benefits from the current law.

The high public profile of the U.S. announcement that it would initiate negotiations with India limited the possibilities for progress on legitimate concerns and made negotiations difficult for both countries. The U.S should avoid overestimating its leverage and sacrificing the positive aspects of Indo-American relations. In the long term, American interests are best served by building support for its concerns within India. This is best accomplished through constructive dialogue and encouraging economic reforms that enhance India's experience with free trade, foreign investment, and the protection of intellectual property.

Conclusion

The international economy has developed a tier of countries that can be characterized as "transitional" economies. India shares the three basic characteristics of this group. *First,* it is undergoing a change from extensive to intensive development; economic growth is no longer driven so much by exploiting new resources as by increasing productivity through the introduction of new technologies. *Second,* India is attempting to re-articulate its economic institutions in ways that promote more efficient utilization of resources. *Third,* India has achieved sophisticated production capabilities in some sectors.

Transitional economies such as India present both opportunities and challenges to the United States. The opportunities come from the opening up of their economies, their eagerness to acquire new technologies, and their growing capabilities in science and technology. The challenges stem from their growing emphasis on export-led growth and their international competitiveness in certain sectors. Finding ways to establish mutually beneficial relations may be trying at times, since these countries have their own agendas and are not about to allow the United States to impose its will upon them. Nevertheless, these relations will become increasingly important since transitional economies such as India are certain to become more consequential global actors.

Notes

Note: The author wishes to thank Jonathan Lipow for his excellent research assistance. He also wishes to thank John P. Lewis and Valeriana Kallab for their comments on an earlier draft of this chapter.

[1]Raj Krishna, "The Economic Outlook for India," in James R. Roach, ed., *India 2000: The Next Fifteen Years* (Riverdale, Md.: Riverdaly, 1986), p. 175.

[2]The figures for other large developing countries are: Brazil, 10.8 per cent; Mexico, 12.7 per cent; Pakistan, 17.8 per cent; and Indonesia, 19.7 per cent. See World Bank, *World Development Report 1988* (Washington, D.C.: The World Bank, 1988), pp. 226–27, 242–43.

[3]FY1987–88 refers to the Indian fiscal year, beginning on April 1, 1987 and ending on March 31, 1988. Further references to fiscal years in this chapter follow this convention.

[4]Sanjaya Lall, "India," in John H. Dunning, ed., *Multinational Enterprises, Economic Structure and International Competitiveness* (Chichester, U.K.: John Wiley & Sons, 1985), pp. 314, 318.

[5]The World Bank, *World Debt Tables, 1987–88, Volume II. Country Tables* (Washington, D.C.: The World Bank, 1988), pp. 182–85.

[6]For instance, see John W. Mellor and Gunvant M. Desai, "Agricultural Change and Rural Poverty: A Synthesis," in John W. Mellor and Gunvant M. Desai, eds., *Agricultural Change and Rural Poverty: Variations on a Theme by Dharm Narain* (Baltimore, Md.: Johns Hopkins University Press, 1985), pp. 194–95.

[7]Government of India, Planning Commission, *The Seventh Five Year Plan, 1985–90, Vol. I* (New Delhi: Controller of Publications, 1985), p. xi.

[8]Government of India, Ministry of Finance, *Economic Survey 1988–89* (New Delhi: Controller of Publications, 1989), p. S–6; *Census of India 1981,* Series 1 India, Part III-A(i), General Economic Tables (Delhi: Controller of Publications, 1987), pp. 238–39; and *Census of India 1951,* Vol. 1, Part I-A (Delhi: Manager of Publications, 1953), p. 92.

[9]V.M. Dandekar, "Indian Economy since Independence," *Economic and Political Weekly,* Vol. 23, Nos. 1 and 2 (January 2–9, 1988), p. 49.

[10]M.L. Dantawala, "Growth and Equity in Agriculture," *Indian Journal of Agricultural Economics,* Vol. 42, No. 2 (April-June 1987), p. 154.

[11]A. Vaidyanathan, "Agricultural Development and Rural Poverty," in Robert E. B. Lucas and Gustav F. Papanek, eds., *The Indian Economy: Recent Developments and Future Prospects* (Boulder, Colo.: Westview Press, 1988), p. 81.

[12]H. K. Paranjape, "Indian 'Liberalization': Perestroika or Salaami Tactics?" *Economic and Political Weekly,* Vol. 23, Nos. 45–47 (November 1988), pp. 2343–58. The gradual pace continued during the second tenure of Indira Gandhi (1980–84) and accelerated under Rajiv Gandhi in 1985. For a good discussion of reforms under Indira Gandhi and their relationship to Rajiv Gandhi's reforms, see Atul Kohli, "Politics of Economic Liberalization in India," *World Development,* Vol. 17, No. 3 (March 1989), pp. 305–28.

[13]See for instance, Yoginder K. Alagh, "Policy, Growth and Structural Change in Indian Industry," *Economic and Political Weekly,* Vol. 22, Nos. 19–21 (May 1987), pp. AN57–AN60; Isher Judge Ahluwalia, "Industrial Policy and Industrial Performance in India," pp. 151–62, and Montek S. Ahluwalia, "India's Economic Performance, Policies and Prospects," pp. 345–60, both in Lucas and Papanek, *The Indian Economy,* op. cit. Not surprisingly, the government of India also supports this position. See *The Seventh Five Year Plan, 1985–90,* op. cit., p. 1.

[14]See, for instance, his foreword to the *Seventh Five Year Plan, 1985–90,* op. cit., pp. v–vii.

[15]*Economic Survey 1989–90,* op. cit., pp. S42–S44.

[16]Raj Chengappa, "Power: Seeking Radical Solutions," *India Today,* January 31, 1989, p. 63; *Seventh Five Year Plan, 1985–90,* op. cit., p. 21; and "Bid to involve private sector fails," *The Economic Times,* December 10, 1988.

[17]See, for instance, the following articles from *The Economic Times:* "Government turns to NRIs for funding energy sector," July 3, 1989; "Private power," June 12, 1989; "Industry status, plan priority for road building activities," May 25, 1989; "Private units to provide telecom equipment," July 9, 1989; "Maharashtra Initiative," May 22, 1989.

[18]All U.S. dollar equivalents are calculated at Rs. 17 = $US 1, the exchange rate approximating the U.S. dollar value of the rupee in December 1988. See "World Value of Rupee," *India Today,* December 31, 1989, p. 68.

[19]"Delicensing, relief package notified," *The Economic Times,* June 4, 1988; and Anand P. Raman, "Industrial Policy: A Bold Initiative," *India Today,* June 30, 1988, pp. 54–55.

[20]Ian M. D. Little, Dipak Mazumdar, and John M. Page, Jr., *Small Manufacturing Enterprises* (New York: Oxford University Press, 1987), p. 27; Anand P. Raman, "Industrial Policy: A Bold Initiative," op. cit.; "Automatic re-endorsement of licenses: New Scheme to boost production," *The Economic Times,* April 9, 1988; and Stanley Kochanek, "Regulation and Liberalization Theology in India," *Asian Survey,* Vol. 26, No. 12 (December 1986), p. 1290.

[21]Kochanek, "Regulation and Liberalization Theology," op. cit., p. 1291; "69 MRTP companies taken out of licensing curbs," *The Economic Times,* July 1, 1988; and Anand P. Raman, "MRTP: Shackles Off," *India Today,* July 31, 1988, p. 62.

[22]*Economic Survey 1987–88,* op. cit., p. 31.

[23]"Statistics," *Economic and Political Weekly,* Vol. 24, No. 47 (November 25, 1989), p. 2580.

[24]*Emerging Stock Markets Factbook* (Washington, D.C.: International Finance Corporation, 1989), pp. 16–17, 89.

[25]The World Bank, *World Development Report 1989* (New York: Oxford University Press, 1989), p. 108.

[26]T. N. Ninan, "Business and the Economy: Reaching Out and Upward," in Marshall M. Bouton and Philip Oldenburg, eds., *India Briefing 1989* (Boulder, Colo.: Westview Press, 1989), p. 44.

[27]"SEBI moots finds to boost capital market," *The Economic Times,* June 9, 1989.

[28]Palakunnathu G. Mathai, "Stock Markets: Changing Times," *India Today,* October 15, 1989; and "Venturing Forth," *The Economic Times,* July 22, 1989.

[29]For a good overview of these new trends see Ninan, "Business and the Economy," op. cit., pp. 48–52.

[30]"$150 million IBRD loan for tech, capital goods import likely," *The Economic Times,* June 23, 1989; "Technical Development Fund scheme: Fresh dose of liberalization," *The Economic Times,* March 18, 1989; and "India Rebuffs IBRD move to study Patents Act," *The Economic Times,* July 2, 1989.

[31]Charan Wadhva, "Import and Export Policy 1988–91: A Provisional Appraisal," *Economic and Political Weekly,* Vol 23, No. 26 (June 25, 1988), p. 1335.

[32]Calculated from Government of India, Ministry of Finance, *Economic Survey 1987–88,* op. cit., pp. S72–S73 and *Economic Survey 1989–90,* op. cit., pp. S72–S73.

[33]Calculated from "Finances of Government of India," *Economic and Political Weekly,* Vol. 24, No. 15 (April 15, 1989), p. 839.

[34]William Blanplied, "Science, Technology, and India's Aspirations," in Marshall M. Bouton and Philip Oldenburg, eds., *India Briefing 1988* (Boulder, Colo.: Westview Press, 1988) p. 149; "Tie-ups with U.S. firm for information network," *The Economic Times,* March 15, 1989; Manju Subramanya, "Lab industry interface increasing," *The Economic Times,* July 10, 1988; and "TDICI to assist projects in rural areas," *The Economic Times,* July 11, 1988.

[35]The contents of the Planning Commission's approach paper were reported in "Plan panel favors FERA reappraisal for investment," *The Economic Times,* June 18, 1989. Days after the contents of the Planning Commission's paper were published, senior government officials denied that India would encourage substantially larger sums of FDI. See "India reluctant to seek foreign direct investment," *The Economic Times,* June 25, 1989.

[36]"Fast channel a slow track," *The Economic Times,* November 29, 1988.

[37]"Foreign Investment Figures Cited," *Xinhua,* 1157 GMT, January 23, 1989. As cited in Rensselaer Lee's chapter in this volume.

[38]Wadhva, "Import and Export Policy 1988–91," op.cit., p. 1333.

[39]The sole exceptions were nine product groups whose import remains controlled by government agencies. See Wadhva, "Import and Export Policy 1988–91," op. cit., p. 1335.

[40]"Diesel at world market prices for export units," *The Economic Times,* June 17, 1988.

[41]The nominal changes were from Rs. 3.99 billion in 1980–81 to 5.18 billion in 1984–45 to a revised estimate of Rs. 9.60 billion in 1987–88. The budget estimate for 1988-89 calls for another 13.6 per cent increase to Rs. 10.91 billion. See *Expenditure Budget 1988–89,* op. cit., p. 107. The nominal figures were deflated by the wholesale price index.

[42]Calculations based on the TT selling rates for rupees supplied by the Bank of Tokyo Limited, New Delhi, on January 15, 1989, and October 21, 1989, as cited in *India Today.*

[43]Priya Ranjan Dash, "Dramatic growth in engg [engineering] exports," *The Economic Times,* June 5, 1989; "Manufacturer's export share rises," *The Economic Times,* June 5, 1989; and *Economic Survey 1988–89,* op. cit., pp. S76–S77.

[44]*Economic Survey, 1988–89,* op. cit., pp. 54, S9.

[45]See Blanplied, "Science, Technology, and India's Aspirations," op. cit., p. 148.

[46]Bal Phondke, "Scientific Projects: How not to manage them," *The Economic Times,* May 15, 1988.

[47]National Science Foundation, "Science and Technology in India," Washington, D.C., n.d., unpublished manuscript.

[48]See Ashok V. Desai, "The Technology Acquisition and Application: Interpretations of the Indian Experience," in Lucas and Papanek, *The Indian Economy,* op. cit., pp. 163–84; Vivek Bharati, "Technology Import: II. Indigenous barriers to self-reliance," *The Economic Times,* May 24, 1988; and Ashok V. Desai, ed., *Technology Absorption in Indian Industry* (New Delhi: Wiley Eastern Ltd., 1988).

[49]The high-profile resistance to the deal negotiated by Pepsico, Voltas, and Punjab State Agro Industries is a good example of this. It delayed approval of the project for more than two years. See Barbara Crossette, "India Allows Pepsi In After 2-Year Debate," *New York Times,* September 20, 1988; and David Devadas, "Pepsi-Cola: Fizzing Again," *India Today,* September 15, 1988.

[50]This problem is best exemplified by the case of Pepsico and Coca Cola. Two years of negotiation with the former resulted in an arrangement that provided substantial benefits to India in terms of technology transfer, research and development, and employment generation. Subsequent policy changes have enabled Coke to apply for production facilities in India on far more favorable terms, at least from Coca Cola's standpoint if not from India's. This has created a dilemma for the government. If it turns down the proposal from high-profile Coca Cola, it raises doubts about its eagerness for foreign investment. If it approves the Coke proposal, Pepsi may renegotiate its proposal on similar terms. See "Coke seeks 600t. capacity for concentrate," *The Economic Times,* November 27, 1988; "Coke may again opt for Pure Drinks as partner," *The Economic Times,* January 17, 1989; and David Devadas, "Soft Drinks: The New Fizz," *India Today,* December 15, 1988.

[51]This is especially true of the International Price Reimbursement Scheme (IPRS). See "Funds for the IPRS," *The Economic Times,* June 17, 1988; "Rs. 40 cr. ad hoc allotment for IPRS," *The Economic Times,* July 13, 1988. At the beginning of 1989 financing for the IPRS was increased to provide enough funding so it will not have to rely on ad hoc funding. See Priya Ranjan Dash, "Industry's gall is exporter's manna," *The Economic Times,* January 10, 1988.

[52]Wadhva, "Import and Export Policy 1988–91," op. cit., p. 1335.

[53]Ibid, p. 1335.

[54]A recent study of large engineering firms found that during 1985–86 their imports were valued at Rs. 8.41 billion while their exports amounted to just Rs. 4.91 billion. See Surajeet Das Gupta, "Export: A Sense of Purpose," *India Today*, October 31, 1988. See also "Big Houses criticized for poor export performance," *The Economic Times*, October 11, 1988; "Future licenses to be linked to exports," *The Economic Times*, October 11, 1988; and Palakunnathu G. Mathai and Parhasarathi Swami, "Export Obligations: Unrealistic Demands," *India Today*, April 15, 1987, pp. 76–8.

[55]"No More a Distant Threat," *Economic and Political Weekly*, Vol. 24, No. 47 (November 25, 1989), p. 2575.

[56]The data for 1984 comes from *World Debt Tables, 1988–89*, (Washington, D.C.: The World Bank, 1989), pp. 186–89. The data for 1989 was given by India's new Finance Minister, Madhu Dandavate, cited in David Housego, "Singh shows flair in distributing cabinet posts," *Financial Times*, December 27, 1989. The Washington D.C.-based Institute of International Finance has also estimated India's foreign debt for March 1989 at $60.2 billion. Ninan, "Business and Economy," op. cit., p. 36.

[57]*Economic Survey 1988–89*, op. cit., p. S-3; and "Finances of Government of India," *Economic and Political Weekly*, April 15, 1989, pp. 838–39. I have estimated India's GNP on the basis of 9 per cent growth and 5 per cent inflation.

[58]India's budget deficit was 7.9 per cent of its GDP in FY1987–88. See *International Financial Statistics Yearbook 1989* (Washington, D.C.: International Monetary Fund, 1989), p. 413.

[59]The data on expenditures is from *Expenditure Budget 1988–89*, op. cit., pp. 106, 108. Data on government deficits comes from *Receipts Budget 1988–89* (New Delhi: Government of India, 1988), p. 70. Conversion of current rupees into constant rupees was calculated using the wholesale price index. See *Economic Survey 1987–88*, op. cit., p. S57, and *Economic News*, Vol. 3, No. 10 (October 1988), p. 187.

[60]The data in this paragraph is taken from Anand P. Gupta, "Financing Public Enterprise Investments in India," *Economic and Political Weekly*, Vol. 23, No. 51 (December 17, 1988), pp. 2697–702.

[61]For similar arguments along these lines, see: Gustav F. Papanek, "Poverty in India," and Robert E. B. Lucas, "India's Industrial Policies," both in Lucas and Papanek, eds., *The Indian Economy*, op. cit., especially pp. 131–33, 188–90.

[62]This and the other data in this paragraph come from "The Economy: Growth Without Employment," *Economic and Political Weekly*, Vol. 24, No. 48 (December 2, 1989), p. 2628.

[63]From 1980 to 1987, 95 per cent of the growth in organized sector employment was in the public sector. Of this, more than 44 per cent came from "community and personal services." *Economic Survey, 1988–89*, op. cit., pp. S46–47.

[64]The data on changes in income in the public and private organized sector are from C. P. Chandrasekhar, "Aspects of Growth and Structural Change in Indian Industry," *Economic and Political Weekly*, Vol. 23, Nos. 45–47 (November 1988), pp. 2365. The figures for per capita income are computed on the basis of per capita net national product. See *Economic Survey 1988–89*, op. cit., p. S–3.

[65]R. Nagaraj, "Growth in Manufacturing Output since 1980: Some Preliminary Findings," *Economic and Political Weekly*, Vol. 24, No. 26 July 1, 1989, p. 1482.

[66]K. J. Joseph, "Bridling Growth of Electronics," *Economic and Political Weekly*, Vol. 24, No. 19 (April 22, 1989), p. 855.

[67]Ashok Rudra, "Luxury-Led Growth Strategy and Its Beneficiaries," *Economic and Political Weekly*, Vol. 23, No. 27 (July 2, 1988), pp. 1370–72; C. T. Kurien, "Indian Economy in the 1980s and on to the 1990s," *Economic and Political Weekly*, Vol. 24, No. 15 (April 15, 1989), pp. 787–98; Prabhat Patnaik, "Recent Growth Experience of the Indian Economy: Some Comments," *Economic and Political Weekly*, Vol. 22, Nos. 19–21 (May 1987), pp. AN49–AN56; and Sukharoy Chakravarty, "India's Development Strategy for the 1980s," *Economic and Political Weekly*, Vol. 19, Nos. 21 and 22 (May 26, 1984), pp. 845–51.

[68]*Economic Survey 1989–90*, op. cit., p. 107.

[69]U.S. Agency for International Development, mimeo, Washington, D.C., 1989.

[70]A. S. Ahmed Meer, "Indo-U.S. science and technology cooperation," *The Economic Times*, July 4, 1988.

[71]See "Indian Scientific Strengths: Selected Opportunities for Indo-U.S. Collaboration," Proceedings of a National Science Foundation Workshop, Washington, D.C., Spring 1987.

[72]Two other programs are in the initial stages of implementation. The Program for Acceleration of Commercial Technologies is designed to develop proposals to commercial-

ize energy technologies. The U.S. Agency for International Development (USAID) has recently formulated a program for establishing a Center for Technology Development. The CDT will promote joint research between academia and the private sector in India.

[73]Supporters of the act declared that its dilution of patent protection would prevent foreign multinationals from dominating Indian markets and stimulate domestic research. India's Minister for Industrial Development described the act as a "landmark in the industrial development of our country." See R. Michael Gadbaw and Leigh A. Kenney, "India," in R. Michael Gadbaw and Timothy J. Richards, eds., *Intellectual Property Rights: Global Consensus, Global Conflict?* (Boulder, Colo.: Westview Press, 1988), p. 200.

[74]See for instance, "Indian drug makers: Brand X is better," *The Economist*, July 1, 1989, p. 58; and S. N. Vasuki, "Pharmaceuticals: Export Surge," *India Today*, April 30, 1989, pp. 64–65.

Chapter 4

The Political Economy of Reform in the Three Giants

John Echeverri-Gent and Friedemann Müller

In an effort to keep pace with an increasingly dynamic and competitive international environment, the Soviet Union, China, and India have each begun to reform their economic and political institutions. Despite having achieved relatively high rates of savings and investment prior to the reforms, the economies of all three Giants have suffered from declining rates of growth. Furthermore, their emphasis on self-reliant development isolated them from rapid technological change in the global economy. This led to widening gaps between technological frontiers and the Giants' domestic capabilities.

Each country is attempting to make a transition from extensive development to intensive development. The former is primarily driven by bringing new resources into production processes; the latter results from improving economic efficiency, productivity, and domestic technological capabilities. Despite the considerable differences in their economic and political systems, this common challenge presents each of these Giants with parallel problems. This chapter analyzes how their distinctive ideological, political, and institutional traits have shaped the Giants' strategies to resolve these problems. In doing so, it attempts to go beyond the sometimes misleading generalizations characterizing communist and democratic political systems to explore the specific mechanisms that shape the dynamics of reform.

The chapter begins by discussing the attempts of each Giant to restructure its political institutions to be more compatible with the

135

requisites of intensive economic development. It then examines the relationship between the reforms and the politics of regionalism. Next, it investigates the Giants' efforts to increase the efficiency of their investment and labor force, and examines the political economy of price reform and inflation in each of the three countries. It then compares the measures that each Giant has taken to open up its economy in order to reap the benefits of international trade and technological development. A discussion of the implications of the political economy of reform in the Giants for U.S. foreign policy concludes our analysis.

Strategies for Political Reform

Despite the diversity of the Giants' political systems, the strategies for reform in each of them have included a degree of political change. Reformers in the Soviet Union have viewed the country's Stalinist political institutions as a major impediment to effective reform. During the 1980s, China's leadership introduced political reforms that were much more limited than those in the USSR, but by the end of the decade, it reverted to authoritarianism despite popular opposition. Efforts at political reform in India are not as concerned with creating new institutions as they are with curbing corruption and ending the erosion of political legitimacy.

The scope of political change in these different systems is better explained by disaggregating it into three dimensions. *Administrative rationalization* refers to the implementation of measures to create a more effective state apparatus. *Political liberalization* represents the process of extending to individuals and social groups rights that protect them from arbitrary or illegal acts committed by the state or third parties. *Democratization* denotes the process by which states are made responsive to the desires of their citizens.[1] Our comparison of these dimensions is intended to give a rough idea of the direction and extent of political change in the Giants. It is not designed to compare their absolute positions. This would be difficult given the problems of quantifying such matters. It also would not be very meaningful, since the three countries start from very different positions.

Administrative Rationalization

Administrative rationalization has been an important objective of political reform in each of the Giants. The Soviet Union and China have been especially concerned with redefining the role of their

Communist Parties. While the Soviets have stressed improving the commitment of their cadres largely by expelling corrupt members, the Chinese have attempted to recruit younger members with more education.[2]

The Soviets, to a much greater degree than the Chinese, have restructured their Communist Party and state bureaucracies in an effort to curtail micro-management of their economy. In 1988, they reorganized the Central Committee apparatus, reducing its departments from twenty to nine. During the summer of 1988, Gorbachev stated that he intended to cut personnel in the Central Committee bureaucracy by half, and by the end of 1988, 40 per cent of Central Committee officials had retired or were transfered. The July 1988 Central Committee plenum resolved to reorganize central and local Communist Party units to eliminate sub-units parallel to administrative branches. It also moved to terminate joint resolutions by Party committees and the executive administrative bodies of the Soviets.

In the USSR, important measures also have been taken to restructure all-union bureaucracies, with the intent of curtailing their involvement in the daily management of the economy and concentrating their focus on strategic management. The most significant move towards this end was Soviet Prime Minister Nikolai Ryzkhov's statement that he planned to reduce the number of branch industrial ministries from fifty to thirty-two.[3]

In China, efforts to improve economic management are primarily reflected in the increased use of empirical analysis in policymaking decisions. Over the past decade, research institutes proliferated and exerted a growing influence over public policy.[4] The state and the Communist Party even began to use surveys to gauge the public's response to policies.[5] In the aftermath of the June 1989 crackdown, however, many of the new institutes have been closed down, and the importance of empirical research has receded in the face of the new emphasis on ideological correctness.

In India, Rajiv Gandhi initiated substantial measures for administrative rationalization, but most of these were short-lived. Soon after becoming Prime Minister, he promised to improve management by delegating more authority to his cabinet ministers. His collegial management, however, soon deteriorated into incessant cabinet reshuffling with little improvement in administrative performance.[6] Rajiv Gandhi also attempted to gain greater control over India's expanding black market economy by allowing his Finance Minister to conduct raids against businesses suspected of violating the country's income tax and foreign exchange laws. But when the zealous V.P. Singh began raiding businessmen with connections to the Congress (I) Party, he was summarily transfered and eventually forced out of the Congress Party.

The ouster of Mr. Singh returned to haunt Rajiv Gandhi. The continuing corruption scandals that plagued the last years of Rajiv Gandhi's rule contributed to V.P. Singh's defeat of Rajiv and the Congress (I) Party in the November 1989 elections. Weeks after becoming Prime Minister, Singh took forceful steps to finally dispose of the scandals and reduce government corruption. At the end of December, his government passed legislation in the lower house of India's Parliament that would establish a national ombudsman with power to investigate the Prime Minister's office in order to curtail government corruption. Curbing this corruption would facilitate India's economic reform since it would refurbish the government's legitimacy and eliminate the illicit ties that have vested powerful actors within the bureaucracy and business community with a stake in the status quo.[7]

Political Liberalization

In the area of political liberalization, the Soviets have brought about remarkable changes. *Glasnost* greatly increased the access of Soviet citizens to non-official points of view. Under Gorbachev, the Soviet regime has shown much greater flexibility in tolerating political organizations outside the Communist Party. It has also enhanced the rights of the Soviet citizens to emigrate. The creation of a Constitutional Commission to write a new Soviet constitution is likely to further extend civil liberties; the Commission is chaired by Mikhail Gorbachev and includes many other prominent reformers.[8]

In China, access to critical sources of information—including foreign sources—increased during the 1980s, even while the Chinese political leadership's tolerance for political organization outside the Communist Party remained low. China's 1982 constitution formally expanded the rights of Chinese citizens. The limited liberalization that occurred was sharply curtailed, however, following the repression at Tiananmen Square in June 1989.

In general, India is far ahead of China and the Soviet Union in the extension of civil liberties to its citizens. The protection of these rights in some areas, however, eroded under Rajiv Gandhi. After initially raising hopes that he would relax controls over the country's government-owned television and radio, Rajiv's government flagrantly used them for partisan purposes during the 1989 election campaigns. His government also harassed the country's largest daily newspaper—the *Indian Express*—in a crude attempt to punish the paper for its anti-government exposés. Rajiv's unsuccessful effort to pass the Defamation Bill in August 1988 threatened to drastically reduce the freedom of India's lively press. And the enactment of the 59th Amendment to the Constitution in 1988 provided the government with the authority to suspend civil liberties in states suffering from internal disturbances. V.P. Singh's government seems intent on reversing the erosion of civil liberties. In its first month in office, it has passed legislation in India's lower house that would repeal the 59th Amendment and set up an autonomous Indian Broadcasting Corporation, removing television and radio from government control.

Democratization

The democratic advances made by the Soviet Union have surprised virtually everyone. While the March 1989 Supreme Soviet elections were structured to facilitate Communist Party control, the persistent efforts of Soviet citizens overcame many of the barriers to electoral responsiveness. In contrast to the old Supreme Soviet, the new one provides a forum for a broad spectrum of opinions and possesses substantial legislative authority. Its fifteen committees exercise the power of oversight over the executive, and it established special committees to investigate such sensitive matters as the violent repression of demonstrators at Tbilisi and the Molotov Ribbentrop Pact.

Even prior to its brutal suppression in May-June 1989, the extension of democracy in China was modest. In 1979, electoral reforms introduced multi-candidate elections at the local level, but nomination procedures largely remained under the control of the Communist Party.[9] Debates in the National Peoples Congress became more substantive, but the NPC remained a consultative body at best.

Governmental responsiveness in India declined under Rajiv Gandhi. Rajiv can claim credit for passing the Anti-defection Bill in 1985 and for his 1989 attempt to rejuvenate *panchayati raj*—India's local government in rural areas, but he failed to arrest a number of long-standing trends that diminished the government's accountability. The political vitality of India's Parliament reached new lows during Rajiv's tenure. Rajiv's poor handling of the Bofors scandal left the impression that he was either inept or attempting to perpetrate a cover-up. As illustrated by his support for the dismissal of the opposition state government in Karnataka in the spring of 1989, Rajiv continued to support central government dismissal of opposition state governments on dubious constitutional grounds. Rajiv also failed in his efforts to reform the inner workings of the Congress (I) Party and hold internal party elections.

Explaining the Differences

Political reform has advanced further in the Soviet Union than in China on virtually all counts. Though India's democracy is far in advance of the Communist Giants on each of the three analytical dimensions, it regressed during the tenure of Rajiv Gandhi. What explains the differences?

The remarkable advances in the USSR result from a variety of factors. In Mikhail Gorbachev's own analysis, the "era of stagnation" produced a profound social crisis as well as severe economic problems. Resolution of the crisis lay in reforming both the economic and the political systems. Ending the pervasive alienation of Soviet citizens was essential for rejuvenating the economy. Gorbachev's political reforms have been designed to encourage individual initiative and creativity by increasing the opportunities for participation. Gorbachev and other Soviet reformers were also acutely aware that the failure of previous attempts at economic reform had been caused in part by neglecting the need for simultaneous political change.[10] When Gorbachev entered office, he was confronted with a divided Politburo and entrenched bureaucracies with little interest in changing the status quo.[11] Strengthening his power and undermining the opposition has been an important motive of his reform strategy. But the pressure for reform is not only from the top down. The Soviet citizenry, once given the opportunity, has also provided substantial impetus. Social progress in the Soviet Union—especially the achievement of higher levels of education and economic well-being—along with the spread of news media and the greater openness to the West have produced a public that has a greater interest in democracy.[12]

China, in comparison, has experienced less political reform; its most substantial reforms have been in the area of administrative rationalization. Part of the explanation of the contrast between China and the Soviet Union in this respect is the different orientation of important segments of their political leaderships. As Gorbachev's call for creating a "common European home" illustrates, Soviet leaders manifest a greater affinity for Western Europe and its democratic values. Democratization in Eastern Europe also places the Soviet leadership under greater pressure for political reform. In contrast, many in China's leadership are attracted to a "new authoritarianism" based on the past experience of Taiwan, South Korea, and Singapore.[13] The impact of the Cultural Revolution is another factor. The social upheaval left China's economic and political institutions in disarray. The absence of deeply embedded institutional interests facilitated economic reform without recourse to political reform. Gorbachev, in contrast, must reform institutions that have had seventy years to entrench themselves. He has a greater need to introduce political reforms in order to overcome the resistance to economic reforms. In China, the trauma of the Cultural Revolution has also shaped the course of political reform. It left many of China's leaders—particularly Deng Xiaoping—with a deep-seated fear of the potential for disorder should the Communist Party lose its monopoly of power.[14] Since the limited experiments with multiple-candidate local elections mentioned previously, most of the pressure for democratization has come from the Chinese public. Until now, however, this pressure has been confined to students and a limited segment of urban workers. China's vast peasantry has yet to throw its weight behind political reform.[15]

The lack of substantial political reforms in India stems largely from the weakness of Rajiv Gandhi's political leadership. The challenge of implementing political reform is no less daunting than in the Soviet Union or China, but Rajiv Gandhi never displayed the capabilities and stature of Gorbachev or Deng Xiaoping. His shortcomings notwithstanding, the outcome of India's November 1989 elections shows the continuing resilience of India's democracy. During its first month in power, the V.P. Singh government has taken important measures to rejuvenate India's political institutions.

Economic Reform and the Politics of Regional and Ethnic Tensions

A distinctive feature of the Giants is that they span vast territories with substantial geographic and ethnic diversity. The immense scale of the Giants means that their regional sub-units often cover territories the size of countries. The size, distinctive cultures, languages, and economies of many regions within the Giants make them potentially viable nation-states. To govern their huge expanses, the Giants add extra administrative layers to their state institutions. Economic reform in the Giants often involves the decentralization of economic decisionmaking power from central governments to local authorities. The overlay of economic decentralization upon regional tensions can have explosive consequences. The heterogeneity and administrative complexity of the Giants greatly complicate the dynamics of their economic reform.

Reforms in the Soviet Union have changed the system of reward and repression that previously ensured national unity.[16] Gorbachev's measures to rationalize administration at the republic level ousted regional political leaders who had maintained order by building up the Soviet equivalent of political machines. The curtailment of some of the more repressive aspects of control has lowered the costs of collective action outside the official channels. The decline of repression and the newly instituted mechanisms of electoral accountability mean that Communist Party and state officials in the republics must be more responsive to the distinctive interests of their republic instead of acting as Moscow's pro-consuls. This has been a source of considerable divisiveness within the Party. Conflict between national Party leaders and regional leaders in Lithuania and Azerbaijan have already complicated the dynamics of Soviet reform.

The Soviets' reevaluation of their past has discredited the principles that previously legitimated the integration of the Soviet nationalities. It has stoked long-simmering resentments. *Glasnost* has led to a flowering of republican presses that report the news from the perspective of the local nationality. Economic stagnation and declining social mobility has intensified rivalry between different nationalities and created a pool of readily mobilizable educated unemployed. Regional tensions have been exacerbated by fiscal strains, budgetary reforms making the subsidies to backward republics more transparent, and efforts to introduce self-financing at the republic level. The considerable disparities in levels of economic development among the republics mean that economic reform has a differential impact. This adds to the stress.[17]

The Soviet political system is currently in a state of transition. The old forms of cohesion have eroded and new ones have yet to take their place. A rebirth of civil society has taken place in the midst of this transition. The success of Gorbachev's efforts to stimulate local initiative has left him with the challenge of containing and channeling local forces.[18] Meeting this challenge is likely to entail negotiating a new social compact with the nationalities. Such an accommodation requires establishing rules that specify limits to the scope of permissible demands and regulating the interaction of different players in a way that convinces leaders of nationalities that participation is worthwhile. The new Supreme Soviet, especially its Council of Nationalities, and the new Constitutional Commission are likely to be important fora for elaborating the rules of a new politics of nationalities.[19]

Though China has much less ethnic diversity than the Soviet Union, it historically has had a more decentralized state. Even at the peak of its administrative centralization, China's economy was less centrally controlled than that of the Soviet Union. In 1957–58, at the end of the period of Soviet tutelage, China's central plan allocated some 500 goods, whereas in the Soviet Union, Gosplan and the all-union ministries controlled the use of some 5,760 commodities.[20] China's small and much more numerous industrial enterprises provide another indication of its relatively greater economic decentralization. These totaled 499,300 in 1986, whereas Soviet industrial enterprises numbered only 45,539 in 1983.[21] The Chinese have historically placed greater reliance on area principles of administration that decentralize control to provincial and local Party committees while the Soviets have emphasized branch principles that concentrate power in all-union ministries and stress vertical channels of control.[22] Control over personnel through Communist Party *nomenklatura* (political appointment) systems is more decentralized in China. According to a recent estimate, the Central Committee's *nomenklatura* in the Soviet Union covers ten times the number of posts as that of the Chinese Central Committee.[23]

Historical political dynamics help explain China's greater decentralization. While Stalin's purges weakened the Soviet Communist Party at the regional level, Chinese regional leaders have exercised powerful influence.[24] Regional leaders have always had an important presence in the Chinese Communist Party's Central Committee, and their support has proved decisive at times when the central leadership was divided. Their backing was especially important during the Cultural Revolution, when Mao cultivated their support in order to challenge his foes in Beijing.[25] According to Susan Shirk, regional leaders have maintained the largest bloc within the Central Committee throughout the 1980s.[26]

A key political strategy of China's reformers has been what Shirk describes as "playing to the provinces." This has involved overcoming opposition in Beijing by designing reforms in a way that will gain the support of provincial leaders. The 1980 budgetary reforms provide a classic example. They introduced profit-sharing arrangements between local governments and the enterprises within their jurisdiction. This increased the revenues under local control and provided local officials with strong incentives to develop the local economy to increase their revenue base. Changes in policies affecting retained depreciation funds, the banking system, and price reform have also increased the share of resources under local control. In China's political system, local leaders frequently attempt to advance their careers by maximizing the economic growth of the unit under their command and protecting their subordinates from misfortune regardless of the broader consequences.[27] As control over resources has been decentralized, many leaders have engaged in what might be called "economic warlordism" by protecting local industry from external competition and constructing duplicative production facilities operating at inefficient economies of scale (see also Chapter 2). The decentralization of control over resources is also an important source of the periodic "overheating" of China's economy. As a consequence, the tension between central government attempts to reassert control, and the local governments' efforts to increase their autonomy is an important dynamic in China's reform process.[28]

While economic reform in China has been accompanied by the decentralization of power, economic reform in India has been implemented as political power has become increasingly centralized. The trend toward centralization began with Indira Gandhi's rise to power. In the early 1970s, she introduced Indian politics to mass mobilization through populist appeals. This freed her from dependence on state and local leaders to mobilize electoral support. Mrs. Gandhi proceeded to concentrate power in her own hands by, among other things, making herself final arbiter for the selection of Congress (I) Party election candidates; picking the chief ministers to head Congress (I) state governments on the basis of their loyalty to her rather than the extent of their popular support; and failing to respect the outcomes of state elections. As Mrs. Gandhi centralized power, she weakened the capacity of the Indian state and her own party to accommodate the manifold interests in India's heterogeneous society. Analysts have found the centralization of Indian political power to be an important cause of the outbreak of terrorism in Punjab.[29] Centralization also contributed to the growing stridency of conflict between the states and the central government over the apportioning of tax revenues.[30]

During the period immediately after he was elected Prime Minister, Rajiv Gandhi appeared determined to resolve India's festering regional conflicts. Atul Kohli's study of the Prime Minister's efforts to resolve the Punjab crisis shows that the concentration of power in his office paradoxically reduced his capacity for ending the conflict. It attenuated information flows to him and concentrated excessive administrative burdens on his shoulders. This impeded judicious decisionmaking and hindered the Prime Minister from following through on his commitments. His ineffectiveness, in turn, undermined his authority.[31]

The experience of the Giants shows that their size and diversity makes finding a proper balance between central and local authority within their political systems an essential element of their reform. Decentralization of political and economic decisionmaking authority is essential if their governments are to adequately account for the heterogeneous social conditions within their territories. Even if it were possible to account for this diversity within a centralized system, such a system would create widespread social alienation—since it could never accommodate the aspirations of people to participate in the economic and political decisions that affect their lives. At the same time, the legitimacy of central authorities must be refurbished. Resolving the social conflicts that are a natural consequence of the Giants' diversity necessitates compromises between competing interests. The legitimacy of the central authorities is essential to securing the sacrifices necessary to reach such compromises. The two developments are obviously interrelated, since decentralization of decisionmaking authority in each Giant is a precondition for enhancing the legitimacy of central authorities.

The Politics of Efficiency and Economic Security

Each of the Giants is confronted with a trade-off between increasing economic efficiency and sacrificing social entitlements that have been created to provide personal economic security. Social guarantees in terms of employment, wages, price stability, etc., have made the Soviet Union and China the world's largest risk-free societies. While somewhat less pervasive in its intervention, the Indian state is also quite paternalistic—especially in its large public sector. Improving economic efficiency in the Giants requires altering ideologies and deeply engrained individual attitudes. It also necessitates extracting immediate sacrifices from concentrated and well organized social groups with vested interests in the status quo in order to reap future benefits for more diffuse social interests. Reformers must find ways to overcome the resistance of the short-term losers without much support from the future beneficiaries.[32]

The Giants' heterogeneity and federal administrative structure further complicate matters[33]—since sacrifices are often concentrated in a particular locality, while the benefits are reaped in another or diffused throughout the system. Thus the federal structure disposes government and political authorities representing that locality to resist the changes. In this section, we examine two types of strategies to increase efficiency: reforms designed to improve efficiency by adjusting investment patterns and reforms that attempt to improve labor efficiency.

In the Soviet Union, the Law on State Enterprises, put into effect in January 1988, was an important early step in Gorbachev's strategy for improving the efficiency of investment. The new law was intended to increase the autonomy of Soviet enterprises by making them self-financing and self-managed. The law's final formulation, however, contained compromises with conservatives that reduced the independence of the enterprises. Central ministries, traditionally responsible for the supervision of Soviet enterprises, have been reluctant to cede their authority. The reforms were introduced in the midst of the 12th five-year plan, and the ministries remained responsible for ensuring that the enterprises met the plan's ambitious output targets. Thus when centrally-mandated output targets (known as "state orders") were reduced, the ministries issued their own state orders, which often occupied an enterprise's entire productive capacity.[34]

By forcing enterprises to become self-financing, the Law on State Enterprises pressures them to take measures to increase the productivity of their workers. These pressures are probably a cause of the reported decline in the number of industrial workers in the state sector by 1.7 million between March 1988 and March 1989. Growing cooperative and private sectors are likely to have absorbed a good number of these workers. Employment in these sectors during the same period increased by 1.5 million and 1.0 million respectively. It totaled 3.6 million as of March 31, 1989.[35]

The growth of private enterprise can potentially make an important contribution to increasing the efficiency of industrial labor in the Soviet Union. Reports already indicate that private entrepreneurs are leasing inefficient industrial plants and improving their performance by cutting their workforce.[36] Expanding the role of private enterprise through the introduction of family contracts and lease arrangements is also an important element in Gorbachev's strategy to resolve the Soviet Union's agricultural problems. However, their expansion continues to be limited by the objections of conservative Party leaders—and of the public at large—to private property and large disparities in personal incomes.

Other efforts to increase the efficiency of labor have met with mixed success. Wage reforms were implemented with the objective of tying increases to productivity growth, but in 1988, wages increased by 7 per cent while productivity rose by only 2.5 per cent.[37] Gorbachev's political reforms have reduced the costs of collective action for the workers. The crippling wildcat strikes of the summer of 1989 express a central problem for Soviet reformers over the next years: They must find a way to direct worker initiative into productive channels and persuade workers who have long suffered under miserable conditions to once again accept short-term sacrifices in order to secure long-term benefits.[38]

In contrast to the Soviet Union, where the power of the central ministries has constrained Soviet efforts to improve investment efficiency, local governments in China have played an important role in shaping the outcomes of Chinese strategies. The 1981 reform enabling enterprises to retain their profits reduced the revenues of the central government and increased the resources of enterprises and local governments. Reforms in 1984 expanded the sale of industrial goods on markets and enabled enterprises to sell their above-quota production at floating prices within 20 per cent of the administered prices. These reforms have increased enterprise autonomy in relation to the center and provided greater incentives for local government intervention. As control over enterprises through *direct* administrative mechanisms recedes, local governments exercise power over local enterprises through *indirect* means. They influence the allocation of the factors of production—especially labor and finance. Local officials also influence appointments of enterprise managers and the determination of profit retention rates.[39]

Local governments and enterprises develop a symbiotic relationship that limits improvements in efficiency. Since enterprises enhance their revenue base and provide jobs to local workers, local officials have considerable incentive to promote them. This is true of local governments in any country. It is the means available to Chinese local government that are extraordinary. Because local governments receive their revenues from both profits and taxes, they often perpetuate the survival of unprofitable firms as long as their tax revenues exceed their losses. By erecting trade barriers, local governments protect inefficient enterprises and impede the expansion of dynamic firms from other regions. They also require enterprises in their jurisdiction to purchase inputs from uncompetitive local suppliers. The intervention of local governments often interferes with realizing efficient economies of scale, and difficulties in creating coordination among them hinders the implementation of inter-regional infrastructural projects. The pervasive intervention of local governments has led one analyst to observe: "Inter-regional competition in Chinese industry may be more akin to competition in international trade than to competition in well-integrated national markets."[40] The parallels extend to strategies for overcoming protectionism, since enterprises interested in breaking into a local market often are obliged to enter into joint ventures with local enterprises.

As in the Soviet Union, the expansion of small-scale collectives and private enterprises in China offers an important means to increase economic efficiency. Collectives and private enterprises were one of the most dynamic sectors of the Chinese economy. In 1988, industrial production in the collective and private sectors was estimated to have grown by 29 per cent and 46 per cent, respectively. Private enterprises, however, have borne the brunt of the Chinese government's retrenchment program initiated in the fall of 1988. As a consequence, a reported 2.2 million of the 14.5 private businesses existing in 1988 were forced to close down by the fall of 1989. While some of these were opportunistic endeavors that could be shut down with little damage to the economy, the use of private enterprise as a means of enhancing economic efficiency has been called into question by the Communist Party's renewed disdain for wealthy entrepreneurs—now labeled "exploiters"—in the aftermath of the 1989 crackdown.[41]

The Chinese have had mixed success in their efforts to increase labor efficiency. The introduction of the production responsibility system has been highly successful in increasing the productivity of agricultural labor.[42] Efforts to increase the productivity of industrial workers by reforming the wage system have been far less successful.

The reestablishment of bonuses in 1979—after their abolition during the Cultural Revolution—and their linkage to enterprise profits have had a negative impact. Managers of enterprises, eager to avoid creating tensions among their workers, have distributed equal bonuses to their workers—thus limiting incentives. Generous bonuses have been distributed even when it has required "cooking the company books."[43] Wage increases in China have outpaced increases in productivity and economic growth. From 1984 to 1988, wages increased by 16–24 per cent annually while the growth of China's GNP averaged only 8–14 per cent.[44] In 1989, the Chinese government was compelled to combat the inflationary impact of wage increases by forcing workers to purchase government bonds.

The Chinese have also introduced a labor contract system to provide managers with the authority to weed out unproductive workers. As it stands now, sacking a worker is "harder than going to heaven" according to one industrial manager.[45] Because housing and welfare benefits are tied to employment, workers continue to prefer secure job tenure to labor contracts at increased wages. Managers of skilled laborers have also been unenthusiastic, since skilled workers are in high demand. The government has attempted to soften the impact of unemployment by creating unemployment insurance funds. But this insurance system, introduced in 1986, has yet to make the labor contract system more popular. Recent estimates indicate that less than 5 per cent of the workforce has signed labor contracts.[46]

Indian public policy, like China's, stresses the broad social responsibilities of its enterprises—and, as in China, the efficiency of investment allocation in India suffers from the resulting rigidities. In the Indian policy environment, a firm is not merely an agent for efficiently transforming resources into commodities, but part of a social contract which provides a secure livelihood to its workers. As a result, Indian laws prevent firms employing over ninety-nine workers from laying off their employees without first obtaining government approval, and an array of public policies impede mergers and bankruptcies. These rigidities have contributed to the proliferation of "sick units"—firms which, after having registered for seven years, have accumulated losses equal to their assets and have incurred losses in the last two years. Between December 1980 and June 1987, the number of sick units rose from 24,550 to 159,938.[47]

The Indian approach to alleviating the problem of sick industries reflects the acute concern of policymakers about providing employment security and the scarcity of capital. Measures such as the establishment of the Industrial Reconstruction Bank of India in 1984 and of the Board for Industrial Financial Reconstruction in 1987 have been taken to sort out viable and non-viable units and to formulate plans to revive the viable ones. Though these institutions have greatly expedited governmental responses to the problems of sick units, they operate in an environment where cultural values and pressures from local politicians, businesses, and trade unions encourage them to salvage firms suffering from critical problems. As one observer noted, they often find themselves in the position of a "doctor trying to revive a corpse."[48]

The Indian state's efforts to improve labor efficiency also reflect its unwillingness to take the political risks necessary for longer-term economic efficiency. The introduction of the Industrial Relations Act in the spring of 1988 was implicit recognition of the need for changes. But the Act, which was introduced without prior public debate, contained so many flaws and met with such vehement opposition from labor and business alike that it was never brought to a vote.[49] Similarly, despite widespread consensus that India's public sector is overstaffed and woefully inefficient, employment in public sector services over the last fifteen years has expanded faster than any other sector. From 1971 to 1986, it grew by 67 per cent from 5.6 million to 9.4 million.[50]

The Politics of Price Reform and Inflation

Price reform is central to the Giants' efforts to set up a mechanism that will efficiently allocate resources. In the Soviet Union and China, determination of virtually all prices by central planners resulted in widespread distortions and inefficiency. Government control over prices in India is less pervasive but still considerable.

Price reform in the Giants has followed one of two strategies. Government authority may be used to change prices so that they more accurately approximate scarcity values, or the state may relinquish its control and allow markets to establish prices. In either case, price reform is likely to result in substantial price increases.

The political leaderships of the Soviet Union and China have both rolled back price reform programs for fear of its inflationary impact. Yet price reform itself is not inherently inflationary. History includes examples of radical price reforms that have been non-inflationary.[51] Our comparison of the politics of reform in the Giants shows that the sources of inflation should be distinguished from price reform. Inflationary pressures in each Giant *preceded* the recent reforms. Prior to the reforms, these pressures were disguised as long lines, immense monetary overhangs, and thriving black markets. The specter of inflation that haunts price reform can be extinguished only after public policy in the Giants satisfactorily disposes of these pressures.

Agricultural price reform provides a good example. Demand has traditionally exceeded supply at the prices set in the communist Giants. Administratively determined prices repressed the inflationary manifestations of this imbalance. Allowing the equilibrium of supply and demand to freely set prices in these circumstances naturally leads to price increases. This is a politically sensitive matter. In each of the three Giants, strategies for reforming agricultural prices are constrained by the political leadership's desire to avoid popular protest. Diverse political circumstances in each country have shaped different strategies to resolve the problem.

In 1988, the Soviets curtailed subsidies on agricultural inputs while increasing state purchase prices by approximately the same amount. Passing on these increases to the public was politically unacceptable, so Soviet leaders avoided raising retail prices by increasing subsidies. These were budgeted for 87.9 billion rubles, or 17.8 per cent of all expenditures in the 1989 budget.[52] The new program for economic reform announced in December 1989 postponed further increases in agricultural purchase prices from 1990 to 1991. Retail prices will not be increased before 1992—and even then only after a nationwide debate.

China has gone much further in revising agricultural prices. This is in part a consequence of the fact that agriculture is a more important sector in the Chinese economy. It may also result from the greater sympathy that the Chinese Communist Party has historically displayed toward the peasantry. The Chinese government stimulated the agricultural production boom of the early 1980s by increasing purchase prices by 20 per cent in 1979 and 8 per cent in

1980. Increasing the share of produce sold on the open market soon superseded raising state procurement prices as the basic strategy for price adjustment. This was in part due to the government's desire to improve the coordination between production and demand by substituting markets for state procurement. But it was also motivated by the state's wish to avoid the budgetary strains that would accompany further increases in procurement prices without comparable increases in retail prices. Pent-up demand drove up market prices for many commodities. At the same time, state purchase prices for foodgrains did not keep up with the rising costs of inputs. Farmers shifted production out of foodgrains, causing shortages. The government attempted to combat this trend by guaranteeing farmers access to scarce inputs at discounted prices, and, more recently, by increasing its purchase prices.[53] Yet the government still faces a dilemma: It must increase the profitability of foodgrain production if it is to provide sufficient incentives to meet the country's foodgrain needs. This means that it must either increase retail prices and confront popular unrest or increase its subsidization of urban foodgrain prices and exacerbate the strain on its budget.[54]

India's problems with agricultural price reform are similar, although its political terrain differs in important ways. In contrast to the Soviet Union but like China, India has a predominantly rural population and a weighty agricultural sector. But India's peasants, unlike China's, cast effective votes. In a democracy where more than 60 per cent of the workforce is employed in agriculture and where demonstrations to demand higher agricultural prices have drawn hundreds of thousands, one might expect the state to be very responsive. Yet state procurement prices in India declined in real terms from the early 1960s to the mid-1980s.[55] Part of the explanation for this lies in the fact that most political parties organized their rural constituencies before widespread commercialization of foodgrain production. They defined the interests of rural voters in terms of caste rather than agriculture. When commercialization generated demands for higher procurement prices, India's caste-based parties were slow to respond. An important factor in the National Front's defeat of the Congress (I) Party in the 1989 elections was its greater responsiveness to the demands of India's farmers. Its campaign pledges included promises to revise the formula for calculating agricultural prices and to increase central government investment in the agricultural sector.[56]

The fact that the deregulation of food prices in China has proceeded much further than deregulation of industrial prices suggests that, in addition to the fear of a public backlash against inflation, other factors impede price reform.[57] In 1985, Zhao Ziyang announced that the State Council would formulate a policy for a comprehensive industrial price reform. While there have been modest adjustments in the prices of a limited number of goods, the Chinese shied away from comprehensive reform, and in the spring of 1989, they began to roll back many of their reforms.[58]

Price reform is inherently redistributive. It is resisted by those who lose. In state managed economies, proposals for price reform generate intense bureaucratic conflict. This has been the case in China, where industrial price reform has proceeded much further than in the Soviet Union. Ministries for heavy industries have put up particularly strong resistance to industrial reforms.[59] These are traditionally among the most powerful bureaucracies in communist systems. Overcoming their resistance was possible only by using various forms of "side payments" to compensate them for their losses. These, however, impede efficient sectoral adjustments and add to the fiscal burdens of reform. In the Soviet case, price reform eventually may create even greater bureaucratic conflict. Since the Soviets lack sufficient industrial competition to prevent producers from taking advantage of the reform to impose monopoly prices,[60] effective price reform will necessitate breaking up the concentration of economic power in different sectors.

The political dynamics of agricultural and industrial price reform in the Giants show that increased subsidies and consequent fiscal strains are an important source of inflation. Economic reform in each Giant has been accompanied by growing budget deficits.[61] Yet the side payments have failed to eliminate the bureaucratic and popular pressures that threaten the reforms. The ad hoc fashion in which they have been doled out prevents the formulation of comprehensive adjustment policies. A more comprehensive approach would ease inflationary pressures and enable better management of the social dislocation that is an inevitable consequence of the reforms.

The contrast between India on the one hand and the Soviet Union and China on the other highlights the communist countries' lack of an effective monetary policy as another source of inflation. The role of monetary policy in the command economies was subordinated to the central plan. Monetary policy and the banking system were not responsible for efficiently allocating investment, since the state budget provided investment funds and minimum levels of working capital. The role of the banking system was to facilitate achievement of the central plan's output targets by providing supplementary working capital and regulating liquidity outside the enterprise sector. Major changes in financial institutions and monetary policy are needed as the economic reforms increase the share of credit allocated outside the state budget.[62]

Comparison with the Indian case highlights the fact that the central banks in the communist countries are recent creations and have yet to develop effective policy instruments. While India's central bank, the Reserve Bank of India (RBI), was founded in 1935, the People's Bank of China (PBC) became China's central bank only in 1984, and the Soviets began to reform the position of Gosbank only at the beginning of 1988. Though India's RBI wields relatively crude monetary policy instruments, they are considerably more effective than those available to the PBC or Gosbank. While the RBI's obligation to finance central government budget deficits puts an upward pressure on the money supply, it retains a limited capacity for managing India's currency through its control over the banking system's cash reserve and statutory liquidity ratios.[63] The PBC and Gosbank have been unable to wield even these rather crude instruments with much effect. The relatively more advanced PBC, for instance, has the power to set interest rates, but the changes it has introduced have been so modest and the rates have remained so low that they fail to deter borrowing. Reserve ratios are ineffective because China's banks often use their political ties to have their targets adjusted retroactively. The PBC's lack of insulation from political pressure has hampered its ability to limit the growth of currency.[64]

China's banking system operates in an environment that encourages rapid credit expansion.[65] Chinese enterprises have soft budget constraints and an insatiable appetite for riskless finance. Local government and party officials often place tremendous pressure on local banks to issue loans regardless of project viability. The banks evaluate loans to enterprises within a distorted price system that makes accurate appraisal difficult. Banking officials lack adequate training. They have personal incentives to extend credit since their salaries and fringe benefits are tied to the volume of loans that they issue. Ultimately, the banks have little incentive to restrict credit because they are not held responsible for bad loans. The provision of excessive credit to inefficient enterprises has contributed to China's budget deficits and the rapid growth of its currency.[66] It has also contributed to economic bottlenecks by diverting state investment from infrastructure. The retrenchment beginning in the fall of 1989 succeeded in curbing the banking system's extension of credit only by imposing administrative controls.

The lack of effective monetary policy shows one of the central weaknesses of the reform process in the USSR and China. As they remove the administrative controls that predominated in their centrally planned systems, they must develop new institutions and macroeconomic policy instruments to regulate their markets and prevent their economies from running out of control. The limitations of

China's efforts to do so have contributed to its oscillations between economic overheating and retrenchment through crude administrative controls. Overcoming this "China syndrome" presents a central challenge for Soviet economic policymakers.

The Politics of Opening Economies to Foreign Trade and Investment

Prior to the reforms, each Giant followed a development strategy that emphasized economic self-reliance. In each case, the strategy was underpinned by apprehensions that global markets were capricious and iniquitous and by the difficulties of reconciling international markets with the extensive bureaucratic controls that regulated their domestic economies. The large, diversified economies of the Giants made autarkic developmental strategies more plausible. Political leaders in each Giant have come to realize that their country's economic isolation prevented them from taking advantage of the opportunities available through greater integration with global markets. Measures to facilitate increased integration have been a central feature of the reforms in the Giants. However, the different institutions and political dynamics that characterize each country have shaped its strategies for economic opening.

China's pre-reform trading system was modeled after that of the Soviet Union, and the countries' strategies for trade reform were confronted with similar initial problems. In both countries, virtually all foreign trade was channelled through foreign trade agencies directly controlled by a central ministry of foreign trade.[67] Both the Soviet Union and China have reorganized their trade bureaucracies at the central government level. The motives for the Soviet's creation of the State Foreign Economic Commission in 1986 and China's establishment of the Ministry of Foreign Economic Relations and Trade (MOFERT) in 1982 were similar. In each case, the objective was to transform the central authority from an agency in charge of a system of administrative trade controls to one concerned with implementing strategic planning through more indirect mechanisms.

At the same time, each country decentralized authority within the trade system and created incentives to increase exports by allowing exporters to retain a percentage of their foreign exchange earnings. The patterns of decentralization within the Soviet Union and China varied according to the distribution of power within their political systems. In the Soviet Union, decentralization initially transfered foreign trade organizations from the Ministry of Foreign

Trade to about twenty other ministries. It also enabled some seventy enterprises to engage in foreign trade. The reforms implemented on April 1, 1989 extended decentralization by authorizing any domestic enterprise to engage in foreign trade *directly*, though licensing and access to foreign exchange continue to limit to some two hundred the number of enterprises conducting foreign trade.[68] The pattern of decentralization in China is quite different. Instead of providing control over trade to individual enterprises, China's trade reform provided provincial and local governments with control over trade by giving them authority over branches of MOFERT's foreign trade corporations as well as the right to establish new foreign trade corporations (FTCs).

The decentralization of authority over foreign trade, coupled with the incentive of retained foreign exchange, have been popular measures in both the Soviet Union and China. The reasons are not difficult to see. Those who lose from the reforms are limited to the bureaucrats in central trade ministries while a broad constellation of interests within each political system reaps an array of benefits (e.g., new technologies, high quality goods, foreign travel) from the greater access to foreign trade.[69]

Since trade reform was initiated earlier in China than in the Soviet Union, the problems China has confronted highlight issues that are likely to be important to the success of Soviet reform. After achieving trade surpluses from 1981 to 1984, China ran unprecedented deficits in 1985 and 1986.[70] An important cause of the problems was the fact that decentralization of trade authority occurred before China developed new mechanisms to guide the decisions of local authorities so that they did not conflict with national interests. Imports surged by 62 per cent from 1984 to 1985. This was in part a result of a "binge" by local authorities who used their newly acquired authority to import for themselves. Free-wheeling local governments liberally supplemented the foreign exchange that they retained from their exports with borrowings from Chinese and foreign banks.[71] Simultaneously, cut-throat competition between different FTCs in markets dominated by Chinese exports drove down prices and reduced revenues.[72]

The Chinese trade deficits in 1985 and 1986 also illustrate the interrelated nature of China's economic reforms. Uncontrolled credits from China's banking system, which was itself reformed in 1984, were an important source of financing for the export binge. The partial nature of Chinese price reform means that domestic prices do not reflect international scarcity values. This distorts the incentives for exports and imports. The rationality of China's trade structure is also distorted by the lack of a *national* market for converting foreign exchange. China's thirty-nine local foreign exchange centers offer substantially different rates. As a result, a high-cost producer in a region with an advantageous exchange rate may displace the exports of lower-cost producers in regions with less favorable rates.[73]

The Chinese curbed their trade deficits in 1987 by devaluing the *reminbi* and increasing the regulation of the FTCs. MOFERT's regulation of the FTCs was strengthened. Controls over the financing of imports were tightened. Requirements for the licensing of imports and exports were extended. Customs duties were increased, especially for what are considered to be unnecessary imports. Export associations were organized to coordinate sales, and export production networks were formed to promote exports.[74]

Reforms introduced in 1988 launched a new round of decentralization. The new "contract responsibility system" transferred much of the responsibility for regulating trade to the provincial governments. The reforms also enabled some enterprises to conduct trade independently of FTCs. Following these reforms, the trade deficit jumped to $7.7 billion in 1988. Since September 1988, the Chinese have re-centralized control and increased the number of products subject to export licenses, quotas, and outright bans and by re-centralizing controls over trading corporations.[75]

Comparing trade reform in China with that in India highlights their different points of departure. While China is building up its licensing and tariff systems, India is beginning to dismantle them. The politics of trade reform in India, like those of China and the Soviet Union, are shaped by the political repercussions of its previous import substitution strategy. But regulation of Indian foreign trade was initiated not by a revolutionary communist regime but by a British colonial government concerned with conserving foreign exchange during World War II. Given this beginning and the political power exercised by private traders, the Indian state never monopolized control over trade as did the Chinese and Soviet states. Instead, it erected an elaborate licensing system and high tariffs to protect its industry.

The major objective of Indian trade reform has been to shift the means of protection from licensing to tariffs and then reduce the level of tariffs. The dynamics of the reform have been shaped by the country's highly organized private sector as well as by the interests of its public sector.[76] Public sector enterprises such as Bharat Heavy Electricals Ltd. and the Steel Authority of India Ltd. have been important forces behind India's protectionism. However, the public sector provided an early impetus for trade reform when the Indian government, in order to counter the trend of declining public investment, attempted to reduce its capital costs by enabling selected industries to import equipment and avoid high domestic costs.[77] Pressures for relaxing import restrictions in cases of domestic availability and reducing the country's extraordinary high tariffs spread, and the government soon announced a strategy to modernize India's industrial base by relaxing restrictions on imports and promoting selected exports (see also Chapter 3).

India's capital goods industry has been a central target of the reforms although it has lobbied to defend its protection. In 1987 it succeeded in rolling back tariff reductions, and in 1988 it pressured the government to modify a new reform package in a way that made it less vulnerable to international competition.[78] Indian trade reform exhibits a pattern that also may develop in the Soviet Union and China. Liberalization of trade restrictions has proceeded much further in new industries (e.g., electronics), where the political lobbies have yet to develop strength, than in older sectors where industries have already established strong lobbies.

Opening to Foreign Investment

In addition to introducing trade reform, each Giant has opened up its economy by reforming policies to facilitate foreign direct investment (FDI). FDI was virtually prohibited in China until 1979 and in the Soviet Union until 1987. Restrictions on convertibility still constrain its scope in the Communist Giants. The Soviets, especially with the implementation of new regulations on April 1, 1989, have shown remarkable eagerness to attract FDI (see also Chapter 1). What explains the Soviet eagerness? Like the other Giants, the Soviets find FDI an attractive source of new technologies. Absorbing advanced technologies is especially important to the Soviets, who cannot resort to a comparative advantage in cheap labor to promote exports. FDI also promises to improve the availability and quality of Soviet consumer goods. In addition, the Soviets desire to develop their managerial skills. Both the Soviet Union and China have been much more isolated from capitalist management strategies than India. While the Chinese have access to those of the overseas Chinese community, joint ventures with OECD multinationals are the primary source for the Soviets.

In contrast to the Soviet Union and China, India has been relatively slow to reform its regulation of FDI. Its Foreign Exchange Regulation Act continues to exercise stricter controls over FDI than regulations in either the USSR or China. Even when it promises thousands of jobs and improvement of technological capabilities in strategic areas, FDI must still overcome political controversy often instigated by domestic competitors.[79] Indian controls began to be relaxed in 1988 (see Chapter 3). However, further reform has been delayed by the 1989 political campaign and the more conservative position taken by the National Front government during its first weeks in office.

The politics of economic opening in the Soviet Union and China appear to be less contested than in India. To a large extent this is due to their different points of departure. In the case of the communist Giants, economic opening still has the traits of an expanding-sum game.[80] In the Soviet Union, this is largely due to the initial stage of the reform process. The Chinese reforms have produced more controversy because they have exacerbated regional disparities, incited conflict among state bureaucracies, and exposed the country to controversial foreign influences.[81] The Chinese leadership's strong commitment to economic opening is reflected in its unwavering adherence to the policy even in the wake of the obvious role played by foreign influence in promoting dissidence from their regime.

Despite the measures taken to open up their economies, domestic industry in both the Soviet Union and China remains highly protected.[82] In the Soviet Union, decentralization of authority over trade and provisions allowing currency retention have had a very limited impact on imports, since most hard currency is earned through energy exports that remain under the control of the central government.[83] The scope for competition from joint ventures is limited because they are usually placed under the supervision of ministries that sponsor competing Soviet enterprises. Despite the advance of reforms in China, domestic industry presents the government with lists of goods whose importation should be denied due to their domestic availability,[84] and China's regulation of FDI favors ventures that export or produce substitutes for imports. In each country, barriers to the convertibility of domestic currency continue to insulate domestic industry. Protection of domestic industry in the communist Giants is likely to continue into the foreseeable future since the social disruption that would result from the introduction of international competition would present their leadership with grave political perils.

Opening up the Indian economy to international competition presents even greater immediate political challenges. The measures India has taken to open up its economy have begun to threaten the protection of domestic enterprises in the public and private sector. Furthermore, India's democratic political system provides these enterprises with more opportunities to oppose the introduction of foreign competition. The resistance of these influential political actors provides an important explanation for the slower pace of India's economic opening.

Conclusion

The reform process has created extraordinary uncertainty in each of the Giants. In the Soviet Union and China, the reforms involve a struggle to create a new social order. In India, reform objectives are more modest—to recast state intervention in the economy and to reform the workings of the country's democratic system to restore the legitimacy of its institutions. In each case, there is uncertainty as to whether new reforms will be permanent or simply temporary steps in a longer transition, and no one can forecast the ultimate destination of the transition.

The uncertainty inherent in the transitions creates problems for their successful culmination. The effective economic reform in each of the Giants requires that substantial segments of their societies sacrifice their immediate interests in order to reshape their institutions in a manner that will increase social welfare over the long term. Yet the uncertainty makes the temptation to maximize short-term welfare difficult to resist. This is especially true in the case of Soviet workers, who have repeatedly been asked to tighten their belts in order to achieve a utopian future that has never materialized. It is also true of Party officials who use their privileged positions to exploit the opportunities presented by the transition.

In each of the three Giants, reform has been accompanied by political crisis. In India, the crisis was less due to the implementation of economic reforms than to the failure to curtail destructive trends in the functioning of the country's political institutions. India's mixed economy has long provided opportunities for corruption that are comparable to those created by the emerging two-track economic systems in the Soviet Union and China. Rajiv Gandhi failed to stop the proliferation of corruption. Furthermore, he continued the trend toward the centralization of power and as a result failed to curb the tensions growing among India's many ethnic and religious communities. The ouster of Rajiv Gandhi in the November 1989 elections demonstrates one of the advantages of democratic systems over the authoritarian systems of the Soviet Union and China. Democracy provides the citizens of the country with an opportunity to reject political leaders whose abilities do not fit the needs of the day.

In the Soviet Union and China, economic and political reforms have undermined the Communist Party's monopoly of power and eroded its legitimacy. The economic crises that have occurred belie the Party's claim to an infallible understanding of social change and undercut the Leninist rationale for its vanguard position. Opening up the societies has intensified the exposure of the Soviet and Chinese people to an influx of foreign ideas—including democratic values. The decentralization of economic decisionmaking authority, especially the promotion of cooperatives and private property, have created sources of power outside the Communist Party as well as alternative avenues of social mobility. In the Soviet Union, *political* reform has made it harder to recruit Communist Party members, since reform has created new channels for public service.[85] In China, *economic* reform made it more difficult to attract new Communist Party members with individual initiative—since it generated more attractive opportunities for achievement outside the Party.[86] In both countries, the co-existence of market and command systems has created tremendous opportunities for graft. Popular disaffection has grown as personal sacrifice by Party members has given way to opportunistic corruption.

By undermining the legitimacy of their Parties and promoting alternative bases of power, the Soviet and Chinese reforms have created conditions conducive to democratization. Our comparison of political reform in the Soviet Union and China identified the differences in their level of economic development as an important factor in determining whether these conditions will lead to greater democracy. Political leadership and the orientation of the military are also crucial.

The nature of the reform process places a premium on political leadership. Reforming social institutions requires a political vision capable of conceiving alternatives that are not only feasible but also sufficiently attractive to inspire popular support even when this means immediate sacrifices. The politics of institutional reform also necessitate extraordinary political skills. New political coalitions that are capable of overcoming powerful groups with vested interests in the status quo must be formed. Differences in the ability of the political leaderships of the Giants are an important factor in explaining the progress of their reforms. The worldviews and strategies of key leaders become increasingly central to explanations of important turns of events.

If the political leaderships are unable to refashion their countries' institutions in ways that revive their legitimacy, the role of the military and paramilitary forces grows in importance. This is most clear in China, where the military has provided a crucial pillar of support after the suppression of the pro-democracy movement, and military connections became crucial in the power struggle within the Party. Should Gorbachev fail to legitimize his reforms, the Soviet military will be an important factor in determining whether he will succeed in repressing popular discontent or be dislodged from power by either a popular revolt or a conservative coup.

Can the United States influence the outcome of the transitions under way in the Giants? The ability of any country to shape the domestic affairs of another is always limited. This is especially true of the Giants, whose immense size dilutes the impact of external factors. In addition, each of the Giants protects its independence with special zeal, and the complexity of its domestic politics makes the impact of outside intervention difficult to predict. Nevertheless, the tendency of the reforms to produce fiscal strains, current-account deficits, and a need for expertise concerning market mechanisms increases the oportunities for outside influence.

The distinctiveness of the reform process in each Giant means that the United States should pursue different strategies toward each country. In India, the World Bank and the IMF have already played an important role in promoting economic reforms. They should be encouraged to increase the availability of their expertise and funding. The multilateral nature of these institutions helps to lessen suspicions concerning ulterior motives. Their experience in promoting structural adjustment in other developing countries endows them with expertise that is especially relevant to the Indian case.

The introduction of market mechanisms into command economies like that of the Soviet Union creates a different set of needs. The effective operation of markets requires not only decentralization of economic decisionmaking and price reform, but also the creation of new national institutions and policy instruments—central banks, an efficient commercial banking system, stock exchanges, new tax systems, and social safety nets—to regulate the operation of the market. The World Bank and the IMF played an important role during the 1980s in advising China on these matters. The United States should encourage Soviet access to Bank and Fund expertise and not oppose eventual Soviet membership in both institutions, if the USSR is willing to abide by their conditions.[87]

The United States government itself possesses considerable expertise in regulating markets. U.S. officials have already visited the Soviet Union to provide advice. This interchange should be expanded and institutionalized through a program of official exchanges. Finally, successful participation in markets requires entrepreneurial skills—e.g. business management, accounting and international trade—that have remained woefully underdeveloped during the Soviet Union's seventy years under a command economy. The United States can play a role in strengthening Soviet skills in these areas by sponsoring educational exchanges. Leading American business schools could not only host Soviet students but also make their expertise available in assisting the Soviets in setting up their own programs.[88]

During the 1980s, China benefited from many of the above measures, but these failed to deter the suppression of the pro-democracy movement in June 1989. How should the United States respond to such reversals in the Giants' reforms? U.S. policy must strike a delicate balance between projecting American values and preserving a basic framework necessary for building relations over the long term with these large and strategically important countries. Despite its muted diplomatic rhetoric, the Bush Administration's initial sanctions—the suspension of military sales, the delay of new loans from the World Bank, and moratorium on all high-level official contacts—appropriately balanced these demands. The Administration's later actions—especially President Bush's veto of the Pelosi bill extending the right of Chinese students to remain in the United States and the Scowcroft visits—appear at this writing (January 10, 1989) to be shortsighted concessions to Chinese hardliners even while the latter continue to repress dissidents and retrench economic reforms.

The case of China shows that reforms in the Giants may lead to polarization between hardliners whose material interests and ideological values are threatened by both a) the advance of reforms, and b) the forces for democracy promoted by the decline in the legitimacy of the ruling party and the creation of a more pluralistic social infrastructure. In such circumstances, the United States will be confronted with the temptation to accommodate hardliners for short-term diplomatic expediency at the expense of democratic forces whose immediate chances for power seem remote. The prospects for democratization will improve, however, if the reforms continue to advance. The long-term interests of the United States are best served by resisting concessions to the hardliners and devising policies to support the democrats.

Notes

Note: The authors wish to thank Jonathan Lipow, Gregory Chen, and Manu Goswani for their research assistance. We would also like to thank Joan M. Nelson, John P. Lewis, Susan Shirk, Valeriana Kallab, and the members of the SAPE Seminar at the University of Chicago for their comments on an earlier version of this chapter. Special thanks are due to John Lewis for his insights about the institutional consequences of country size.

[1]The definitions for liberalization and democracy are derived from Guillermo O'Donnell and Philippe C. Schmitter, *Transitions from Authoritarian Rule: Tentative Conclusions about Uncertain Democracies* (Baltimore, Md.: Johns Hopkins University Press, 1986), pp. 7–8. The dimension of administrative rationalization is suggested by Nina Halperin in her "Economic Reform and Democratization in Communist Systems: The Case of China," *Studies in Comparative Communism*, Vol. 22, Nos. ⅔ (Summer/Autumn 1989), pp. 139–52.

[2]Donna Bahry and Brian Silver, "Public Perceptions and the Dilemmas of Party Reform in the USSR: Insights from Soviet Emigrants," Paper presented at the Annual Meeting of the American Political Science Association, Atlanta, Georgia, August 31–September 3, 1989, pp. 1–2; and Bohdan Harasymiw, "The CPSU in transition from Brezhnev to Gorbachev," *Canadian Journal of Political Science*, No. 21 (1988), pp. 249–66.

From 1984 to 1986, the Chinese recruited six million new Party members and significantly lowered the average age level of cadres and increased their average educational qualifications. Stanley Rosen, "The Chinese Communist Party and Chinese Society: Popular Attitudes Toward Party Membership and the Party's Image," a Paper presented at the Annual Meeting of the American Political Science Association, Atlanta, Georgia, August 31–September 3, pp. 5–6. See also Richard Baum, "Introduction: Beyond Leninism? Economic Reform and Political Development in Post-Mao China," *Studies in Comparative Communism*, Vol. 22, Nos. ⅔ (Summer/Autumn 1989), p. 116; and Harry Harding, *China's Second Revolution* (Washington, D.C.: The Brookings Institution, 1987), pp. 206–7.

[3]Archie Brown, "Political Change in the Soviet Union," *World Policy Journal*, Vol. 6, No. 4 (Fall 1989), pp. 490–94; and Jeffrey W. Hahn, "Power to the Soviets?" *Problems of Communism* (January 1989), pp. 41–42, 45.

[4]Kenneth Lieberthal and Michel Oksenburg, *Policy Making in China: Leaders, Structures and Processes* (Princeton, N.J.: Princeton University Press, 1988), pp. 158–60.

[5]Stanley Rosen, "Public Opinion and Reform in the People's Republic of China," *Studies in Comparative Communism*, Vol. 22, Nos. ⅔ (Summer/Autumn 1989), pp. 153–70.

[6]By one estimate, Rajiv made twenty-six changes in his cabinet in his first four years in government. See Babhani Sen Gupta, "The Fourth Year," *Economic and Political Weekly*, January 7, 1989, p. 13.

[7]For the illicit links between the Congress (I) Party and India's business community, see Stanley A. Kochanek, "Briefcase Politics in India: The Congress Party and the Business Elite," *Asian Survey*, Vol. 27, No. 12 (December 1987), 1278–1301. For arguments that these liaisons have limited India's economic reforms, see Atul Kohli, "Politics of Economic Liberalization in India," *World Development*, Vol. 17, No. 3 (March 1989), pp. 305–28; John Harriss, "The State in Retreat? Why Has India Experienced Such Half-Hearted 'Liberalisation' in the 1980s?" and James Manor, "Tried, then Abandoned: Economic Liberalisation in India," both in *IDS Bulletin*, Vol. 18, No. 4 (November 1987), pp. 31–38, 39–44.

[8]Brown, "Political Change in the Soviet Union," op. cit., pp. 486–88.

[9]See Barrett McCormick, "Leninist Implementation: The Election Campaign," in David Lampton, ed., *Policy Implementation in Post-Mao China* (Berkeley, Calif.: University of California Press, 1987), pp. 383–413; and Andrew Nathan, *Chinese Democracy* (Berkeley, Calif.: University of California Press, 1985), Chapter 10.

[10]According to Gorbachev's report to the 19th All-Union Conference, June 28, 1988, "The existing political system proved incapable of protecting us from the growth of stagnation phenomena in economic and social life in the later decades, and doomed the reforms undertaken at the time to failure." *Moscow News*, July 3, 1988, Supplement, p. 5. This was also the conclusion of a conference of Soviet economists chaired by Leonid Abalkin held in Moscow in 1987 to assess the implications of previous reform experience for *perestroika*. See Anders Aslund, *Gorbachev's Struggle for Economic Reform* (Ithaca, N.Y.: Cornell University Press, 1989), p. 180.

[11]See Aslund, *Gorbachev's Struggle*, op. cit., for an excellent overview of the compromises imposed upon Gorbachev by opponents in the Politburo and the resistance put up by various bureaucracies.

[12]Gail W. Lapidus, "State and Society: Towards the Emergence of Civil Society in the Soviet Union," in Seweryn Bialer, ed., *Politics, Society, and Nationality Inside Gorbachev's Russia* (Boulder, Colo.: Westview Press, 1989), pp. 121–47.

[13]Nicholas D. Kristof, " 'New Authoritarianism' Seen in Chinese Actions," *The New York Times*, February 28, 1989.

[14]For the impact of the Cultural Revolution on Deng's attitude towards democracy, see Stuart R. Schram, "China After the 13th Congress," *China Quarterly*, No. 114 (June 1988), pp. 182, 196–97.

[15]David Zweig documents the lack of peasant support for political reform. Nevertheless, he contends that peasant unrest will grow rapidly if the Chinese regime is unable to resolve the problems in China's rural sector. See David Zweig, "Peasants and Politics," *World Policy Journal*, Vol. 6, No. 4 (Fall 1989), pp. 633–45.

[16]The following paragraphs draw from Paul Goble, "Ethnic Politics in the USSR," *Problems of Communism* (July-August 1989), pp. 1–14; Gail W. Lapidus, "Gorbachev's Nationalities Problem," *Foreign Affairs*, (1989), pp. 92–108; Ronald Grigor Suny, "Nationalist and Ethnic Unrest in the Soviet Union," *World Policy Journal*, Vol. 6, No.4 (Fall 1989), pp. 503–28; and Patrick Cockburn, "Dateline USSR: Ethnic Tremors," *Foreign Policy*, No. 74 (Spring 1989), pp. 168–84.

[17]For an excellent account of the impact of the economic reforms on republican finances and the subsequent controversies, see Donna Bahry, "Perestroika and the Debate over Territorial Economic Decentralization," *The Harriman Institute Forum*, Vol. 2, No. 5 (May 1989), pp. 1–8. For background to these issues see Donna Bahry's *Outside Moscow: Power, Politics, and Budgetary Policies in the Soviet Republics* (New York: Columbia University Press, 1987).

[18]Lapidus, "Gorbachev's Nationalities Problem," op cit., p. 107.

[19]Cockburn, "Dateline USSR: Ethnic Tremors," op. cit., especially pp. 183–84.

[20]Christine Wong, "Material Allocation and Decentralization: Impact of the Local Sector on Industrial Reform," in Elizabeth J. Perry and Christine Wong, eds., *The Political Economy of Reform in Post-Mao China* (Cambridge, Mass.: Harvard University Press, 1985), p. 261.

[21]The Chinese data is from State Statistical Bureau, People's Republic of China, *Chinese Statistical Yearbook, 1987* (Longman, 1988), p. 187. The Soviet data is from Ed A. Hewett, *Reforming the Soviet Economy: Equality versus Efficiency* (Washington, D.C.: The Brookings Institution, 1988), p. 115. Much (though not all) of the difference is explained by the rapid growth of China's collective enterprises since 1970. China's 96,000 state owned industrial enterprises are still double the total of all Soviet industrial enterprises.

[22]Franz Schurmann, *Ideology and Organization in Communist China* (Berkeley, Calif.: University of California Press, 1966), pp. 175–76. For a discussion of branch and area principles of administration in China see Jonathan Unger, "The Struggle to Dictate China's Administration: The Conflict of Branches vs. Areas vs. Reform," *The Australian Journal of Chinese Affairs*, No. 18 (July 1987), pp. 16–45.

[23]John P. Burns, "China's Nomenklatura System," *Problems of Communism* (Sept-Oct 1987), p. 46.

[24]Ibid., p. 174.

[25]Barry Naughton, "The Decline of Central Control over Investment in Post-Mao China," in Lampton, ed., *Policy Implementation in Post-Mao China* op. cit., p. 71.

[26]Susan L. Shirk, "The Chinese Political System and the Political Strategy of Economic Reform," Paper presented to the conference on "The Structure of Authority and Bureaucratic Behavior in China," sponsored by the Joint Committee on Chinese Studies of the American Council of Learned Societies and the Social Science Research Council, Tucson, Arizona, June 19–23, 1988.

[27]See David Lampton, "Chinese Politics: The Bargaining Treadmill," *Issues and Studies*, Vol. 23, No. 3 (March 1987), p. 14; and Lieberthal and Oksenberg, *Policy Making in China*, op. cit., pp. 346–47.

[28]Shirk, "The Chinese Political System," op. cit., pp. 25–30; Naughton, "The Decline of Central Control," op. cit., pp. 57–59; Wong, "Material Allocation and Decentralization," op. cit., pp. 253–280; and Christine Wong, "Between Plan and Market: The Role of the Local Sector in Post-Mao China," in Bruce L. Reynolds, ed., *Chinese Economic Reform: How Far, How Fast?* (Boston, Mass.: Academic Press, 1988), pp. 95–108.

[29]See especially Paul R. Brass, "The Punjab Crisis and the Unity of India," in Atul Kohli, ed., *India's Democracy: An Analysis of Changing State Society Relations* (Princeton, N.J.: Princeton University, 1988), pp. 169–213; and Lloyd I. Rudolph, "India and Punjab: A Fragile Peace," *Asian Issues 1985* (Lanham, Md: University Press of America, 1986), pp. 33–53.

[30]For instance, see Salamat Ali, "Delhi's Dictat," *Far Eastern Economic Review*, April 6, 1989, pp. 19–21; and Hemlata Rao, "Financial Relations," *Seminar 357* (May 1989), pp. 31–35.

[31]Kohli, "Centralization and Powerlessness in India," op. cit., pp. 13–34.

[32]For a similar formulation concerning the politics of structural adjustment see Joan M. Nelson, "Comparative Perspectives: The Politics of Economic Adjustment in Developing Nations," in Joan M. Nelson, ed., *Economic Crisis and Policy Choice: The Politics of Economic Adjustment in the Third World* (Princeton, N.J.: Princeton University Press, forthcoming).

[33]While the Chinese polity is technically not a federal system, provincial and local-level officials within the Communist Party and state institutions in fact exercise considerable power as noted above. Thus, we feel that the observations hold true for China as well as the other Giants.

[34]See the Central Intelligence Agency and the Defense Intelligence Agency, "The Soviet Economy in 1988: Gorbachev Changes Course," Report presented to the Subcommittee on National Security Economics of the Joint Economic Committee, April 14, 1989, pp. 9–10; Daniel Thorniley, "Reforming the Soviet Foreign Trade Structure and Adapting to Change," Paper presented at the colloquium on "Soviet Economic Reforms: Implementation Under Way," sponsored by NATO Economics Directorate, Brussels, March 15–17, p. 6; and Anders Aslund, *Gorbachev's Struggle for Economic Reform,* op. cit., pp. 104–5.

[35]See *PlanEcon Report,* Vol. 5, No. 17 (April 28, 1989), p. 5. In addition, this source reports that employment in the Kolkhoz sector declined by 1.1 million and unemployment increased by one million.

[36]Gorbachev himself has observed, "Just look at what is happening in industry, comrades. People are leasing low-performance workshops and factories, and the first thing they do is cut the work force by a third." *Moscow News,* No. 33 (August 14, 1988), Supplement, p. 4.

[37]Central Intelligence Agency and the Defense Intelligence Agency, "The Soviet Economy in 1988," op. cit., pp. 8, 12b, 41.

[38]For an interesting account of the role of trade unions in Gorbachev's Soviet Union see Peter Hauslohner, "Democratization From the Middle Out: Soviet trade Unions and Perestroika," *The Harriman Institute Forum 10,* No. 10 (October 1988), pp. 1–8.

[39]Wong, "Between Plan and Market," op. cit., pp. 101–2.

[40]See William Byrd, "The Role and Impact of Markets," in Gene Tidrick and Chen Jiyuan, eds., *China's Industrial Reforms* (New York: Oxford University Press, 1987), pp. 256–59.

[41]Central Intelligence Agency, "The Chinese Economy in 1988 and 1989: Reforms on Hold, Economic Problems Mount," Report presented to the Subcommittee on Technology and National Security of the Joint Economic Committee, U.S. Congress, Washington, D.C., 1989, p. 19; Sheryl WuDunn, "China Cracks Down on Private Work," *The New York Times,* November 8, 1989; and Nicholas Kristof, "Beijing Party Calls for Purge in Capital," *The New York Times,* October 16, 1989.

[42]Jeffrey R. Taylor, "Rural Employment Trends and the Legacy of Surplus Labor, 1978–86," *China Quarterly* (December, 1988), p. 25.

[43]Andrew G. Walder, "Wage Reform and the Web of Factory Interests," *China Quarterly,* No. 109 (March 1987), pp. 22–41; and W. Gary Vause and Georgia Bush Vrionis, "China's Labor Reform Challenge: Motivation of the Productive Forces," *Stanford Journal of International Law,* Vol. 24, No. 2 (Spring 1988), especially pp. 459–60.

[44]Bernard Stavis, "The Political Economy of Inflation in China," *Studies in Comparative Communism,* Vol. 22, Nos. ⅔ (Summer/Autumn 1989), p. 242.

[45]Jamie P. Horsley, "The Chinese Workforce," *The China Business Review* (May-June 1988), p. 52.

[46]Lowell Dittmer, "China in 1988: The Continuing Dilemma of Socialist Reform," *Asian Survey,* Vol. 29, No. 1 (January 1989), pp. 12–28. For a good account of the implementation of the labor contract system see: Gordon White, "The Politics of Economic Reform in Chinese Industry: The Introduction of the Labor Contract System," *China Quarterly* (September 1987), pp. 365–89.

[47]Government of India, *Economic Survey 1987–88* (New Delhi: Controller of Publications, 1988), p. 40; and Government of India, *Economic Survey 1988–89* (New Delhi: Controller of Publications, 1989), p. 56.

[48]See "Dealing with Sickness," *The Economic Times,* May 6, 1988.

[49]"Industrial ties amendment bill introduced in RS," *The Economic Times,* May 14, 1988; C. V. Pavaskar, "Industrial Disputes Act: Proposed Amendment," *The Economic Times,* May 16, 1988; "Industrial Disputes Bill: Action plan by TUs," *The Economic Times,* May 27, 1988; R. J. Mehta, "IDA: Old wine in new bottle," *The Economic Times,* June 16, 1988; and "New labour bill flayed," *The Economic Times,* August 3, 1988.

[50]Mrinal Datta-Chadhuri, "Indian Workers and Their Conditions of Work," a Paper presented at a joint Overseas Development Council/U.S. Department of Labor symposium, December 1988, p.6.

[51]In 1948, the Federal Republic of Germany conducted comprehensive price reforms that not only did not cause inflation but had deflationary repercussions.

[52]Morris Bornstein, "Problems of Price Reform in the USSR," Paper presented at the NATO Economics Colloquium, "Soviet Economic Reforms: Implementation Under Way," Brussels, March 15–17, 1989, p. 13.

[53]Prices were raised in 1988 and again in March 1989. In many areas, these increases remained insufficient to cover growing costs. For a fascinating journalistic account of the current situation, see James L. Tyson, "China's Farm Policies Roil Peasants," *The Christian Science Monitor*, April 14, 1989.

[54]For one of the best recent treatments of China's agricultural reforms, see the special issue "Food and Agriculture in China during the Post-Mao Era," in *China Quarterly*, No. 116 (December 1988), particularly the articles by Robert F. Ash, "The Evolution of Agricultural Policy," pp. 529–55, and Terry Sicular, "Agricultural Planning and Pricing in the Post-Mao Period," pp. 671–705.

[55]P. S. George, "Costs and Benefits of Food Subsidies in India," in Per Pinstrup-Andersen, ed., *Food Subsidies in Developing Countries: Costs, Benefits, and Policy Options* (Baltimore, Md.: Johns Hopkins University Press, 1988), p. 231.

[56]For an excellent analysis of India's new agrarian politics see Ashutosh Varshney, "Organizing the Countryside: Peasant Mobilization in the 1980s," unpublished paper, Massachusetts Institute of Technology, 1989. See also the special issue of *Seminar*, No. 352 (December 1988) on the new agrarianism and Lloyd I. Rudolph and Susanne Hoeber Rudolph *In Pursuit of Lakshmi: The Political Economy of the Indian State* (Chicago: University of Chicago Press, 1987), pp. 333–92.

[57]Susan L. Shirk, "The Chinese Political System and the Political Strategy of Economic Reform," Paper presented to the Conference on "The Structure of Authority and Bureaucratic Behavior in China," sponsored by the Joint Committee on Chinese Studies of the American Council of Learned Societies and the Social Science Research Council, Tucson, Arizona, June 19–23, 1988.

[58]*The Washington Post*, March 22, 1989; and *Journal of Commerce*, March 27, 1989.

[59]Ibid., pp. 21–25; and Dorothy J. Solinger, "The Fifth National People's Congress and the Process of Policymaking: Reform, Readjustment and Opposition," *Issues and Studies*, Vol. 28, No.8 (August 1982), pp. 63–106.

[60]Soviet reformers are well aware of the lack of competition in Soviet industry. For instance, according to Leonid Abalkin, Deputy Prime Minister of the Soviet Union, economic reform "requires resolute struggle against monopolistic trends and phenomena that inevitably lead to inhibition and stagnation." "Restructuring the Management of the Economy," *Problems of Economics* (August 1988), p. 20. Nikolai P. Shmelyov, head of the economics department at the Institute for the USA and Canada in Moscow, has asserted, "In our present situation the market is highly monopolized. It is much more monopolized than the markets in the United States—very much more. In this situation, it is really dangerous to decontrol prices because the first response of the monopoly organizations will be to raise their prices." "Perestroika: The View From Moscow," *The New York Times*, April 30, 1989. See also Ed A. Hewett, *Reforming the Soviet Economy: Equality versus Efficiency* (Washington, D.C.: The Brookings Institution, 1988), pp. 352–53.

[61]Under Gorbachev, Soviet budget deficits have steadily risen from roughly 2 per cent of the GNP in 1984 to 9 per cent in 1988. Central Intelligence Agency and the Defense Intelligence Agency, "The Soviet Economy in 1988," op. cit., p. 12. In China, budget deficits have corresponded to the country's reform cycle. According to IMF statistics, they started at 2.6 billion yuan in 1981 and rose to 4.4 billion yuan in 1984 before returning to a 2.2 billion yuan surplus in 1985. They rose to a plateau of between seven and eight billion yuan between 1986 and 1988. This is slightly less than one per cent of China's GNP. See *International Financial Statistics Yearbook 1989* (Washington, D.C.: International Monetary Fund, 1989), p. 291. The CIA, in contrast, estimates that China's budget deficit grew by almost 50 per cent between 1987 and 1988, reaching 2.5 per cent of its GNP. Central Intelligence Agency, "Chinese Economy in 1988 and 1989: Reforms on Hold, Economic Problems Mount," op. cit., pp. 26–27. India's budget deficit grew steadily from 5.5 per cent of its GDP in the Fiscal Year ending in March 31, 1982 to 9.1 per cent of the GDP in FY1987 before declining to 7.9 per cent in FY1988. See *International Financial Statistics Yearbook 1989*, op. cit. p. 413.

[62]In China, for instance, budget investment grew at an annual average of 2.3 per cent from 1979 to 1986 while extra-budget investment rose at an annual average of 20.6 per cent. See Li Yunqi, "China's Inflation: Causes, Effects, and Solutions," *Asian Survey*, Vol. 29, No. 7 (July 1989), p. 663. For a good description of the transition necessary in transforming China's monetary policy, see Luc De Wulf and David Goldsbough, "The Evolving Role of Monetary Policy in China," *IMF Staff Papers*, Vol. 33, No. 2 (June 1986), pp. 209–43. For the Soviet Union see: Hewett, *Reforming the Soviet Economy*, op. cit, pp. 298–299, and Aslund, *Gorbachev's Struggle*, op. cit. pp. 134–35.

[63]Vijay Joshi and I. M. D. Little, "Indian Macro-Economic Policies," unpublished paper, Nuffield College, Oxford University, 1988, pp. 30–34.

[64]For descriptions of the Chinese banking system see: Zhou Xiaochuan and Zhu Li,

"China's Banking System: Current Status, Perspective on Reform," *Journal of Comparative Economics*, Vol. 11 (1987), pp. 399–409; On-Kit Ta, "The Development of China's Financial System," *The Australian Journal of Chinese Affairs* (January 1987), pp. 95–113; and On-Kit Ta, "Reform of China's Banking System," *World Economy* (December 1986), pp. 427–40.

[65]Strict application of commercial criteria in India's banking system has also been diluted with the 1975 initiation of Regional Rural Banks whose lending is targeted to "weaker sections," and the 1979 requirement that all banks allocate 40 per cent of their credit to "priority sectors" at concessional interest rates by 1985. For an interesting presentation of the trade-offs between "commercial banking," "development banking," and "social banking," see James Copestake, "The Transition to Social Banking in India: Promises and Pitfalls," *Development Policy Review*, Vol. 6 (June 1988), pp. 139–64.

[66]According to IMF estimates, China's currency grew at an average rate of 28 per cent from 1983 to 1987. See Li Yunqi, "China's Inflation," op. cit., p. 658.

[67]For descriptions of the pre-reform trade system in the Soviet Union, see: Ed A. Hewett, "Foreign Economic Relations," in Abram Bergson and Herbert S. Levine, eds., *The Soviet Economy: Toward the Year 2000* (Boston, Mass.: Allen and Unwin, 1983), especially pp. 291–95. For a description of the pre-reform trade system in China see The World Bank, *China: External Trade and Capital* (Washington, D.C.: The World Bank, 1988), pp. 95–98.

[68]*Novoe Vremya*, No. 19 (1989), p. 16, as cited in Radio Liberty, *Report on the USSR*, Vol. 1, No. 24 (June 16, 1989).

[69]Aslund notes that the Soviets' Ministry of Foreign Trade was an especially easy target since it was notorious for its corruption. See his *Gorbachev's Struggle for Economic Reform*, op. cit., p. 137.

[70]China's trade deficit leaped to $13.1 billion in 1985 and $9.1 billion in 1986. *IMF Balance of Payments Statistics*, Vol. 39, Part 1 (Washington, D.C.: IMF, 1988).

[71]The increase was also in part a result of a decision by the Chinese government to run down what it considered to be an excessive accumulation of reserves. For explanations of the causes of the import surge, see *China: External Trade and Capital*, op. cit., pp. 69–70; and Harding, *China's Second Revolution*, op. cit., pp. 149–50.

[72]This was true in the case of commodity markets such as tungsten where competition among Chinese FTC's contributed to a 70 per cent drop in world prices. See Madelyn Ross, "Foreign Trade Offensive," *The China Business Review* (July-August 1987), pp. 31–32. It also took place in geographical markets like Hong Kong where China is a dominant exporter of relatively homogeneous commodities (e.g. agricultural goods, textiles and handicrafts) and demand is relatively inelastic. See *China: External Trade and Capital*, op. cit., p. 107. The decline of petroleum prices beginning at the end of 1985 also contributed to the reduction of China's exports. See Nicholas R. Lardy, *China's Entry into the World Economy* (Lanham, Md: University Press of America, 1987), pp. 30–31.

[73]Nicholas R. Lardy, "Debate over Reform of China's Foreign Trade System," Paper prepared for the 41st Annual Meeting of the Association for Asian Studies, Washington, D.C., March 17–19, 1989.

[74]Madelyn C. Ross, "Foreign Trade Offensive," op. cit., pp. 30–35.

[75]See Central Intelligence Agency, "The Chinese Economic Reform in 1988 and 1989: Reforms on Hold, Economic Problems Mount," op. cit., pp. 3, 5. For the 1988 reforms, see: Madelyn C. Ross, "Changing the Foreign Trade System," *The China Business Review* (May/June 1988), pp. 34–36. See also *China: External Trade and Capital*, op. cit., pp. 134–42.

[76]Pervasive state economic intervention in India has led to widespread political organization among the country's business community.

[77]See Ashok V. Desai, "The Politics of India's Trade Policy," in Henry R. Nau, ed., *Domestic Trade Politics and the Uruguay Round* (New York: Columbia University Press, 1989), pp. 102–3.

[78]Since 1987, the value of capital goods imports has declined in dollar terms. "Capital Illusion," *India Today*, December 31, 1989, p. 57. See also Charan Wadhva, "Import and Export Policy 1988–91: A Provisional Appraisal," *Economic and Political Weekly*, Vol. 24, No. 25, June 25, 1988, pp. 1331, 1335.

[79]The joint venture among Pepsico, Volta, and Punjab State Agro Industries incited popular controversy and took two years to gain approval despite its promise to provide 20,000 jobs in the troubled state of Punjab and its arrangement to undertake research and development in the priority food processing sector. The controversy was in part fueled by the opposition of local soft drink manufacturers. See Barbara Crossette, "India Allows Pepsi in After 2–Year Debate," *The New York Times*, September 20, 1988; and David Devadas, "Pepsi-Cola: Fizzing Again," *India Today*, September 15, 1988.

[80]David Bachman, "Domestic Sources of Chinese Foreign Policy," in Samuel S. Kim, ed., *China and the World: New Directions in Chinese Foreign Relations* (Boulder, Colo.: Westview Press, 1989), especially p. 47.

[81]Susan Shirk, for instance, argues that China's economic opening has exacerbated tensions between regions and economic sectors. The argument here is that these tensions have shaped the course of China's economic opening in a manner that preserves protectionism, (see below) but they have not stemmed the impetus driving it. See Susan Shirk, "The Domestic Political Dimensions of China's Foreign Economic Relations," in Samuel S. Kim, *China and the World* (1st ed.) (Boulder, Colo.: Westview Press, 1984), pp. 60–70. For a good discussion of the impact of historical and contemporary resentment against foreign cultural influences, see Harding, *China's Second Revolution*, op. cit., pp. 20–24, 134–36.

[82]Harry Harding and Ed A. Hewett, "Socialist Reforms and the World Economy," in John D. Streinbruner, ed., *Restructuring American Foreign Policy* (Washington, D.C.: The Brookings Institution, 1989), pp. 171–74.

[83]According to Soviet economists quoted in the weekly *Novoe Vremya*, No. 19, 1989, p. 16, "there are only 200 Soviet enterprises that are capable of establishing links with foreign partners. The number could increase to 40,000 if the enterprises had access to hard currency reserves." Cited in Radio Liberty, *Report on the USSR*, Vol. 1, No. 24 (June 16, 1989), p. 15.

[84]Shirk notes that the Chinese Ministry of Machine Building has been a particularly strong source of protectionist pressures. It has won the right to veto equipment import. See "The Domestic Political Dimensions of China's Foreign Economic Relations," op. cit., pp. 65–66.

[85]Bahry and Silver, "Public Perceptions and the Dilemmas of Party Reform in the USSR," op. cit., p. 18.

[86]Rosen, "The Chinese Communist Party and Chinese Society," op. cit., pp. 2–3.

[87]See Richard E. Feinberg, "The Soviet Union and the Bretton Woods Institutions: Risks and Rewards of Membership," Public Policy Paper, Institute for East-West Security Studies (New York), 1989 (New York, 1989).

[88]For some interesting proposals along these lines, see Thomas Naylor, "Economic Reforms and Changes In Patterns of International Relations," Unpublished paper, Duke University, May 1989, pp. 20–21.

Chapter 5

Science and Technology and Reform in the Giants

Richard P. Suttmeier

Introduction

Science and technology figure prominently in the reform programs of China, India, and the USSR. The ideology of each Giant speaks to the transformative and modernizing properties of science and technology (S&T), and national leaders have consciously identified themselves with their nations' S&T reforms. In spite of past technical achievements, each of the three Giants has fallen far short of realizing its S&T aspirations, especially as these relate to technological innovation. Thus, reform of the Giants' S&T policies is central to their broader reforms. The United States faces intriguing challenges and opportunities both to assist in the Giants' national reform efforts and to build innovative relationships with them that are adapted to a rapidly changing international environment.

Each of the three Giants has a community of scientists and engineers that is among the largest in the world, and each has invested heavily in the development of scientific and technological resources in the past. While cross-national indicators must be used with care, Table 1 illustrates the numerical strength of high-level research and development (R&D) manpower in the Giants relative to that of selected other countries. Were we measuring the *total* number of scientists and engineers, China would rank second and India, with 2.2 million scientists and engineers in 1985, would rank third or fourth.

Table 1. Numbers of Scientists and Engineers in R&D in Selected Countries

Country	Estimated Number of Scientists and Engineers in R&D	
USSR (low estimate)	1,485,000	(1985)
(high estimate)	1,710,000	(1985)
United States	806,200	(1987)
China	450,000	(1988)
Japan	418,300	(1987)
Germany	151,500	(1987)
France	108,200	(1987)
United Kingdom	98,700	(1986)
India	85,309	(1986)

Source: National Science Foundation. Figure for China is author's estimate based on various sources.

All three Giants are spending an increasing share of their GNP on research and development, with China recently rising above the 1 per cent figure and India coming close to it. In absolute terms, however, Indian and Chinese national expenditures are far below the world's leaders (see Table 2).

The aspirations of the three countries are often discussed in terms of concern within the Giants that they are falling hopelessly behind the West technologically. Gaining access to advanced Western technology is thus seen as a central part of their reform programs. Yet the Giants themselves remain ambivalent about Western technology. They want and need it; they fear dependence on it; and their ability to absorb it is highly variable. Their attitudes toward foreign technology are also conditioned by a sense of technological nationalism, grounded in beliefs that national technical needs should be satisfied by a country's own scientists and engineers.

Thus while issues of *commercial technology transfer* are clearly important, U.S. responses to reform should recognize the desirability of more *comprehensive technical relationships* with the Giants. Such relationships involve science as well as technology. They also encompass questions of the transfer of institutional models as well as the transfer of technology, and they entail a recognition of the institutional complexities of technology transfer. This more comprehensive view also includes the relationships among science, technology, and the future of the "global commons,"[1] and it inevitably is linked to national security considerations.

Table 2. National Expenditures on Research and Development (billions and percentages)

Country	Domestic Currency		$US		Percentage of GNP
USSR	–		–		3.8
China	RMB	15.37	4.2		1.5
India	rupees	18.14	1.5		.9
Japan			39.1	(1987)	2.9
United States			100.8	(1987)	2.6

Source: National Science Foundation. Figure for China is author's estimate based on various sources.

The notion of comprehensive technical relationships, initiated by governments, may also be a workable response to the problem of integrating the Giants into a world economy of ever more complex commercial technology flows. As countless students of international technology transfer have noted, *companies*—not countries—transfer technology. Much of the technology desired by the Giants is private property—part of a bundle of assets that private firms use to advance their economic interests. Companies transfer technology *when they consider it in their interest to do so*—not out of altruism, and typically not at the behest of governments. In many industries with technologies desired by the Giants, these interests increasingly are defined by strategies for global operations in which the Giants have *not* figured prominently.

Thus the technology transfer policies of governments are limited; privately owned technology is not a direct or immediate policy asset. Instead, "technology transfer policy" usually refers to policies of denial, such as unilateral or multilateral export controls. Yet when export controls are combined with a variety of other trade policies, with public sector S&T programs, and with educational exchange activities, governments do have the potential for shaping the kind of comprehensive technical relationship noted above.

In an age when science and technology are becoming more central to foreign affairs, relations with the Giants could indeed be seen as test cases of how well that potential can be realized. The challenge of forging comprehensive technical relationships with the Giants requires attention to the institutional resources available in the United States to devise creative responses to reforms. At issue is the enhancement of a capability to formulate and coordinate policy across fields—trade, security, science, education, human rights, foreign assistance, etc.—areas that until recently had little to do with one another.

Reform Strategies in the Giants

Many of the conditions prompting reform in the three countries are similar. Each has serious problems using human and material resources in R&D efficiently; each suffers from serious gaps between research and production; and, in varying degrees, each has been relatively isolated from the technological dynamism of the industrialized market economies. The factors that affect technological performance in the three different country settings—domestic economic structures, foreign trade policies, the nature of the domestic R&D systems, heavy commitments to military and high-prestige projects—are surprisingly similar.

In all three countries, the national R&D agendas have been tightly controlled by central planners, who both set the directions of research and are chiefly responsible for its material support. The great bulk of national research in each of the three Giants is conducted in centralized national research institutes.

The centralizing design of these nations' R&D institutions and the lack of strong incentives to pursue research and development within enterprises have resulted in underdeveloped R&D activity at the enterprise level. Only 3 per cent of the holders of the *kandidat* degree, for instance, work in Soviet industrial enterprises.[2] With enterprises protected from national and international competition, innovation of all sorts, including that coming from R&D, has not been high on the list of managerial priorities. Patterns of R&D expenditures reflect this tradition.

In India, for instance, private industry funded only 13 per cent of the nation's R&D in 1985 (with 77 per cent coming from the national government and 10 per cent from the states). This contrasts with the United States, where approximately 50 per cent of funding comes from the private sector, and with Japan, where the figure approaches 80 per cent.[3] Especially interesting in contrast to the Giants is the case of South Korea. Between 1970 and 1986, the burden of supporting South Korea's national research efforts shifted from a government/private ratio of 77:23 to one of 26:74.[4]

The underdeveloped level of R&D in enterprises in the three countries has led to a search for mechanisms to transfer research results to production. Generally these have not been successful. The organizational separation of research from production has also shaped the cultures of the research communities in ways that reinforce elitism and contempt for practicality. As the Chinese sometimes put it, "To work in industry is a sign of a failed career."

Research in the university sector has also been neglected in all three countries. In the Indian case, while some centers of excellence have emerged, university research generally has not enjoyed the priority attention and investments accorded government institutes. In the USSR, the design of the R&D system deemphasizes university research in favor of centralized institutes of the Academy of Sciences and the ministries. China has shared the Soviet design philosophy, but in the post-Mao period, university research is being encouraged as a result of exposure to Western models and help from the World Bank.

China

Prior to the political upheavals of May-June, 1989, which now make the short-term future of reform more uncertain, the S&T reform process in China was further along than in the other two Giants. The Chinese began to confront the problems of their R&D system in the late 1970s and started to implement a multifaceted reform strategy in earnest in the early 1980s.[5] The opening to the outside world has had profound effects on S&T and on the reform environment. Party influence within institutes, a product of radical Maoist politics in the past, has been reduced as a result of reform. Military R&D has been directed to serve civilian industry. As in the Soviet Union, leadership positions were monopolized by the aged; under reform, a substantial rejuvenation has occurred during the 1980s.

Perhaps the three most significant areas of reform have been (1) those in the personnel system (designed to increase mobility and improve the matching of training with responsibilities), (2) those affecting the economic status of technology, and (3) those pertaining to the funding of research.

In spite of some significant changes in the personnel area during the 1980s—especially the growth of employment opportunities outside the state sector—the reform of the personnel system has been one of the most difficult.[6] Even after several years of implementation, less than 2 per cent of China's technical personnel have opportunities to change jobs.[7] Considerably more success is evident in reforms designed to attach commercial value to technology. A patent system has been introduced to allow for proprietary claims to technical knowledge, and the widespread use of "technology markets" has accelerated trade in technology.

Funding reforms are altering the past practice of "entitlement support," in which centralized budgetary allocations were made to institutes without regard to the quality and productivity of the research work done. Reform has involved the ratcheting down of central budget allocations, the encouragement of contract research with industry, and the introduction of new national programs and funding mechanisms that link financial support from the state to success in a competitive process of evaluating research proposals.

Funding reforms have had a variety of consequences. They have changed the way research institutes behave, forcing them to seek support from industry and to take industrial needs more seriously. Reforms in funding have also been criticized by Chinese and foreign observers for being too applications-oriented. They are seen as damaging to basic research and education and as harmful to Chinese scientific development over the long term.[8]

Although direct financial support from the state has been reduced substantially, the overall level of funding for research has increased as sources have become more diversified. In addition to increased industrial funding, new sources of support include a National High Technology Program that has targeted seven key areas—biotechnology, space, informatics, automation, lasers, energy, and materials—for priority funding to be allocated on a competitive project basis. The National Natural Science Foundation was established in 1986 to support basic research.

One of the unanticipated consequences of reform has been the establishment of new companies spun off from research institutes and universities. While some companies only offer limited technical services or market hard-to-get imported equipment, others are doing R&D and manufacturing—in some cases with foreign partners. In addition to the new companies spun off from research institutes, individual technical entrepreneurs have also started new firms.[9] Consulting and individual "moonlighting" have become widespread. To further the aims of commercialization, the government has supported the establishment of high-technology zones, science parks, innovative financing schemes, and "technology incubators," and it is attempting to offer comprehensive support for such activities through the initiation of its new "Torch Program" for high-technology industrialization.[10]

The entrepreneurial burst of the past few years marks a significant new direction for China's technical community. Even before the May-June 1989 student demonstrations, however, the start-up company phenomenon was entering a shakedown phase.[11] The reimposition of tight political controls in China and the purging of the more daring reformers are likely to smother the spirit of technical entrepreneurship and set back the innovative experiments in commercialization that had become so central a part of the reform agenda.[12]

Under its "open door" policy, China has been seeking to acquire science and technology as well as investment from abroad. As of 1988, it had entered into fifty agreements with foreign governments for S&T cooperation, the largest and most extensive of which is with the United States. Since the late 1970s, some 70,000–80,000 students and scholars (a large majority in technical fields) have gone abroad for advanced education and training.[13] While most sent out in the late 1970s and early 1980s have returned, large numbers remain abroad. Their return is now in doubt as a result of the political upheaval of May-June 1989, and their immigration status has become a contentious issue in U.S.-China relations.

Although China spent some $US 14.5 billion to import technology between 1979 and 1985,[14] the coherence of its technology import strategy has been questioned.[15] Despite clear policy directives that technology imports should be focused on the acquisition of "know-how," the overall value of imports continues to be biased toward the procurement of complete sets of equipment. Technology transfer to China is conditioned by the business climate (as it affects foreign participation in the economy), China's financial capabilities and foreign exchange holdings (as these affect its ability to pay for foreign technology), and the course of further changes in the domestic economy (as these affect assimilation). There has been considerable volatility in each of these areas.

While progress has been made in creating a more hospitable foreign investment climate, fundamental issues of profit repatriation and foreign exchange responsibilities, extensive bureaucratism and an uncertain political climate made China a less than preferred business destination even prior to the events of early 1989. Although China's leaders continue to encourage foreign business activities, confidence in the Chinese business climate has clearly been damaged during the past year.[16]

India

Like China, India has not been without industrial and S&T achievements. But, also like China, it is now setting its sights on a 21st-century world of high technology, preparation for which requires reform.[17] The government sees a need to increase state expenditures for S&T by as much as 50 per cent, but in return seeks significant quality improvements in research and improved links between research and production. The reform strategy calls for new facilities for agricultural and industrial R&D, improvements in scientific and technical education, and rationalized research management. Laboratories under the Council of Scientific and Industrial

Research (CSIR), for instance, are to be de-linked from CSIR and reassigned to "user" departments. In a strategy reminiscent of Chinese reforms, CSIR-industry links are to be strengthened by requiring that the latter assume more responsibility for financing the activities of the former.[18]

The reform agenda recognizes the need for foreign technology and provides for the liberalization of its importation. Changes here are expected to influence the quality of domestic research as well; by general agreement, one of the constraints limiting quality improvements has been the poor state of instrumentation and computerization. With reform, it will be easier to import sophisticated instruments. However, India's technology-acquisition strategy (like those of China and the USSR) can be derailed by an unattractive business climate. Although the atmosphere has improved, the U.S. direct foreign investment in India of $US 466 million in 1987 is hardly comparable to the $3 billion invested in China.[19] Strong disincentives include the 40-per-cent limit on foreign ownership (although this is waived under certain conditions), strict requirements for the indigenization of component supplies, weak patent protection for product innovations, and excessively complex investment approval procedures.[20] In the promising area of software production, ways have been found to overcome the disincentives. Compared with the explicit legal frameworks and welcoming business climates offered elsewhere in Asia, however, much remains to be done.

India's reform plans, like China's, call for priority attention to certain fields of science and technology deemed critical for a high-tech future. These include solid-state electronics, lasers, integral optics, digital telecommunications, advanced machine tools, and biotechnology. With India's growing capabilities in space technologies, complementary technologies to support a domestic satellite-based telecommunications system are also being emphasized.

India aims to upgrade the technological levels of the private industrial sector and to encourage a more positive attitude of the latter toward R&D. Attention is focused on the wider applications of microelectronic devices to production processes, improved efficiency in the use of energy, and expanded use of new materials.[21] Protection of domestic industry is to be reduced to stimulate greater innovation. The private sector is expected to "upgrade technology and management, attain economies of scale, pursue greater value-added activities and selectively launch an export drive."[22] While public-sector research institutes and enterprises will still bear the main responsibility for stimulating new high-technology industry, private-sector expectations have clearly increased. The new emphasis has been given high-level expression with the restructuring of the cabinet's Science Advisory Committee to include representatives from private industry (as well as from higher education).

In light of past patterns of resource allocation, reform will not be easy for India. Some 50 per cent of central budget allocations for R&D goes to the seven large S&T-related departments (the lion's share going to Atomic Energy and Space). Within private industry, 46 per cent of R&D is in the electronics, chemical, pharmaceutical, and industrial machinery industries. Only 2 per cent is in telecommunications, non-nuclear energy, and fertilizers—industries singled out for priority attention in the Seventh Plan.[23]

Only 18 per cent of the nation's R&D manpower is employed in the private sector, and indeed only one-third or so of the nation's 2.2 million scientists and engineers are engaged in R&D.[24] One of the more hopeful signs of better manpower utilization is the appearance of as many as one hundred new consulting organizations employing some 20,000 technical personnel. Many of these are based in the Indian Institutes of Technology and thus also act as a stimulus to the university sector.

India's relative weakness and inexperience in industrial research may also limit the effectiveness of an expanded foreign-technology acquisition strategy. Morehouse and Gupta, for instance, note the neglect of "absorptive" research and engineering in India when the country has acquired technology from abroad in the past. By contrast, Japan focused much of its research on assimilation during the period of high-technology imports.[25]

India—like China and unlike the USSR—has the advantage of a large overseas population with ethnic ties to the country. In the United States alone, there are some 600,000 "nonresident Indians" (NRIs), many of whom are scientists and engineers.[26] Long seen in brain-drain terms, this pool of technical talent is now being viewed as an Indian asset. Ethnic Indians (like ethnic Chinese abroad) are playing increasingly important bridging roles between the local and foreign technical communities, and successful overseas Indian entrepreneurs have become active in forging commerical links with India in high-technology areas.

The Soviet Union

Soviet reform impulses are in many ways similar to those in China. In both cases, the design of research and economic institutions biases support in favor of highly centralized research, but yields weak linkages to the economy. The research systems in both countries have been inefficient and unaccountable, highly bureaucratized, and filled with superannuated leaders. In both, a protected and uncompetitive domestic economy, responding to planned targets biased toward physical output, has produced an industrial economy lacking a strong capacity for technological innovation.

Though many of the impulses for reform thus are the same, the *dynamics* of reform have been different. The trauma of the Cultural Revolution is a powerful background factor for Chinese reforms. The strong commitment to and the successes of agricultural reform in China also sets it apart. The policy of sending abroad large numbers of students and the existence of networks of overseas Chinese businesspeople, scientists, and engineers have resulted in an infusion of human and material resources into China for which there is no counterpart in the case of the Soviet Union. On the other hand, the commitment to political reform in the USSR seems to be firmer and has tended to rally Soviet intellectuals around the regime. The slowness of political reform in China has had disastrous consequences, and the worsening alienation of the intellectuals has become a major obstacle to modernization.

Given the similarities, however, it is not surprising that Soviet reform efforts in S&T echo those in China. To address the "research to production" problem, new attention is being given to the "Science-Production Associations" (NPOs) (a pre-*perestroika* innovation), new engineering research centers are being established and "Inter-branch Scientific-Technical Complexes" (MNTKs) have been established in biotechnology, machine tools, computers, robotics, fiber optics, chemical catalysis, lasers, welding, automation, and petrochemicals.

Unlike the NPOs, which are based in the production ministries and have had at best a mixed record of success, the majority of MNTKs (twelve of twenty-one) are under the USSR Academy of Sciences. The Academy is assumed to be more sensitive to the importance of science-based technology and more willing to push for its commercialization. As with the new companies established under the Chinese Academy of Sciences, however, the lack of business management experience in what had been a research organization is a constraint on the success of the MNTKs.[27]

In the USSR as in China, the reforms have included more liberalized treatment of private and collective economic activities. Technical intellectuals have responded by forming a number of technical "collectives," and interest in private consulting is growing. The establishment of a stable legal and institutional environment for technical entrepreneurship—again, as in China—remains unclear, although talk of establishing a licensing system to facilitate the emergence of independent software writers indicates that a start has been made.[28]

Central to reform thinking about S&T is the information industry. Computerization in the Soviet Union is far behind that of the OECD countries; reportedly, only 10 per cent of Soviet enterprises have management information systems, and there are only 6,000 educational computers in the entire country.[29] Soviet dilemmas with the information revolution are a function of the systemic nature of the information industry, which presumes the availability of a bundle of know-how—hardware, software, and communications capabilities—*and* a culture that recognizes the value of information and its free flow. Arguably, the Soviet Union has serious deficiencies in all the necessary parts of the system, and efforts to structure the industry according to different assumptions do not seem to be promising.[30]

Soviet (and to a lesser extent, Chinese) S&T reforms reflect ambivalence over whether reform is essentially a process of modifying the operation of central planning to make "top-down" approaches to innovation work better, or whether it should create the conditions—through decentralization and marketization—necessary for the flourishing of "bottom-up" innovations. The record in informatics seems to support the former interpretation.[31] Indeed, some analysts maintain that Soviet S&T reforms are best understood as efforts to transfer the military innovation model (highly centralized and directed from the top) to the civilian economy.[32]

The Soviet reform program also calls for significant changes in foreign trade practices—decentralization of foreign trade decision-making, and the licensing of an expanding number of organizations to conduct foreign trade—as means to acquire foreign technology. Some 170 joint ventures with Western firms had been established by the end of 1988, though only twelve of these were with U.S. firms.[33] Majority shareholding by foreign partners has now been sanctioned to spur investment. However, Soviet efforts to attract foreign participation in its reform and economic modernization again echo much of the Chinese experience. Shortages of foreign exchange and a nonconvertible currency, an extensive bureaucracy, an underdeveloped infrastructure, labor issues, etc., all limit the appeal of the Soviet Union as a market for investment. Chinese experience throughout the 1980s, however, suggests that progress can be made on these problems, and thus Soviet potential for attracting foreign investment should not be underestimated.

Yet, in words that could describe China and India as well, Loren Graham has observed:

> The Soviet authorities see these [technology transfer] agreements as ways to obtain foreign technology, but are anxious not

to become dependent on foreign sources for that technology, or to expend large amounts of hard currency on it. They would prefer to find ways in which they can learn about the technology, possibly through limited sales for joint ventures, and then produce it on their own. The Westerners are primarily interested in gaining access to the potentially huge Soviet market.[34]

U.S. Science and Technology Relations with the Giants

The United States has been responsive to the wishes of the Giants for closer links in science and technology. Science and technology have figured prominently in improved ties with both China and India and are likely to become more important in relations with the Soviet Union as well.

China

Science and technology were used boldly in the process of restoring U.S. relations with China in the 1970s. The two countries signed an umbrella S&T agreement in 1979. Over a decade, this agreement has led to thirty protocols (involving hundreds of projects) for cooperation between agencies of the two governments. These have been conducted on the principle of mutual cost sharing; and, with few exceptions, agencies on the U.S. side have not had special budgets for their relations with China. In the absence of an official foreign assistance program, U.S. government S&T activities in China have had to be justified on technical merit in service to agency missions.

On the other hand, U.S. support for Chinese S&T development has been substantial in the area of the exchange of students and scholars. Almost 60,000 Chinese students and scholars have come to the United States over the last decade, and the costs of educating these individuals has fallen increasingly on the United States.[35] The United States has also sought to facilitate the transfer of technology to China—both within the U.S. government and at the Paris-based Coordinating Committee for Multilateral Export Controls (COCOM)—by gradually liberalizing export controls. While China is still a controlled destination, it is among the most privileged of them.

In spite of a decade of remarkable progress, the U.S.-China relationship needed rethinking even before the recent political crackdown. The U.S. role as supplier of technology and partner in S&T cooperation was being eroded by aggressive initiatives from other

OECD countries. Chinese S&T had changed markedly during the last ten years; it had new needs and offered new opportunities.[36] Whether a workable S&T relationship can exist in the face of the recent changes in Chinese politics remains to be seen.

India

The U.S.-Indian S&T relationship is also extensive.[37] A joint Science and Technology Subcommission provides the umbrella for cooperation between fifteen U.S. and Indian technical agencies in such fields as energy; materials and physical sciences; atmospheric, earth, and marine sciences; health and life sciences; environment and ecology; and information sciences. A separate Agricultural Subcommission oversees cooperation in agricultural S&T.[38]

The Science and Technology Initiative (STI), launched during Indira Gandhi's 1982 visit to Washington (and extended during Rajiv Gandhi's 1987 visit), is a high-visibility, mutually funded program (with approximately $7 million contributed by each side) for cooperative research in areas of high priority for both countries. It was under STI that the United States, by presidential determination, agreed to the sale of a supercomputer to India for monsoon research.

The U.S. Agency for International Development (USAID), involved in India since the 1950s, has long sponsored active programs in health, agriculture, and science education. Though its work in India is now greatly scaled down, USAID has begun working with India on innovative programs to speed the commercialization of research. One such effort is the Program for the Advancement of Commercial Technology (PACT), begun in FY1987. By providing seed money, PACT encourages Indo-U.S. joint ventures in high-technology industries. USAID has also been active in stimulating the commercialization of energy and telecommunications technologies—two priority areas of India's Seventh Plan.

The U.S.-India S&T relationship gained further momentum in 1987 with the establishment of the U.S.-India Fund (USIF)—a rupee account worth some $US 110 million that is expected to generate the equivalent of $US 200 million over the course of its ten-year life. Limited research cooperation also exists between the defense establishments in the area of materials science (funded by the United States through the National Bureau of Standards and the Office of Naval Research), signal processing, and other basic technologies.

There are signs that closer Indo-U.S. S&T relations are beginning to yield commercial payoffs in high-technology fields. The number of approved licenses for exports to India rose dramatically—from 710 to 3,916, representing a 400-per-cent increase in value terms— between 1983 and 1987. Commercial cooperation in the computer and software industries has been particularly promising.[39]

The Soviet Union

Prior to the current reform era, programs with the USSR were adversely affected by tensions in U.S.-Soviet relations during the late 1970s and early 1980s. Eleven specialized bilateral agreements were in force in the early 1970s; by 1983, there were only seven. Thus the S&T relationship with the Soviet Union is currently in the process of being rebuilt.

As with programs with China and India, S&T cooperation with the USSR has been helped along by high-level political attention. The December 1987 Reagan-Gorbachev Washington Summit produced agreement on expanded cooperation in the fields of transportation, global climate and environmental change, and oceans research. A new outer space agreement was signed at the Shultz-Shevardnadze meeting in April 1987. New agreements, or renewals of old ones, are evident in such areas as nuclear fusion, reactor safety, environmental protection, health, and housing. A new basic sciences agreement has been signed to replace one that had lapsed, and memoranda of understanding are now being negotiated for specific projects. Non-governmental programs that had been important during the earlier détente period, such as those of the National Academy of Sciences, are also expanding.

Implications for the United States

Distinct U.S. interests vis-à-vis the individual Giants will dictate separate S&T-related policies toward each in such arenas as export controls, intellectual property protection, trade financing, foreign assistance, access to the U.S. market, and human rights.[40] At the same time, the reforms do raise a number of generic issues associated with the growing importance of S&T in relations among nations. As the United States confronts these, it must recognize that its relations with the Giants already show signs of interdependence. The future of many science and engineering graduate programs at American universities, for instance, would be much in doubt were it not for the research assistance provided by large numbers of Chinese and Indian (and other foreign) students.

Defining an appropriate U.S. response to the reforms typifies the problems of U.S. foreign policy in a complex and uncertain world. Both bilateral and multilateral issues are at stake, and they range across *security, commercial* and *environmental* concerns. The challenge to U.S. policy is to achieve a balance among these. Science and technology crosscut the range of concerns.

Implications for the United States stemming from reform in the Giants must be seen in light of the following considerations:

1. However consistent reform may seem with U.S. security, commercial, and environmental interests, the potential problems of reform must not be forgotten. The three Giants all aspire to "great power" status, and successful reform will enhance their military capabilities.[41] China's recent political experiences illustrate the difficulty of understanding and controlling the interactive effects of rapid socio-economic and political changes resulting from reform. In the absence of imaginative institutional innovation in the political realm within the Giants, such changes can lead to forms of political instability that can both undo reform progress and harm foreign interests that have developed a stake in the reform process. While U.S. policy can assist the reform process, there is little it can do when reforms go awry.

2. The reforming Giants have become arenas of competition among the countries of the OECD world for commercial, technological, and cultural influence. Competitive instincts to pursue national advantages can work against the maintenance of multilateral understandings designed to serve the common interests of the countries of the OECD world—understandings pertaining to, for instance, export controls, trade finance, foreign assistance, intellectual property protection, and human rights.

The United States thus faces a dual challenge. It will seek to compete with its OECD partners for influence with the Giants, but it also should assume a leadership role in seeing that multilateral understandings are upheld. The pursuit of the latter—for instance, with regard to human rights in the Soviet case, and to export controls and concessional trade financing in the Indian and Chinese cases—have conflicted with the pursuit of the former.

3. U.S. strengths in science and technology, and the fact that S&T figures so prominently in the reform programs of the Giants, nevertheless put the United States in a good position to work with the Giants in mutually beneficial ways. With the diffusion of S&T capabilities to other countries, however, the

United States can no longer assume that its technical assets have hegemonic consequences. It must therefore become smarter in their use—through more focused policy attention, more active inter-agency coordination, and increased government-private sector cooperation. The United States must, of course, also do considerably more to maintain its strengths; the international importance of domestic science education and of research and development policies has increased dramatically.

4. **U.S. capabilities in S&T remain important resources for responding to the challenges ahead.** Relations with China and India during the past decade have demonstrated the utility of programs of S&T cooperation for the achievement of U.S. unilateral and multilateral foreign policy goals. The management of U.S. S&T resources, however, requires further attention.

In particular, in spite of the considerable access that S&T programs provide to key technical leaders and industrial decisionmakers in the countries involved, the potential commercial benefit from them generally has not been realized. More attention should be given to the staffing of S&T programs—in Washington and at embassies abroad—to ensure that the individuals recruited have technical competence and a good sense for commercial opportunities.[42] In addition, S&T programs with China and the USSR have been constrained by funding limitations, and the considerable information generated by them has not been well captured and utilized to advance the multiple objectives of U.S. policy.

More generally, there is a need for sustained, high-level political commitment to international S&T—one that reflects a clear vision of U.S. security, commercial, and environmental interests in comprehensive technical relationships with the Giants. Such a commitment, and the ongoing interpretation of its meaning, will also require enhanced analytical capability as well as more focused coordination among diverse but relevant policy areas. The Bush Administration's naming of a new Science Advisor, the establishment of a new Technology Administration at the undersecretary level within the Department of Commerce, and the creation of the National Institute of Standards and Technology (out of the old National Bureau of Standards), provided an occasion for a thorough reassessment of the roles of S&T in U.S. foreign relations. It appears, however, that the opportunities offered by this occasion have not been seized.

Placing the establishment of comprehensive technical relationships at the center of its policies toward the Giants would allow the United States to respond to the cardinal issues of reform. In the area of export controls, for instance, pressure to liberalize is mounting rapidly, since the full integration of the Giants into the world economy will not be possible without facilitated East-West technology flows.[43] However, in light of the great uncertainties surrounding reform (noted above), it would be prudent to maintain unilateral and multilateral control regimes. Liberalization within these regimes is unavoidable, however. The consideration of decisions to liberalize will be more intelligent if done in a forum that accurately assesses both the risks *and* the benefits from liberalization in a comprehensive fashion—one that cuts across commercial, scientific, and environmental as well as security issues. Decisions to liberalize can also be made with greater confidence once a web of technical relations of the sort discussed above is in place.

The encouragement of comprehensive technical relations would facilitate the engagement of the Giants on issues of global importance, and it would further open access to human resources and key decisionmakers in the Giants, which in turn could serve U.S. interests. To maximize the opportunities afforded by reforms in the Giants, however, international S&T policy must be given a much higher profile—and more powerful organizational resources—in the U.S. policy process. The reforms in China, India, and the Soviet Union, in short, remind us of the need for change in the fourth Giant.

Notes

[1]Even apart from Bhopal and Chernobyl, the intensity of human activities in the Giants, their size, and their topography make them critical for global ecological understanding and environmental management.

[2]Loren R. Graham, "Gorbachev's Great Experiment," *Issues in Science and Technology,* Vol. IV, No. 2 (Winter 1988), p. 25.

[3]William Blanpied, "Science, Technology, and India's Aspirations," in Marshall M. Bouton and Philip Oldenburg, eds., *India Briefing, 1988* (Boulder, Colo.: Westview Press, 1988), p. 140.

[4]Richard P. Suttmeier, "The Role of Science and Technology in South Korean Development." Unpublished paper presented at the Conference on Korean Challenges and American Policy, the Washington Institute for Values in Public Policy, December 6–8, 1988.

[5]Tony Saich, *China's Science Policy in the 80's* (Atlantic Heights, N.J.: Humanities Press International, Inc., 1989); and Denis Fred Simon and Merle Goldman, eds., *Science and Technology in Post-Mao China* (Cambridge, Mass.: The Council on East Asia Studies, Harvard University, 1989).

[6]The reasons for this are complex, centering on the hold that the work unit has on personnel and the non-availability of housing, welfare, and other services from sources other than the work unit.

[7]*China Daily,* March 3, 1989.

[8]C.F.V. Mason, *The Future of Chinese Science,* LA-11561-MS, UC-100 (Los Alamos, N.M.: Los Alamos National Laboratory, 1989).

[9]In the city of Wuhan alone, the number of nongovernmental research centers grew from 92 in 1987 to 455 in 1988, with the total number of technical personnel employed in them rising from 860 to 6,005. *China Daily*, March 8, 1989.

[10]State Science and Technology Commission, *Torch Program: A Program for China's High Technology Industries* (Beijing: SSTC, 1988).

[11]Many of the start-ups faced a cash crisis as a result of the tightening of credit in early 1989. See *China Daily*, March 13, 1989.

[12]Wan Runnan, founder and president of the most successful start-up (the Stone Corporation), is now in exile as a result of his support of the democracy movement. In the summer of 1989, he joined with four other exiled dissidents to establish the Federation for a Democratic China, of which he is now Secretary General.

[13]Leo A. Orleans, *Chinese Students in America: Policies, Issues and Numbers* (Washington, D.C.: National Academy Press, 1988), Chapters 4–5.

[14]Some $US 5 billion have been spent on foreign technology for the iron and steel industry alone. *China Daily*, March 8, 1989.

[15]Office of Technology Assessment, *Technology Transfer to China* (Washington, D.C.: U.S. Government Printing Office, 1989); and Denis Fred Simon, "Technology Transfer and China's Emerging Role in the World," in Denis Fred Simon and Merle Goldman, eds., *Science and Technology in Post-Mao China* (Cambridge, Mass.: The Council on East Asia Studies, Harvard University, 1989), pp. 289–318.

[16]It should be noted that China seeks to *export* as well as import technology. The value of its technology exports in 1988 was expected to reach $US 200 million (up from $US 150 million in 1987), with hopes of reaching $US 1 billion by the year 2000. During the first nine months of 1988, the value of Chinese-produced software alone reached $US 10 million. *China Daily*, November 24, 1988.

[17]Blanpied, "Science, Technology, and India's Aspirations," op. cit.

[18]National Science Foundation, *Indian Scientific Strengths: Selected Opportunities for Indo-U.S. Cooperation.* Unpublished workshop proceedings, 1987.

[19]Data from the Office of the U.S. Trade Representative (1989).

[20]Gopal Ramaswamy, "The Halting Pace of Gandhi's Reforms," *The Asian Wall Street Journal Weekly*, March 6, 1988, p. 16.

[21]National Science Foundation, *Indian Scientific Strength*, op. cit.

[22]Ibid.

[23]Blanpied, "Science, Technology, and India's Aspirations," op.cit., pp. 140–41.

[24]Ibid., p. 149.

[25]Ward Morehouse, Brijen K. Gupta, and Anil Deolalikar, *The Political Economy of Science and Technology in North-South Relations. An Assessment of U.S.-Indian Science and Technology Relations: An Analytical Study of Past Performance and Future Prospects* (Springfield, Va.: National Technical Information Service, 1980), Vol. IV, No. 4.

[26]John Echeverri-Gent, "From Autarchy to Interdependence: The Dilemmas in Liberalizing India's Computer Industry." Unpublished paper, 1988.

[27]Graham, "Gorbachev's Great Experiment," op. cit., pp. 26, 27.

[28]Ibid, p. 26.

[29]John Markoff, "Soviet Computing: An Insider's View," *The New York Times*, March 25, 1989, p. 33.

[30]See the collection of papers in *Gorbachev's Economic Plans*, Study Papers presented to the Joint Economic Committee, Vol. 2, 1987, pp. 141–219.

[31]Ibid.

[32]Paul Cocks, "Soviet Science and Technology Strategy: Borrowing From the Defense Sector," in Ibid., pp. 145–60.

[33]Charles E. Hugel, "Trade is the Real Road to Peace," *The New York Times*, June 4, 1989. Estimates on the total number of joint ventures vary. In November 1989, for example, the Chairman of the Economic Commission of the USSR announced that there were 1,050 joint ventures (Radio Liberty, *Report on the USSR*, Vol. 1, No. 46, November 17, 1989).

[34]Graham, "Gorbachev's Great Experiment," op. cit., p. 31.

[35]Orleans, *Chinese Students in America*, op. cit., p. 11.

[36]Richard P. Suttmeier. "Listening to China," *Issues in Science and Technology* (Fall 1989), pp. 42–51.

[37]Unlike programs with the People's Republic of China, contemporary programs with India grow out of decades of interactions, including those supported by USAID, The Rockefeller Foundation, and The Ford Foundation.

[38]The discussion in this section is based on U.S. Congress, *Science, Technology, and American Diplomacy, FY1987*, U.S. House of Representatives, Committee on Foreign Affairs, 1988; and Department of State, "Science, Technology, and American Diplomacy, FY1988," unpublished report to U.S. Congress, 1989.

[39]Echeverri-Gent, "From Autarchy to Independence," op. cit., p. 11.

[40]In relations with China, for instance, the United States must now find the narrow path between condemnation of the retrogressive behavior of the leadership and continued encouragement of reform and engagement with the reform process.

[41]India's recent test of a mid-range missile, criticized by the United States, illustrates how S&T development in the Giants can complicate the search for global security. *The New York Times*, May 23, 1989, p. A9. China's missile program has also been a source of concern to the United States.

[42]Of interest in this connection is the fact that, unlike most of the other OECD countries (as well as the Giants themselves), the United States places the management and coordination of international S&T programs in the hands of its foreign affairs specialists in the State Department, rather than in a technical agency.

Chapter 6 _____

The Geopolitical Consequences of Reform

Elena B. Arefieva

_____

The Relationship Between Economic Reforms and Geopolitics

The preceding chapters depict remarkable changes in the domestic economic policies and foreign economic ties of the three Giants. The geopolitical situation in the world, and particularly in Asia, has changed dramatically, and many aspects of each Giant's foreign policy have been radically revised. These changes pose questions as to whether new geopolitical interests derive from the economic reforms under way in the Soviet Union, China, and India, and whether it is possible to project shifts in geopolitics on the basis of economic policy trends.

Politics is generally considered to be correlated with economics, and the recent changes in the foreign policies of the Giants are widely believed to result directly from their new economic interests. If we limit the examination of the new foreign policies and geopolitical interests of the Giants to economic rationales, it is clear that:

- In the Giants, as everywhere in the world, military confrontation is giving way to economic competition, or even cooperation; this is also reflected in the reshaping of the geopolitics of the Giants, which is now increasingly influenced by their economic interests.

- The Soviet Union and China need resources to carry out their economic reforms, and this makes them interested in reducing defense spending. India, too, is attempting to make more resources available for economic development by limiting defense expenditures.

- The need for economic resources is making the Soviet Union and China change their foreign policies so as to achieve better understanding with prospective developed-country economic partners. At the same time, basing their geopolitics on recognition of an interdependent world makes them not lose sight of the Third World.[1]

It should of course be acknowledged that the world is witnessing a tendency toward eliminating military-strategic bipolarity; that this process coincides with the reduction of international political tensions; and that, as a result, economic power and foreign economic policies are gaining preeminence in international relations. Thus, as many have noted, worldwide concern is now focused on "geo-economics" rather than geopolitics. It is also true that domestic economic reform in the Giants necessitates essential changes in their geo-economic interests, which inevitably influence their geopolitics. But the widespread opinion that the Soviet Union, China, and India need their new foreign policies solely for their economic modernization is an oversimplification. Such a rationale would hardly be in keeping with their national interests—or with those of developed countries, since it would imply that the Giants will abandon their present foreign policies when their economies achieve momentum and their need for outside economic resources subsides.

The major overlooked point is that geopolitical interests do not stem only from economic needs. They are also based on domestic political factors and on the external political situation. Historically, the role of domestic non-economic factors in Asia and in Russia has been considerable. The present foreign policies of the Soviet Union and China are determined, among other things, by the prevailing tendencies of domestic social and political development.

In the Soviet Union, political development can be recognized as a democratization process. It is reflected in a new type of elections leading to real social responsibility on the part of political institutions such as the Supreme Soviet and the standing Committee for Foreign Affairs formed of its members. More broadly, these structures display "democratization of the process of foreign policy decisionmaking"[2]—or, to be more realistic, its very beginning. Other manifestations of such change are open discussions of foreign policy issues in the press[3] and at conferences, and consultation with research institutes in the process of decisionmaking. At the same time, democratization has not produced an upsurge of any social force interested in preserving the old type of *foreign* policy. The military is of course still rather conservative, since its members would not like to lose in terms of their living standards. But never has the army been as unpopular as it is today,[4] and it is not military policy that determines the leadership's course. It is this process of democratization that supported the general trend toward a revision of the whole set of ideological and political goals that necessitated the new thinking in foreign policy[5] and the introduction of a new military doctrine that is more clearly defense-oriented.[6]

In China, several ideological and political innovations were introduced that may be regarded as elements of a future continuation of the course started in the late 1970s. First among these is recognition of the possibility of the coexistence of various modes of economic activity even within the country—and (as it was initially justified) as a basis for unification with Taiwan and Hong Kong.[7] Another important innovation with ideological accents is economic liberalization, which encourages productivity growth through *economic* means—substituting the goal of national economic consolidation for the ideology of militarism as a basis for such consolidation. Thus the concept of a hostile international environment is no longer necessary to justify calls for hard work and the restriction of consumption, and this eliminates the internal function of militarism.

Although the cruel repression by the Chinese leadership of the youth democratic movement in June 1989 undoubtedly marks a step backward from the previous achievements of social liberalization, it should not be viewed as a total turn backwards. The course aimed at economic pluralism is still valid, and political reforms have been put on hold but not dismantled. Moreover, in my view, the June events seem a natural reaction to distortions in Chinese society resulting from a lack of balance in changes in economic and political structures. That is why those events do not entirely undermine the general trend toward the renewal of the society (though they of course postpone it), or of Chinese external relations—both economic and political.

In any case, the new societies that are being constructed according to the present agendas of the two countries (which are quite different, of course) do not rely on a militaristic ideology, which was diagnosed with striking exactness by George Orwell as a disease of an anti-democratic, totalitarian society.[8] This shift should be mentioned especially in connection with the revision of the army's role in the domestic political life of China. China's military spending cuts after 1986 appear to have been determined not only by the move toward technological modernization of the army, but also by conceptual change.[9] This change is likely to have been rooted in the new principles of societal organization in China, which set the country on the difficult and gradual course away from totalitarianism.

In India, the past ten to fifteen years have been marked by the dramatic growth of Indian big business and a deepening of socioeconomic differentiation, which influenced the domestic political situation and the character of its connection with foreign policy. Thomas Thornton's explanation of former Prime Minister Rajiv Gandhi's foreign policy as based on the rivalry among parties and movements in India is probably accurate. The drive toward external *economic* expansion—closely linked to the desire to reinforce the *political* role of the country in the Third World—resulted from pressure of the pragmatically minded wing of parties and movements that represents Indian big business.[10]

As a result of these various economic and non-economic domestic factors, the importance of the military balance is diminishing and a multipolar system is emerging in the Asian Pacific Region (APR). A tendency toward a lesser real role for arms arsenals in the assurance of national security is as clear in Asia as in other parts of the world, and here too, political possibilities for providing international security have begun to prevail over the pressure of the military balance.[11] Moreover, the polarization of forces is geographically more complex in Asia than, say, in Europe, and presents a puzzle from the point of view of the further development of the military balance and the distribution of economic power. It is not irrelevant that Japan's Prime Minister Nakasone has compared this situation to oriental "sumie"—drawings most of whose surface is left uncovered by paint.[12]

It is essential to acknowledge that the restructuring of the balance of forces and the dynamics of economic development of the three Giants are interconnected in an extremely complex way. Before starting the examination of this intricate connection, it may be helpful to confirm the thrust of this analysis as applied to U.S. interests. The hypothesis of this chapter, as the reader may have guessed, is that the evolving geopolitical situation contains new potential advantages for the United States:

- in the form of long-term reduction of international tensions and the achievement of political stability;

- in the growth of economic interdependence in the contemporary world; and

- in areas where U.S. interests coincide with those of the three Giants along the whole spectrum of international political, ecological, and humanitarian problems—including the resolution of pressing Third World development issues.

Possible Influences of Domestic Reforms on the Geopolitical Situation

The Soviet Union

The behavior of the Soviet Union as a participant in the geopolitical situation—in the world in general, and in Asia in particular—has been changing in tandem with the economic reform to which it is indirectly connected. The new foreign policy leaves behind the former confrontational view of the world and is based instead on a combination of economic needs and an appreciation of generally accepted humanitarian values.

There has been a major change in the concept of national security, which is now visualized from the point of view of an indivisible world. This new view is closely connected with the understanding of global security reflected in the concept of a "comprehensive system of international security" put forward by Foreign Minister Eduard Shevardnadze during the 43rd U.N. General Assembly session in September 1988. Simultaneously, traditional criticism of the militarism of the Western countries obviously is being softened. Attention should be paid to an article by Georgy Kunadze, a member of the staff of the Institute of World Economy and International Relations (IMEMO)—recently published in a prestigious Moscow journal—about the urgent need to revise the Soviet concept of the so-called militarism of the developed countries and to reassess the presumed menace of a Japanese military strike at the Soviet Union (as a result of Japan's alliance with the United States.)[13]

The most important moves taken in this direction by the Soviet government have been the conclusion of the Intermediate Nuclear Forces (INF) treaty with the United States in May 1988 and the steps taken to "give the military doctrine of the USSR concrete, clearly defense-oriented features," through the development of this doctrine "on the . . . basis of a reasonable defense sufficiency." In particular, a decision was made to cut the armed forces of the Soviet Union during 1989–90 by 500,000 men, or 12 per cent of the army contingent—a move that implies, among other reductions, the withdrawal and disbanding of six tank divisions from East Germany,

Czechoslovakia, and Hungary (that is, from the zone of confrontation between the Warsaw Treaty and NATO). General military spending cuts are to be considerable, and armaments production is to be reduced by 19.5 per cent.[14]

Of course one could object that arms cuts do not affect missiles targeted at the United States, and this argument should not be disregarded. But the point here is that the process has just started, and we may find grounds to expect a deeper arms reduction (most likely on a reciprocal basis). At any rate, at last the system of decisionmaking concerning defense in the USSR has become explicit along with the forces influencing it.

A series of significant steps concerning regional conflicts merit mention. Outside Asia, the Soviet Union has supported Cuba's initiative to resolve the problem of Southwest Africa and to withdraw Cuban troops from Angola. In Asia itself, the shift is indicated by the withdrawal of Soviet troops from Afghanistan; by a new and flexible policy course regarding Kampuchea and a pragmatic policy toward two Korean states; by energetic measures aimed at the normalization of relations with China notwithstanding the June events; by participation in resolving the Iran-Iraq conflict; and by the activation of Soviet diplomacy in the Middle East.

Asia is also affected by the commitment taken by the Soviet Union on unilateral arms reduction: Troops in the Asian part of the country will be cut by 200,000 men, with most of the contingent from Mongolia withdrawn during 1989-90. In general, relations with the APR countries are based on the program of action set out in President Gorbachev's speeches in Vladivostok (1986) and Krasnoyarsk (1988). The essence of the program is to reduce international tensions in the region and to raise the level of cooperation to correspond to the increased economic potential of the Asian countries.

Soviet foreign policy regarding China has changed greatly due to the new approach toward security issues in the APR. The "three obstacles" to the restoration of relations with China were removed with the withdrawal of troops from Afghanistan, progress on the Kampuchean problem, and the withdrawal of Soviet forces from Mongolia. But policy changes toward China also resulted from the new political thinking, which led to a realistic assessment of internal political and economic restructuring in China. It became possible for the Soviet Union to abandon discussion of Chinese economic reform in purely negative terms[15]—and, in line with Russian tradition, to rush to the other extreme, overestimating every aspect of the Chinese reform, even after June 1989.

All of this of course influenced practical policies toward China, as evidenced by President Gorbachev's visit to Beijing in May 1989.

The purpose of the visit was to normalize political relations with China and to expand economic contacts. It is worth noting that the Soviet leadership's satisfaction with the visit surpassed disappointment with the setback of political liberalization. On the other hand, the results of the visit should not be overestimated; they are limited to a reduction of tensions, enabling a decrease in military expenses and further economic exchange. There is no question of any new influence in China; U.S.-Chinese relations remain unaffected both politically and economically.

The strong willingness of the Soviet leadership to expand political and economic linkages with China has been manifested by an obviously reserved official reaction to the youth disturbances in May-June 1989, followed by cruel repression and considerable changes in the upper echelon of power. The further development of economic relations with China will most probably become another significant factor in the creation of a healthier political situation in Asia. The main achievements in the area of Soviet-Chinese economic relations thus far have been trans-border exchange and the conclusion of the first medium-term trade agreement for 1986–90. Other forms of economic relations, such as the establishment of industrial enterprises by Soviet organizations in China, were resumed in 1984 and exhibited rapid growth through 1988.[16] In addition, the USSR and China are investigating prospects for common use of the border sections of the Argun and the Amur rivers for energy production, fisheries, and navigation; the establishment of a joint enterprise zone is under consideration in the Soviet Far East; joint ventures in the USSR and China are being negotiated.

At the same time, the shaping of a new role for the USSR in Asia and in the Third World as a whole is still hampered by a number of unresolved problems. For example, abandoning the ideological orientation of international relations, announcing the principle of freedom of choice of development strategy, and recognizing the possibility of various types of development[17] all mean that revision is needed in the practice of extending support to regimes mainly for ideological reasons. It seems likely that the political and ideological motivation of Soviet relations with Third World countries will be relegated to the past, yielding to the rationales of commercial advantage or humanitarian principles. Accordingly, arguments for concessional economic assistance will be related to the human or purely economic needs of Third World countries and distanced from ideological or political rationales.[18] In the course of reform, the main area touched upon so far is relations with *developed* countries. There has been a sharp increase in the willingness of ministries, enterprises, and cooperatives to import machines and equipment balanced by exports of know-how, R&D, and intermediate products. Practically the same expectations are emerging toward developing countries. But such a combination of demand for imports and supply of exports can hardly be realized within the framework of present relations with the Third World.[19] That is why the future division of labor with developing countries is still unclear and why it is difficult to project future geographical priorities in trade and investment flows that will eventually shape the geo-economic and, to a great extent, the geopolitical interests of the Soviet Union.

The main shifts in the geo-economic interests of the Soviet Union in Asia are most likely to be the following:

• The expansion of economic relations with developing countries that can provide high-tech imports (both consumer goods and investment). In Asia, these countries are South Korea and the other newly industrialized countries (NICs), India, and, perhaps in the future, China.

• The development of various forms of economic relations with border countries: China, Turkey, and, insofar as possible, the other adjacent nations.

• The attraction of foreign direct investment and imports of turn-key projects from any developing countries able to offer them at a sufficiently competitive level.

India, which ranks among the highest in both the first and second groups mentioned, has a major advantage as a USSR partner: Soviet organizations are well aware of its management structure, and mutual trust exists between the two countries. Suffice it to mention that even today, India is the Soviet Union's major trade partner among Third World countries.

Maintenance of the achieved level of relations with India to a large extent defines Soviet foreign policy in South Asia. For instance, it is believed that the preservation of peace between India and Pakistan can be supported by the development of relations between the Soviet Union and Pakistan—despite the latter's involvement in the military conflict in Afghanistan.[20]

The most vivid example of *economic* incentives for the modification of Soviet foreign policy is provided by relations with South Korea, which still lack official diplomatic status but are evolving successfully in the economic realm. The maintenance of friendly relations with North Korea induces the Soviet Union "not to treat South Korea as its diplomatic or even political partner," but nevertheless "to take reality into account."[21] The fact that political relations remain unsettled does not interfere with economic contacts: Trade relations with South Korea have been established by the Soviet Chamber of Trade and Industry, the Marine Ministry, and the Ministry for the fishing industry.

An important new thrust of Soviet foreign policy is the improvement of relations with Japan. In this case as in many others, the goal is the enhancement of security in Asia, but economic reform in the USSR also generates a need for ties with Japan. Today the Soviet Union has a clear interest in attracting Japanese capital and technology for the development of its own Far Eastern economic region.[22] Economic relations with Japan, like those with South Korea, are gaining momentum notwithstanding complex political relations. There is as yet no solution to the problem of the "Northern Japanese territories" (several southern islands in the Kuril archipelago that are currently under Soviet control but are claimed by Japan), but the Soviet side is working to maximize the independence of economic cooperation from the resolution of that contentious issue.

In its Far Eastern region, the USSR intends to encourage Indian investment (for the production of clothes, footwear, and food products), joint enterprises with North Korean organizations (for growing vegetables and soybeans, woodprocessing and furniture factories, and processing medicinal plants), and the joint participation of North and South Korea in the development of infrastructure. The intended role of China in the development of the Far Eastern region already has been mentioned. But none of these countries is capable of supplying high-tech equipment for natural resource processing, which is expected to be this region's specialization in the near future. This equipment can be supplied by Japan.

Another new aspect of the changes in the USSR relates to new attitudes toward ecological issues. This is a direct result of the freeing up of the press, the development of *glasnost,* and a new understanding on the part of the Soviet people of their rights and responsibilities as "owners" of national resources. As recently as the early 1980s, ecological problems were treated with indifference by the bureaucracy. The abnegation of responsibility for nature was displayed in the elaboration of an expensive plan to reverse the flow of major Siberian rivers southward—an idea worthy of the writings of Jonathan Swift or Francois Rabelais. Today such a proposal would be unthinkable. Issues of environmental protection are now discussed widely and included as an integral part of state programs for economic development; the State Committee for Environmental Protection has been established specifically to deal with such issues.

The Soviet Union's recognition of its share of responsibility for the global environment is now reflected in its participation as a new member of international organizations for environmental preservation. The Montreal Protocol of 1987 has been ratified, and appropriate decisions have been taken to reduce detrimental industrial production involving freon in the USSR. In 1988, the Soviet Union joined the Convention Concerning the Protection of the World Cultural and Natural Heritage (Paris 1972) and announced its intention to extend its participation to other international conventions. As of November 1989, the USSR was a member of 55 conventions out of an existing total of 140.[23] It is also becoming more active as a member of the U.N. Environment Programme (UNEP), where it has put forward proposals for a series of conferences on ecology, including a summit, and for the establishment of a center for international ecological assistance within the framework of the United Nations system.

A further important innovation in the international practice of the USSR is its movement toward a more active role in the work of the United Nations and its encouragement of a strengthened U.N. role in reaching solutions to international issues. President Gorbachev's presentation at the 43rd U.N. General Assembly in December 1988 reflected this new approach.[24] The purpose of such a move is dual: to share responsibility with other nations for resolution of the global problems and to use participation in international relations and the world economy for the national progress of the Soviet Union.

In conclusion, it should be emphasized that a stable geopolitics is essential to assuring the irreversibility of Soviet reform. On the other hand, sustaining the present foreign policy of the Soviet Union increasingly depends on the leadership's ability to overcome internal *economic* difficulties and thus retain popular support for the present course of *perestroika*. That is why two major instruments of external support of the reform are the continued reduction of international tensions (based on reciprocal steps taken by the superpowers) and economic assistance. In Asia, the two may be combined through the backing of the new geo-economics that is taking shape in the region.

The emerging economic relations in Asia appear to represent quite tangible common interests for the United States and the USSR. From the point of view of enlarging potential markets for U.S. goods and investments, prospective gains from intra-Asian economic exchanges merit attention. Their main function now is to encourage the opening up of the economies and to increase their absorptive capacities.

In addition, however, in the framework of USSR-China relations, a trade flow might be shaped that would serve as a safety valve for competition from the cheap Chinese light industrial products and electronics made in special economic zones. The need for such goods in the Soviet market is great. Of course, the problem of financing such imports is still not quite clear and most probably would require loans to be taken by the Soviet government. Though the Soviet government is reluctant to do this, it will soon be left without a choice, given the present decline in consumer goods supply and its social consequences. And if we look ahead to the beginning of the next century—assuming that the reforms have won support and have yielded fruit—the absorption of Chinese and other Asian goods will grow manyfold. This would enable the United States to preserve its position as a major exporter of high-tech products to both markets. Similarly, one could hardly imagine any adverse implications of two other linkages: between the USSR and India, and between the USSR and the newly industrializing countries (NICs). As in the case of China, it is likely that exports of electronics and light industrial products from India and the NICs to the USSR will grow—but this most probably will be a relief for the United States. To put it another way, new geo-economic behavior on the part of the USSR in Asia is unlikely to *damage* U.S. interests and is capable of *enhancing* them.

China

The changes in foreign policy and in the concept of national security that took place in China in the first half of the 1980s had a great deal in common with recent changes in the position of the Soviet Union. China's new approach to foreign policy issues was based primarily on abandonment of the idea of a world of ideologically hostile blocs and the confrontational view of many international problems associated with such an outlook. Consequently, China revised its defense doctrine and shifted away from exaggerating external dangers to assuming the absense of any "big war" threat. This approach was supported by concrete measures taken in the military sphere and resulted in a noticeable change in relations with the United States, the USSR, Japan, and the NICs, including South Korea.

Evidence that the aggressive concept of national security is no longer valid in China includes the remarkable decline in the importance attached to military topics in internal propaganda and ideology, a lower role of the military in decisionmaking, and cuts in spending for military purposes in the national budget. Defense spending was cut from 17.5 per cent of the budget in 1979 to 8 per cent in 1988.[25] Beginning in 1985, the size of the army has been gradually reduced by one million men. It is important to note that this reduction affected troops located along the border with the USSR and in provinces sharing a marine border with Taiwan.[26]

Unfortunately, there is also evidence to the contrary: First, it is no secret that a program of nuclear buildup has begun. Submarines equipped with launching devices are under construction, and professional retraining of the armed forces is under way. However, the optimization of the Chinese military potential can, it seems, be treated in terms of a concept of reasonable defense sufficiency—which has never been declared officially, although it apparently is being implemented.[27] Another set of facts—the abrupt termination of the process of political liberalization and the direct use of the armed forces to suppress the youth demonstrations in June 1989—is rather difficult to interpret. The question is how this step back from political liberalization is likely to influence Chinese foreign policy. In the author's view, *foreign* policy—the result of long-term social and economic restructuring—will remain unaffected.

In China's case, the main rationale for innovations in foreign policy should be sought in the needs of economic reform—although the initial change in the geopolitical approach would not have occurred without two dramatic shifts in ideology and internal politics of the early 1980s: the abolition of the system of people's communes (which had been used as a tool of the totalitarian state), and the introduction of the concept of "one country, two socio-economic systems," with recognition of the possibility of the coexistence of different economic modes of production. Later the restructuring of the domestic political system was initiated (through the program of political reforms adopted by the XIIIth Congress of the Chinese Communist Party and other moves—perceived as small steps from outside, but significant if assessed in historical perspective).[28] All this encourages changes in the course of foreign policy.

A Western observer is certainly perplexed by the parallel development of the decrease of militarism and armed attack on democratic actions by students, who demanded to speed up the political reform of Chinese society. But it should be stressed that we are witnessing a society attempting to rid itself of ancient and deeply rooted political traditions at the moment of transition to a modern-style democracy. That painful transition implies truly unprecedented stages of reforming a domestic political system based on new relations between central power and the individual—or, even more generally, between society and the individual. At the present moment, when the political transformation is lagging behind the economic one, many totalitarian features continue to prevail. While the latter still dominate in the domestic social system, the need to coexist with the outside world forces the society to diminish militarism and intolerance in its foreign policy.

But the major source of change in China's foreign policy is still its new understanding of its economic needs and interests, which have not undergone any recent revision. The Chinese leadership exhibited a purely pragmatic approach when it announced in the early 1980s that the implementation of economic modernization in the country required a tranquil international environment. The further development of China's geopolitical interest is likely to have the following features:

- Even if the budget deficit is overcome, expenditures on the maintenance and modernization of the army will seem less and less justifiable; the security factor will gradually lose its significance in comparison with external economic interests; and geopolitical priorities will be shaped on the basis of geo-economic ones.

- Foreign economic relations will have to be expanded to include the countries of Southeast Asia, the NICs, Japan, the USSR, and the United States.

- External economic interests, as well as the revised security concept, will eventually influence policy toward the United States, but China will stick to balanced relations with the USSR and the United States, or a "policy of equal distance" from both superpowers, maintaining a "big triangle" balance. Although Beijing seeks restoration of neighborly relations with the Soviet Union, it emphasizes that ideological similarities alone will never make them preferable to economic relations with the United States.[29]

New geo-economic interests result from the need to satisfy import demand for modern technology and to balance imports with exports. To meet demand for R&D-intensive and high-tech products, China would like to find partners among Japan, the United States, the Western European countries, and the Asian NICs.

The need to obtain capital and technology resources from Japan most probably will urge China to eliminate as many points of contention as possible to improve the political climate of its relations with Japan. Similarly, the NICs (primarily South Korea and Singapore) will seek to enlarge their share in Chinese imports and thus develop bilateral relations—at first economic, and later perhaps even political—with China.[30]

A critical role in Chinese external interests will be played in the near future by the problem of exports.[31] China needs to diversify its export markets because its products cannot be absorbed indefinitely by its major outlets, Japan and the United States—as evidenced by their protectionism against Chinese goods. Besides, Chinese exports often are not competitive enough to enter Japanese or U.S. markets. It is clear that China's modernization will take years and that the radical reshaping of its export production is still distant.[32]

This suggests that a market much better suited to Chinese exports might eventually be found in the USSR. The Soviet Union is a potential consumer of huge volumes of Chinese light industrial products, food products, and electronics from special economic zones. Especially vital for China, with its labor-abundant economy, is the possibility of exports of labor-intensive goods and even of direct labor exports. The attractiveness of this prospect was stressed by China's Foreign Minister Qian Qichen during his visit to Moscow in late 1988.[33] If it succeeds in accelerating the growth of its export earnings, China may become a substantial outlet for exports from the NICS and Japan, thus removing pressure from the U.S. market.[34] Other steps, such as the development of the domestic market, improvements in the standard of living, etc.—indeed the accomplishment of all of the main goals of economic reform—are of course essential for enlarging the absorptive capacity of the Chinese market. Today the United States has a tool at its disposal to encourage those processes. Leaving aside the *indirect* impact of many aspects of the international activities of the United States, there is the potential leverage of *direct* participation in Chinese economic development—of direct capital investment in special export zones and coastal cities, which, unlike bilateral commerce, does not require balancing.[35] U.S. policymakers urgently need to decide what type of China is more beneficial to the United States—one that builds up armaments and has hostile relations with its neighbors, absorbing U.S. military hardware exports and presenting a growing threat to Asia and the United States, or one that intensively implements its economic reform—not without Western support, but also to the West's benefit, including indirect advantages gained through the development of mutual contacts in the APR.

In any case, it seems likely that both the military doctrine and (to a lesser degree) the totalitarian features of domestic policy—which eventually impact on foreign policy—can be influenced externally. The shortest and the most realistic way to achieve this is by encouraging economic interdependence.

India

The likely impact of domestic economic reform on the geopolitical situation in Asia is even less clear in the case of India than in those of the USSR or China. In some respects it would be more logical to examine the geopolitical *impediments* to a realization of reform than to discuss reform's geopolitical *consequences*. Yet the geopolitical situation is more important for India than for many other countries—and, until the second half of 1988, this situation was unfavorable for the country. Besides the direct threat from a Pakistan under former President Mohammed Zia ul-Haq, India was kept under strain by the generally disturbing situation in Asia. External conditions have substantially changed with the withdrawal of Soviet troops from Afghanistan and of the Vietnamese from Kampuchea, improvement of Sino-Soviet contacts, and a new civilian government headed by Prime Minister Benazir Bhutto in Pakistan. These changes provided Indian Prime Minister Rajiv Gandhi with latitude to deal with his mounting budget deficits by curbing military spending for FY1989–90. It can even be said that the geopolitical implications for India have resulted not so much from its own economic reform as from economic and political reforms in the USSR and China, which have changed "big triangle" relations and altered the overall situation in Asia.[36]

Of the *internal* factors that have until recently impacted on the geopolitical interests of India, the dynamics of political struggle have been the most important. Recent years have been marked by the outbreak of separatist movements in Punjab, Kashmir, and Assam, and by the growing influence of regional parties based on ethnic and religious movements. Losing popularity and lacking levers of control over the situation in the country, Prime Minister Rajiv Gandhi resorted to foreign policy moves, including efforts to enlarge India's political role in South Asia, as means of achieving domestic stability and increasing the prestige and position of the Indian National Congress (I). In the November 1989 elections, the Indian National Congress (I) lost to the National Front, composed of five opposition parties and led by Vishvanath P. Singh. During the election campaign, the basic strategy of the five opposition parties concentrated on criticism of the record of the INC (I). At this writing, the National Front has not completed the development of its economic and political program. However, some changes seem likely. V.P. Singh's evident concern to reduce ethnic tensions within India also makes likely an effort to reduce tensions with India's neighbors. A new agreement has been reached between India and Sri Lanka:

India has agreed to withdraw its troops by March 31, 1990. There are unresolved disputes with other neighbors. With Bangladesh, the problem concerns refugees (who seriously complicate the situation in Tripura state), and the use of waters of the river Ganga. The dispute with Nepal relates to the transit of Chinese goods through this state and the need to develop energy potential by building multipurpose dams—which Nepal argues should be done by India.

It seems likely that India will now be able to devote more attention to *economic* goals in its relations with other South Asian countries. Much will depend on the way cooperation is pursued within the framework of the South Asia Association for Regional Cooperation (SAARC). The international situation in South Asia will be affected critically by the evolving normalization of relations between India and Pakistan begun with the Gandhi-Bhutto summit in Islamabad in 1988.[37] The relaxation of tensions in bilateral relations also has had a direct *economic* effect. It is vitally important for India—when inflation is at about 10 per cent and when budgetary expenditures are rising—to cut military spending from Rs. 132 billion in FY1988–89 to Rs. 130 billion in FY1989–90.[38] Military spending cuts might have been even more substantial had the United States not supplied modern offensive weapons to Pakistan. Those supplies were identified by Zail Singh, then President of India, as one of three obstacles to the normalization of Indo-Pakistani relations (along with Pakistan's nuclear ambitions and its support of Sikh separatists.)[39] Improvement in Sino-Soviet relations strengthens India's attempts to normalize its relations with China. The Western press has frequently implied that disagreements with China and Pakistan formed the basis of India's adherence to close relations with the Soviet Union.[40] It seems likely indeed that India's normalization of relations with China and Pakistan may lessen the importance of military assistance from the Soviet Union. But this would not mean a loss of India's interest in contacts with the USSR—as these contacts take place under conditions of the growing significance of economic priorities. India's participation in the international division of labor, like China's, is currently characterized by a divergence between the orientation of its imports (the West) and the locus of its export potential (the USSR and neighboring countries in South Asia). At the same time, economic reform in the USSR implies expanded prospects for goods and capital imports, especially light industrial products and electronics from India.[41]

As the military factors behind its relations with the countries of Asia diminish, India's geopolitical decisions will relate more closely to a selection of approaches linked to the international economic situation.[42] Hence India is likely to intensify its economic relations with:

- South Asian countries (relations with these states can develop in combination and balance with traditional political contacts);
- Southeast Asian countries (primarily the NICs);[43]
- The Soviet Union (as was already mentioned); and
- Western Europe, the United States, and Japan. (It will, however, be difficult to balance the exports of the OECD countries to the Indian market in the very near future. The prospects are most favorable for those countries that can solve the credits problem. Ideally, commercial exports should be accompanied by a substantial tranfer of concessional resources).[44]

On the whole, the climate of U.S.-Indian bilateral relations so far has been determined by the development of political, military, and economic relations of the United States with China and Pakistan. In that context, it is a strange logic that underlies arguments that it is in the U.S. interest first to arm Pakistan (and thus form a threat to stability on the continent) and then to support the military ambitions of India in an attempt to make it a counterbalance to Pakistan.[45]

Instead, it would seem that India might today be the *focus* of U.S. economic policy in Asia. It would make sense to open up a new option for India—a choice between its own military and economic expenditures (rather than the old one between different military and political allies)—while creating conditions making the new option more attractive for India.

New Prospects and Challenges for the United States

The emerging geopolitical situation appears to favor U.S. interests, as military threats are likely to diminish due to the changing political interests of the three Giants. The Giants' new understanding of global interdependence leads to a unique coincidence of political interests—including the political interests of the United States: All parties need a peaceful international environment. In an atmosphere of gradually lessening geopolitical tensions in Asia, where the existing balance of power is conducive to a stable peace, the United States and other powers have an opportunity to support efforts that seek to further reduce tensions and allow for deeper cuts in military expenditures. Any aggravation of tensions would be resented by the three Giants—and not in the interest of the United States—either in short-term perspective (as a burden on the budget) or in the long run, as other countries' losses from their growth resources would, in an interdependent world, eventually hurt every member of the world community.

Taking a "geo-economic" perspective, the new situation in the APR raises two important questions:

• Is it in the U.S. interest to support the economic reforms in the Giants—and what *economic* results can such support be expected to bring?

• And if the United States does consider support for the Giants to be in its interest, what *forms* of support are likely to be most effective?

The first issue is closely connected with the possibility that the reforms might be reversed. Of course political instability in China and India and national difficulties and ever-growing economic problems in the Soviet Union should be taken into consideration, since eventually, in the worst possible scenario, they might affect the Giants' foreign policies. But however huge these problems may be, it would be strange to look upon them as the rationale for a policy of containment—or even for being in a hurry to get U.S. interests satisfied as soon as possible, as Francis Fukuyama advises.[46] In my view, that kind of international attitude would hinder reforms in the Giants, which in turn would delay the achievement of the truly international benefits of the reforms. In contrast, a course supportive of the reforms—with its potential of the Giants becoming more developed, more economically open, and more integrated into the global economy—could strengthen world trade and other types of economic relations for the benefit of all participants.

Such a long-term argument may be beyond the normal realm of policy decisionmaking, but it should not be ignored; its potential direct benefits to the United States may seem distant, but they are strikingly attractive. While U.S. policymakers are engaged in heated discussions on every aspect of the Giants' reforms and see no reason to respond to the reforms directly, an unexpected issue is taking shape: economic competition in Asia from Japan, which has been implementing an exceptionally rational strategy in the region while the United States has not even joined the game. In the long run, Japanese economic influence in Asia may prove very important, since it affects all of the geopolitically important players: China, India, South Asia, the NICs, and even the USSR.

In summary, the emerging geopolitical and geo-economic situation of the Giants creates new opportunities for the United States:

- The relaxation of international tensions makes it possible to decrease military involvement in Asia and assistance to armies participating in regional conflicts (Afghanistan, Pakistan, Kampuchea); this can yield not only limited savings in the military budget but also savings in foreign military assistance—as well as, last but not least, further *political* gains.

- New prospects are opening up for enhancing U.S. economic influence to the advantage of all of the participants (except possibly Japan); since major geopolitical changes are linked to the new geo-economics in Asia, further political dialogue with the Giants can be treated as a derivative of expanded economic interdependence.

- The general reduction of political tensions and the gradual evolution of the Giants' external economic relations increase the possibility of (as well as the need for) U.S. encouragement of the positive trends in Asia through economic support for the reform process in the Giants.

- The same developments enable a rather wide choice among the potential forms of support; these need not be limited to loans, the encouragement of direct private investment, or even the removal of constraints on bilateral trade. It is important to draw the Giants into the world economy through international institutions and to enable the opening up of their economies. That, in turn, could speed up internal political reform in China and the Soviet Union, and it might help stabilize the political situation in India. To reconcile the U.S. national interest with the Giants' progress, it would be reasonable to formulate mutually acceptable "conditionality" through unofficial discussions with the Giants' research and business representatives.

In conclusion, it should be stressed that the new circumstances, actions, and potential of the Giants await policy response. Being far from simple, the situation admittedly requires extremely prudent treatment. But the players have to decide whether it is more prudent to step aside or to get involved for the sake of averting a turn for the worse in the area of geopolitics and losses in geo-economics.

Notes

[1] It should be noted that huge resource transfers are still involved in economic relations of the Giants with the Third World (though these might be used in new, more efficient ways). The USSR does not intend to write off the Third World "as of limited importance in the American-Soviet competition"—as suggested by Zbigniew Brzezinski in "Sentiment and Strategy: The Imbalance in America's Third World Policy," *The National Interest* (Summer 1988), p. 141.

[2] Interview with Eduard A. Shevardnadze, *Izvestiya*, March 22, 1989. It is in these institutions that the issue of assistance to the Third World will be discussed—to decide what portion of GDP may be diverted and with what specific purposes.

[3] As recently as two to three years ago, no newspaper would have published critical material on the controversial Soviet aid policy in the Third World; yet this became possible in the summer of 1989 ("Interview with Elena B. Arefieva," *Izvestiya*, July 10, 1989). The highest achievement of *glasnost* in foreign policy, however, was making public the military budget of the USSR in June 1989 ("Oboronnyi budget SSSR," *Pravda*, June 11, 1989).

[4] This sentiment has been demonstrated in numerous articles in the press as well as in published letters of readers, in discussions on television, and by the fact that many army representatives lost to their competitors during the spring 1989 elections of the People's Deputies of the Soviet Union (from among whom the Supreme Council was later elected).

[5] Mikhail S. Gorbachev, *Perestroika and the New Thinking for Our Country and for the World* (New York: Harper & Row, 1987).

[6] See M. Moiseev, "Sovetskaya voyennaya doktrina; realizatsia yeye oboronitelnich napravleniy," *Pravda*, March 13, 1989. It is implicitly admitted in the article that special efforts are needed to free the doctrine from its offense-oriented character.

[7] It was declared in 1982 as a slogan—"one nation, two systems"—aimed at resolving the problem of Taiwan and Hong Kong, but recently it has often appeared in Party documents as an admission of the possibility of the coexistence of different types of property and economic modes of production.

[8] George Orwell, *1984*.

[9] Starting in 1986, the growth in military spending steadily diminished; by 1988, it was only 2.6 per cent, while inflation was over 16 per cent. *Asian Security 1988–89* (Tokyo: Research Institute for Peace and Security, 1988), p. 66; and *Pravda*, December 17, 1988.

[10] Thomas P. Thornton, "India's Foreign Relations: Problems Along the Borders," in Marshall M. Bouton and Philip Oldenburg, eds., *India Briefing, 1988* (Boulder, Colo.: Westview Press, 1988), pp. 57–84.

[11] Michael Renner, "Enhancing Global Security," *State of the World* (New York: Worldwatch Institute, 1988).

[12] Yashuhiro Nakasone, "Zalozhit osnovi novogo mezhdunarodnogo soobshestva," *Mirovaya ekonomika i mezhdunarodniye otnosheniya (MEMO)* (Moscow) No. 10, 1988, p. 76.

[13] Georgy Kunadze, "Militarism v. Yaponni: voprosy metodologii analiza," *MEMO,* No. 2, 1989, pp. 117–21, 127.

[14] Moiseev, "Sovetskaya voyennaya doktrina," op. cit.

[15] Now whole pages in newspapers and articles in journals are devoted to analysis of the Chinese experience, and economists—most frequently experts in external economic relations—refer to it in their proposals on the development of *perestroika*. See, for example, S. Manezhev, "Foreign Investments in the Socialist Economy (as exemplified by the PRC)," *Foreign Trade* (Moscow), No. 12, 1988.

[16] For example, Soviet supplies of complete plants and services connected with them in 1988 surpassed the 1987 level by 2.5 times. See M. Kiryanova, "USSR-China: Prospects for Developing Trade and Economic Relations," *Foreign Trade*, No. 11, 1988, p. 3.

[17] See the interview with E. M. Primakov, *Pravda*, October 8, 1988.

[18] An entirely new direction in relations with the Third World has emerged as a result of the decentralization of economic management in the Soviet Union; the launching of the system of self-financing and hard-currency self-repayment of enterprises; granting enterprises and cooperatives the right to enter the world market on their own; growing freedom of action in agriculture, where rent relations can change the whole production structure; permission to apply new forms of external economic ties; a decentralized system of decisionmaking (the establishment of joint ventures, border trade, etc.).

[19]It does refer to the NICs to some extent, as mentioned correctly by Paul Wolfowitz in "Southeast Asia—Deferring Hard Choices," *The National Interest*, No. 12 (Summer 1988), p. 125.

[20]Despite the uneasy situation caused by Pakistan's violation of the Geneva accords dealing with Afghanistan, the Soviet leadership is doing its best to improve relations and remains hopeful that Pakistan will revise its foreign policy and military strategy as a result of the efforts of Prime Minister Banazir Bhutto. High expectations are placed on the Prime Minister's ability to countervail the influence of the army leadership, which is opposed to her on the situation in Afghanistan.

[21]Alexander K. Kislov, "Novoye myshleniye i regionalniye konflikti," *Pravda*, September 29, 1988.

[22]Japan has been quite active in this respect. In particular, there are agreements providing for buy-back supplies of mining equipment exchanged for timber and coal. Even more decisive steps were taken by Japan in Western Siberia; an agreement has been signed by Soviet organizations and the Japanese consortium headed by Mitsubishi about a joint venture to produce engineering plastics in the town of Nishnevartovsk amounting to 4 billion rubles. Two other Japanese firms from the Mitsui group, together with McDermot International, will take part in a joint venture for the processing of raw gas in localities of the town of Urenghoi (*European Chemical News*, November 21, 1988, p. 29; November 28, 1988, p. 25). It is widely believed in the Soviet Union that still more cooperation is ahead.

[23]Eduard A. Shevardnadze, "Ecologiya i diplomatiya", *Literaturnaya gazeta* (Moscow), November 22, 1989, p. 10.

[24]This course has been made evident by the transfer of resources (amounting to $600 million) for assistance to Afghanistan to the U.N. Emergency Relief Fund for Afghanistan, by Soviet participation in deliveries of goods, and by the adoption of a Decree of the Presidium of the USSR Supreme Council concerning recognition by the Soviet Union of the obligatory jurisdiction of the U.N. International Court regarding a number of major multilateral conventions.

[25]*Beijing Review*, Vol. 31, No. 24 (June 1988).

[26]Still earlier, in 1984, Deng Xiaoping called upon the airforce, the navy, and the Commission for Defense Science, Technology, and Industry to allot a part of their resources "for support to development of the national economy," to hand over military airfields and ports for civilian use, and to convert the defense industry to civilian production. Deng Xiaoping, Osnovnije voprosi sovremennogo Kitaya (*Moscow: Politizdat, 1988*).

[27]A conclusion reached by an expert of the Stockholm International Peace Research Institute (SIPRI), Richard W. Fieldhouse, seems to reflect the same approach. In his opinion, China could be induced to launch a new-generation nuclear program only in the case of intensive competition between the United States and the USSR in nuclear and strategic defense weapons; in the absence of such a competition, China will not need such a program. Richard w. Fieldhouse, "Chinese Nuclear Forces: Overview and Ambitions," in Carl G. Jacobsen, ed., *The Uncertain Course: New Weapons, Strategies and Mind-sets* (Stockholm: SIPRI, 1987), p. 265–66.

[28]For instance, democratic methods were applied to the organization of the 1988 session of the All-China Congress of People's Representatives, where real elections of the Standing Committee took place for the first time. In October 1988, discussion within the Secretariat of the CPC touched on the question of whether developments in government need to be controlled by non-Party organizations and public opinion. *Beijing Review*, Vol. 31, No. 44 (October 31–November 6, 1988).

[29]The conclusion that ideological proximity cannot lay the ground for China's foreign policy is reached by Wu Jin in "China, USSR to Normalize Ties: A Trend," *Beijing Review*, Vol. 31, No. 44 (October 31–November 6, 1988), p. 24.

[30]The pressure of economic priorities clearly has influenced the Chinese attitude toward the problem of the Korean peninsula: Despite the disapproval of North Korea, China has maintained quite intensive trade relations with South Korea and has exchanged non-governmental commercial missions. This provided a basis for President Roh Tae Woo to state that he was hopeful of visiting Beijing officially. *Asian Security*, op. cit., pp. 60–61.

[31]Export growth is still inadequate due to domestic difficulties (internal demand pressure, the short supply of materials, insufficient incentives for exporters) as well as limited of external demand. At the same time, according to the seventh five-year plan, the growth of exports will have to overtake import growth (annual rates of 8.1 and 6.1 per cent annual rates respectively). *Beijing Review*, Vol. 29, No. 17 (April 1986).

[32]It is reasonable, however, to join Dwight H. Perkins in his view that China is very

likely to follow the route of the NICs if the democratization of society is continued, productivity growth supported, and, based on this growth, accelerated and the production structure changed. Dwight H. Perkins, *China: Asia's Next Economic Giant?* (Seattle: University of Washington Press, 1986), pp. 49–60, and 85.

[33]*Izvestiya,* December 4, 1988.

[34]Japan itself has become a significant export market for the NICs as a result of market restriction in the United States (in just one year, 1987, exports from South Korea and Taiwan to Japan grew by 50 per cent). However, Japan is now considering protective measures, starting with barriers to textiles from the NICs. (*Asian Security,* op. cit., pp. 8–9).

[35]It should be stressed that, in the case of China, in addition to the usual contribution of direct investments to the economic development of a recipient country, direct investments are capable of influencing the very economic mechanism providing feedback. The reason lies in the fact that the economic transformation is still going on and necessitates the adaptation of the national economy to more developed incomers: foreign companies. It has been noted, for instance, that foreign investment induces a cyclical reaction of removal of market restrictions, such as obstacles to supplying foreign enterprises with materials and to marketing their products. T. Chan, E. K. Y. Chen, and S. Chin, "China's Special Economic Zones: Ideology, Policy, and Practice," in Y. C. Jao and C. K. Leung, eds., *China's Special Economic Zones: Policies, Problems, and Prospects* (Oxford: Oxford University Press, 1986), pp. 99–100.

[36]It should be noted that the normalization of Soviet relations with China is favorable for India due to the overall reduction of tensions in Asia. While there do not appear to be any adverse consequences for relations with India, the opposite (that China will be drawn into a still closer relationship with the Soviet Union) is also unlikely. On this matter, see Bhabani Sen Gupta's generally interesting book, *The Gorbachev Factor in World Affairs: An Indian Interpretation* (Delhi: B. R. Publishing Corporation, 1989), p. 19.

[37]Under Rajiv Gandhi, some observers thought that the menace was exaggerated for domestic political reasons. See R. Rikhye's article in *Economic and Political Weekly* (Bombay), Vol. XXIV, No. 12 (March 12, 1989), p. 606. For his own political reasons, Prime Minister Singh may see the issue differently. However, it must be noted that, currently, the conflict in Kashmir and the apparent Pakistani support for the Kashmiri secessionists is an aggravated source of Indo-Pakistani tensions.

[38]*Izvestiya,* March 13, 1989.

[39]*Asia Yearbook 1988,* Supplement to Far Eastern Economic Review (Hong Kong, 1988), p. 71.

[40]See, for example, Leo E. Rose, "United States and Soviet Policy Towards South Asia," *Current History* (March 1986), p. 134.

[41]The realization of this potential is complicated by difficulties on the Soviet side such as restricted export resources and the inconvertibility of the ruble. Both countries are looking for a way out of this situation.

[42]The problem of export earnings is aggravated as migrant workers return from the Persian Gulf countries and their currency remittances dry up, and also by expenses connected with the repayment of a 1984 IMF loan. The problem is that progress on economic reform depends on India's ability to provide resources for imports of equipment and technology. As Gerald Helleiner has noted, to achieve the planned growth of GNP, India has to have a rate of export growth higher than that of international trade, although an alternative may be found in an increased concessional aid flow. See Gerald K. Helleiner, "Balance-of-Payments Experience and Growth Prospects of Developing Countries: A Synthesis," *International Monetary and Financial Issues for the Developing Countries* (New York: UNCTAD, 1987), p. 161.

[43]Indian businesses fear that competition from Chinese industry may interfere with that perspective; however, it may be that, under conditions of less hostile relations, an understanding (unofficial, of course) could be reached concerning each country's interests in Southeast Asia. This would only intensify the traditional divisions in the sub-region's entrepreneurial orientation toward either China (mostly by ethnic Chinese living outside China) or other Asian countries.

[44]Japan has indicated great willingness to increase assistance to Asian countries, whereas economic assistance from the United States has decreased from $149 million in FY1986–87 to $99 million in FY1987–88. Thornton, "India's Foreign Relations," op. cit., p. 81.

[45]This was said to be the rationale used in Washington to approve Rajiv Gandhi's military operations in Sri Lanka—as he told the Consulting Parliamentary Committee for Foreign Affairs after returning from the United States in 1987. Such action may have

been motivated by concern to contain Pakistan's nuclear plans. It is a fact that Pakistani nuclear plans took shape without U.S. participation, but undoubtedly the general umbrella of U.S. support for Pakistan's military build-up reinforces the country's military strategy. Yet it remains unclear whether it is in the interest of the United States to urge India to play a "more expanded role," when this role is understood primarily as military and political. (*Asia Yearbook*, op. cit., p. 70).

[46]Francis Fukuyama, "Discord or Cooperation in the Third World? Coping with Gorbachev's Soviet Union," *CSIS Significant Issue Series*, Vol. X. No. 9, 1988.

Statistical
Annexes

Table 1. The Giants' GNP
(1987 $ billions and percentages)

	Gross National Product (GNP)				Average Annual Real GNP Growth, 1975–1987	Share in World GNP, 1987	Share in World Population, 1987
	1975	1980	1985	1987			
Soviet Union	1,862	2,110	2,287	2,375	2.0%	13.9%	5.6%
China	121	162	252	294	7.7	1.7	21.2
India	144	172	217	231	4.0	1.4	15.8
Giants	2,127	2,444	2,756	2,900	2.6	17.0	42.6

Source: CIA, *Handbook of Economic Statistics, 1988* (Washington, D.C.: Central Intelligence Agency, Foreign Assistance Center, 1988).

Table 2. The Giants' Share of World Trade,[a] 1981 and 1987
($ billions and percentages)

	1981				1987				Average Annual Growth of Trade[a] 1981–87
	Exports	Imports	Exports and Imports	Percentage Share of World Trade	Exports	Imports	Exports and Imports	Percentage Share of World Trade	
World	1,856.0	1,926.0	3,782.0	100.0%	2,356.0	2,427.0	4,783.0	100.0%	4.0%
Soviet Union	41.2	45.2	86.4	2.3	38.9	42.7	81.6	1.7	0.9
China	19.6	22.5	42.1	1.1	39.6	45.7	85.4	1.8	12.5
India	11.4	12.2	23.6	0.6	15.7	17.2	32.9	0.7	5.7
Giants	72.2	79.9	152.1	4.0	94.2	105.6	199.9	4.2	4.7

[a]Exports and imports are average values of *Direction of Trade Statistics* and *International Financial Statistics*.

Source: IMF, *Direction of Trade Statistics* (Washington, D.C.: IMF, 1988).

Table 3. The Giants' Trade[a] and GNP, 1986
($ billions and percentages)

	Trade[a]	GNP	Trade as Percentage of GNP
Soviet Union	93.0	2,361	3.9
China	37.4	272	13.8
India	12.5	228	5.5

aExports plus imports divided by two.

Source: CIA, *Handbook of Economic Statistics, 1988* (Washington, D.C.: Central Intelligence Agency, Foreign Assistance Center, 1988).

Table 4. Soviet Union's Trade with OECD[a] Countries ($ billions)

Soviet Union's Trade with:	1975		1980		1985		1987		1988	
	Exports	Imports	Exports	Imports	Exports	Imports	Exports	Imports	Exports	Imports
OECD Countries	8.84	12.53	24.79	21.60	23.06	20.94	22.88	20.62	23.66	24.80
United States	0.25	1.84	0.35	2.44	0.41	2.42	0.42	1.48	0.65	2.77
EEC	4.64	6.11	15.44	10.54	15.89	9.52	14.96	10.61	15.31	11.94
Japan	1.17	1.63	2.02	2.77	1.43	2.77	2.36	2.59	2.77	3.13

[a]Member nations of the Organisation for European Co-operation and Development.

Source: OECD, *Statistics of Foreign Trade, Series A* (Washington, D.C.: OECD, 1988); and U.S. Bureau of the Census, *Highlights of U.S. Export and Import Trade (FT 990)* (Washington, D.C.: U.S. Bureau of the Census), December of various years.

Table 5. China's Trade with OECD Countries ($ billions)

China's Trade with:	1975 Exports	1975 Imports	1980 Exports	1980 Imports	1985 Exports	1985 Imports	1987 Exports	1987 Imports	1988 Exports	1988 Imports
OECD Countries	2.82	4.97	8.78	13.28	14.34	24.55	21.66	21.53	28.57	25.50
United States	0.16	0.30	1.06	3.76	3.86	3.85	6.30	3.49	9.27	5.04
EEC	0.80	1.33	2.64	2.41	2.96	5.48	5.86	6.38	7.70	6.79
Japan	1.52	2.26	4.31	5.03	6.55	12.59	7.48	8.34	9.86	9.49

Source: OECD, Statistics of Foreign Trade, Series A (Washington, D.C.: OECD, 1988); and U.S. Bureau of the Census, Highlights of U.S. Export and Import Trade (FT 990) (Washington, D.C.: U.S. Bureau of the Census, December of various years.

Table 6. India's Trade with OECD Countries
($ billions)

India's Trade with:	1975		1980		1985		1987		1988	
	Exports	Imports	Exports	Imports	Exports	Imports	Exports	Imports	Exports	Imports
OECD Countries	2.53	3.64	5.06	6.77	6.22	8.69	7.93	11.48	9.36	13.34
United States	0.55	1.30	1.10	1.69	2.29	1.64	2.53	1.46	3.17	2.50
EEC	1.09	1.36	2.47	3.23	2.29	4.38	2.36	6.55	3.88	6.64
Japan	0.66	0.71	1.02	0.91	1.20	1.61	1.55	1.98	1.81	2.08

Source: OECD, *Statistics of Foreign Trade, Series A* (Washington, D.C.: OECD, 1988); and U.S. Bureau of the Census, *Highlights of U.S. Export and Import Trade (FT 990)* (Washington, D.C.: U.S. Bureau of the Census), December of various years.

Table 7. The Giants' Shares in OECD Trade[a] (percentages)

	1975	1980	1985	1987	1988
Soviet Union	1.85	1.80	1.68	1.23	1.20
China	0.67	0.85	1.48	1.22	1.34
India	0.53	0.46	0.57	0.55	0.56
Giants	3.05	3.11	3.73	3.00	3.10

[a]Exports and imports.

Source: Calculated from Tables 4-6 in this Statistical Annex. OECD, *Statistics of Foreign Trade, Series A* (Washington, D.C.: OECD, 1988).

Table 8. Average Annual Growth of OECD Countries' Trade[a] with Giants, Compared to OECD Trade with World (percentages)

OECD Trade[a] with:	1975–1985	1980–1988	1985–1988
Soviet Union	7.5	0.5	3.2
China	17.4	11.9	11.6
India	9.2	8.5	15.0
World	8.5	5.2	14.2[b]

[a]Exports and imports.
[b]The high growth rate of OECD countries' total trade is partially due to the growing value of most OECD countries' currencies relative to the dollar.

Source: OECD, *Statistics of Foreign Trade, Series A* (Washington, D.C.: OECD, 1988).

Table 9. Structure of OECD[a] Trade with the Soviet Union, 1987 ($ millions and percentages)

Exports to and Imports from Soviet Union:	EXPORTS			IMPORTS		
	U.S.	EEC	Japan	U.S.	EEC	Japan
Raw Materials (SITC 0-4)	971 (66%)	1,182 (11%)	70 (3%)	180 (38%)	10,991 (81%)	1,185 (62%)
Chemicals (SITC 5)	264 (18%)	1,821 (17%)	329 (13%)	118 (25%)	690 (5%)	43 (2%)
Manufactured Products (SITC 6-8)	222 (15%)	7,203 (68%)	2,084 (81%)	158 (34%)	1,827 (13%)	683 (35%)
Total	1,477 (100%)	10,614 (100%)	2,563 (100%)	470 (100%)	13,642 (100%)	1,922 (100%)

[a]U.S., EEC, and Japan data only, as shown.

Source: OECD, *Statistics of Foreign Trade, Series C (1987)* (Paris: OECD, 1989).

Table 10. Structure of OECD[a] Trade with China, 1987 ($ millions and percentages)

Exports to and Imports from China:	EXPORTS			IMPORTS		
	U.S.	EEC	Japan	U.S.	EEC	Japan
Raw Materials (SITC 0-4)	700 (20%)	392 (6%)	232 (3%)	1,012 (15%)	1,668 (28%)	4,501 (61%)
Chemicals (SITC 5)	807 (23%)	865 (14%)	745 (9%)	216 (3%)	495 (8%)	404 (5%)
Manufactured Products (SITC 6-8)	1,929 (56%)	5,030 (79%)	7,210 (87%)	5,609 (81%)	3,623 (62%)	2,322 (31%)
Total	3,460 (100%)	6,351 (100%)	8,249 (100%)	6,910 (100%)	5,855 (100%)	7,386 (100%)

[a] U.S., EEC, and Japan data only, as shown.

Source: OECD, *Statistics of Foreign Trade, Series C (1987)* (Paris: OECD, 1989).

Table 11. Structure of OECD[a] Trade with India, 1987
($ millions and percentages)

Exports to and Imports from India:	EXPORTS			IMPORTS		
	U.S.	EEC	Japan	U.S.	EEC	Japan
Raw Materials (SITC 0-4)	271 (19%)	378 (6%)	51 (3%)	734 (27%)	622 (19%)	1,042 (68%)
Chemicals (SITC 5)	187 (13%)	653 (10%)	118 (6%)	46 (2%)	108 (3%)	17 (1%)
Manufactured Products (SITC 6-8)	941 (65%)	5,241 (80%)	1,778 (91%)	1,928 (71%)	2,509 (77%)	465 (30%)
Total	1,431 (100%)	6,528 (100%)	1,957 (100%)	2,725 (100%)	3,256 (100%)	1,530 (100%)

[a] U.S., EEC, and Japan data only, as shown.

Source: OECD, *Statistics of Foreign Trade, Series C (1987)* (Paris: OECD, 1989).

Table 12. U.S. Trade with Giants, Compared to U.S. Trade with World, 1975–1988 ($ billions)

U.S. Trade with:	1975		1980		1985		1987		1988	
	Exports	Imports	Exports	Imports	Exports	Imports	Exports	Imports	Exports	Imports
Soviet Union	1.835	0.280	1.513	0.484	2.423	0.443	1.480	0.469	2.768	0.649
China	0.304	0.171	3.755	1.161	3.856	4.224	3.497	6.912	5.039	9.270
India	0.760	0.621	1.689	1.209	1.642	2.478	1.463	2.725	2.498	3.167
World	107.6	103.4	220.7	252.8	213.1	361.6	252.9	424.1	320.4	459.9

Source: U.S. Bureau of the Census, Highlights of U.S. Export and Import Trade (FT 990) (Washington, D.C.: U.S. Bureau of the Census), December of various years.

Table 13. The Giants' Share in U.S. Trade[a]
(percentages)

	1975	1980	1985	1987	1988
Soviet Union	1.00	0.42	0.50	0.25	0.44
China	0.23	1.04	1.41	1.54	1.83
India	0.65	0.61	0.72	0.62	0.73
Giants	1.88	2.07	2.63	2.41	3.00

[a]Exports and imports.

Source: Calculated from Table 12.

Table 14. Average Annual Growth of Giants' Trade with the United States, Compared to Growth of U.S. Trade with World
(percentages)

U.S. Trade with:	1975–1985	1980–1988	1985–1988
Soviet Union	3.1	6.9	6.0
China	32.8	14.3	21.0
India	11.6	8.7	11.2
World	10.5	6.4	10.7[a]

[a]Exports and imports.

Source: Calculated from Table 12.

Table 15. U.S. Share in OECD Countries' Trade with the Giants (percentages)

U.S. Share in OECD Trade with:	1975		1980		1985		1988	
	Imports	Exports	Imports	Exports	Imports	Exports	Imports	Exports
Soviet Union	2.9	14.7	1.4	11.2	1.8	11.6	2.7	11.2
China	5.7	6.0	12.0	28.3	26.9	15.7	32.4	19.8
India	21.8	35.6	21.8	25.0	36.8	18.9	33.9	18.7

Source: Calculated from Tables 4–6.

Table 16. Ranking of Giants Among U.S. Trade Partners, 1988 (percentages)

Country	Average Share of Exports and Imports with United States	Share of U.S. Imports	Share of U.S. Exports
EEC	22.0%	19.0%	24.0%
1. Canada	20.0	18.0	22.0
2. Japan	16.0	20.0	12.0
3. Mexico	5.9	5.3	6.4
4. Germany	5.3	6.0	4.5
5. U.K.	4.9	4.1	5.7
6. Italy	4.7	2.6	2.1
7. Taiwan	4.7	5.6	3.8
8. South Korea	4.1	4.6	3.5
9. France	3.0	2.8	3.1
10. Netherlands	2.1	1.0	3.2
11. Hong Kong	2.1	2.3	1.8
12. China	**1.8**	**1.9**	**1.6**
13. Singapore	1.8	1.8	1.8
14. Belgium/Lux	1.7	1.0	2.3
15. Brazil	1.7	2.1	1.3
16. Australia	1.5	0.8	2.2
17. Saudi Arabia	1.3	1.3	1.2
18. Venezuela	1.3	1.2	1.4
19. Switzerland	1.2	1.1	1.3
20. Sweden	1.0	1.1	0.8
21. Spain	1.0	0.7	1.3
22. Israel	0.9	0.7	1.0
23. Malaysia	0.8	0.8	0.7
24. India	**0.8**	**0.7**	**0.8**
25. Thailand	0.7	0.7	0.6
26. Soviet Union	**0.5**	**0.1**	**0.9**
27. Indonesia	0.5	0.7	0.3
28. Nigeria	0.4	0.7	0.1

Source: U.S. Bureau of the Census, *Highlights of U.S. Export and Import Trade (FT 990)* (Washington, D.C.: U.S. Bureau of the Census), December of various years.

Table 17. Soviet Union's Trade Balance, Debt, and Debt/Export Ratio, 1975–1987 ($ billions)

	1975	1978	1980	1981	1982	1983	1984	1985	1986	1987	1988
Total Exports	33.3	52.2	76.4	79.0	86.9	91.3	91.6	87.3	97.3	n.a.	n.a.
Total Imports	37.0	50.5	68.5	73.0	77.8	80.4	80.7	83.1	88.9	n.a.	n.a.
Trade Balance	-3.7	1.7	7.9	6.0	9.1	10.9	10.9	4.2	8.4	n.a.	n.a.
Hard Currency Exports	n.a.	n.a.	28.7	28.7	31.5	32.1	31.7	26.9	24.1	28.7	n.a.
Hard Currency Imports	n.a.	n.a.	27.4	29.4	29.7	29.1	27.9	26.8	25.3	25.1	n.a.
Hard Currency Balance	n.a.	n.a.	1.3	-0.8	1.8	3.0	3.8	0.2	-1.2	3.7	n.a.
Debt Outstanding	n.a.	n.a.	23.5	25.3	26.2	24.5	21.4	25.2	35.2	40.1	41.5
Debt/Export[a] Ratio	n.a.	n.a.	0.82	0.88	0.83	0.76	0.68	0.94	1.46	1.40	n.a.

[a] Hard currency exports.

Source: U.N., *International Trade Statistics Yearbook 1986* (New York: United Nations, 1988) (for total trade); and WIIW (Vienna Institute for Comparative Economic Studies), *Reprint Series*, No. 115, January 1989, pp. 80-85 (for hard currency trade and debt).

Table 18. China's Trade Balance, Debt, and Debt/Export Ratio, 1975–1987 ($ billions)

	1975	1978	1980	1981	1982	1983	1984	1985	1986	1987
Total Exports	7.3	9.7	18.3	22.0	21.9	22.2	24.9	27.3	31.1	n.a.
Total Imports	7.5	10.9	19.6	22.0	18.9	21.3	26.2	42.5	42.6	n.a.
Total Trade Balance	-0.2	-1.2	-1.3	0.0	3.0	0.9	-1.3	-15.2	-11.5	n.a.
Current Account Balance	-0.3	-0.8	-3.2	1.3	5.8	4.4	2.5	-11.4	-7.0	0.3
Debt Outstanding	n.a.	n.a.	4.5	5.8	8.3	9.6	12.1	16.7	21.9	30.2
Debt/Export Ratio	n.a.	n.a.	0.25	0.26	0.38	0.43	0.49	0.61	0.70	n.a.

Source: U.N., *International Trade Statistics Yearbook 1986* (New York: United Nations, 1988) (for trade data); and The World Bank, *World Debt Tables, Volume II* (Washington, D.C.: World Bank, 1989) (for current account and debt data).

Table 19. India's Trade Balance, Debt, and Debt/Export Ratio, 1975–1987 ($ billions)

	1975	1978	1980	1981	1982	1983	1984	1985	1986	1987
Total Exports	4.4	6.7	8.4	8.4	8.8	8.7	9.9	8.7	9.2	n.a.
Total Imports	6.4	7.9	14.1	15.7	14.4	13.4	15.6	15.6	14.9	n.a.
Total Trade Balance	-2.0	-1.2	-5.7	-7.3	-5.6	-4.7	-5.7	-6.9	-5.7	n.a.
Current Account Balance	0.3	0.1	-2.2	-2.7	-2.5	-2.2	-2.5	-4.9	-3.7	-3.8
Debt Outstanding	13.3	16.5	19.3	21.1	25.6	28.8	31.3	36.6	41.3	46.4
Debt/Export[a] Ratio	3.0	2.5	2.3	2.5	2.9	3.3	3.2	4.2	4.5	n.a.

Source: U.N., *International Trade Statistics Yearbook 1986* (New York: United Nations, 1988) (for trade data); and The World Bank, *World Debt Tables, Volume II* (Washington, D.C.: World Bank, 1989) (for current account and debt data).

Table 20. Soviet Union's Trade with World, Developing Countries, and Other Two Giants, 1986 ($ billions and percentages)

Soviet Union's Trade with:	Exports	Imports
World	97.3 (100%)	88.9 (100%)
Developing Countries (excluding socialist countries)	19.0 (20%)	12.1 (14%)
Socialist Countries (including Eastern Europe	57.0 (59%)	50.4 (57%)
China	1.5 (1.5%)	1.2 (1.4%)
India	1.4 (1.4%)	1.7 (1.9%)

Source: U.N., *Statistical Yearbook for Asia and the Pacific 1986–87* (New York: United Nations, 1987); and GATT, *International Trade 1986–87* (Geneva: GATT, 1987).

Table 21. China's Trade with World, Developing Countries, and Other Two Giants, 1986 ($ billions and percentages)

China's Trade with:	Exports	Imports
World	31.37 (100%)	43.50 (100%)
Developing Countries	16.22 (52%)	10.33 (24%)
Soviet Union	1.23 (4%)	1.47 (3.3%)
India	0.09 (0.3%)	0.04 (0.1%)

Source: U.N., *Statistical Yearbook for Asia and the Pacific 1986–87* (New York: United Nations, 1987).

Table 22. India's Trade with World, Developing Countries, and Other Two Giants, 1986 ($ billions and percentages)

India's Trade with:	Exports	Imports
World	10.32 (100%)	18.83 (100%)
Developing Countries	2.06 (20%)	5.09 (27%)
Soviet Union	1.72 (17%)	1.35 (7%)
China	0.04 (0.4%)	0.10 (0.5%)

Source: U.N., *Statistical Yearbook for Asia and the Pacific 1986–87* (New York: United Nations, 1987).

Table 23. OECD Countries' Trade[a] with Giants, Compared to OECD Trade with World: Projections to Year 2010 ($ billions and percentages)

OECD Trade[a] with:	1980	1988	2000	2010
World	2,592.0 (100%)	3,903.0 (100%)	7,212.0 (100%)	12,030 (100%)
Three Giants	80.2 (3.1%)	125.3 (3.2%)	451.0 (6.3%)	981 (8.2%)
Soviet Union	46.4 (1.8%)	48.5 (1.2%)	185.0 (2.6%)	399 (3.3%)
China	22.1 (0.9%)	54.1 (1.4%)	206.0 (2.9%)	445 (3.7%)
India	11.8 (0.5%)	22.7 (0.6%)	60.4 (0.8%)	137 (1.1%)

[a]Exports and imports.

Note: The assumptions underlying the projections are:

(1) The OECD countries' trade with the world will continue to grow at an average annual rate of 5.2 per cent through 2010—as it did between 1980 and 1988.

(2) OECD trade with the Soviet Union and China will grow at an average annual rate of 11.8 per cent between 1988 and 2000 (the rate of growth of OECD trade with China between 1980 and 1988); from 2000 to 2010, it will grow at an average annual rate of 8 per cent. The rationale behind these assumptions is the following: The opening up of the Soviet economy is at about the point that China had reached by 1980—two years after its reform process had started. Domestic as well as external demand for the USSR's integration into the world trade system is now at about the same level as in China's case at the beginning of the 1980s. Soviet import demand is high, and export potential includes a well-educated labor force and rich natural resources. Extremely high growth rates will, however, be blocked by poor infrastructure. After the year 2000, trade growth will still be above the OECD countries' average, but lower than in preceding years, due to demand saturation in some sectors. China's trade with the OECD countries has a good chance of regaining its growth rates of 1980-88 if the political damage of the June 1989 events can be overcome. The integration of Hong Kong into China in 1997 can contribute to opening up the economy further. Like the USSR's OECD trade, China's OECD trade probably will be lower during the first decade of the next century (due to demand saturation in some sectors) but still above the growth rate of the OECD's world imports.

(3) OECD trade with India will continue to grow at an average annual rate of 8.5 per cent through 2010—as it did between 1980 and 1988. India's reform process is more gradual than the Soviet Union's and China's, and there is no significant reason why the growth rate of its OECD trade should change compared to the period 1980-88, when the rate was 8.5 per cent.

Source: Overseas Development Council projections. Data for 1980 and 1988 from *Statistics of Foreign Trade, Series A* (Paris: OECD; December 1982 and September 1989), respectively.

Table 24. U.S. Trade with Giants, Compared to U.S.-World Trade: Projections to Year 2010
($ billions and percentages)

U.S. Trade[a] with:	1980	1988	2000	2010
World	473.50 (100%)	780.30 (100%)	1,643.0 (100%)	3,055.0 (100%)
Giants	9.82 (2.1%)	23.40 (3.0%)	89.7 (5.5%)	242.0 (7.9%)
Soviet Union	2.00 (0.4%)	3.42 (0.4%)	30.5 (1.9%)	94.7 (3.1%)
China	4.92 (1.0%)	14.31 (1.8%)	44.9 (2.7%)	116.5 (3.8%)
India	2.90 (0.6%)	5.67 (0.7%)	14.3 (0.9%)	30.8 (1.0%)

[a]Exports and imports.

Note: The assumptions underlying projections are:

(1) U.S.-World trade will continue to grow at an annual average rate of 6.4 per cent through 2010—as it did between 1980 and 1988.

(2) U.S.-Soviet trade will grow at an annual rate of 20 per cent between 1988 and 2000, and 12 per cent between 2000 and 2010. While high, these growth rates begin from a very low base, artificially depressed by official trade restrictions that are expected to be lifted. After the year 2000, trade growth will still be above the projected U.S. world average, but it will be lower than in previous years due to demand saturation in some areas.

(3) U.S.-Chinese trade will grow at an annual average rate of 10 per cent until 2010. This rate is somewhat lower than the 14 per cent annual average achieved between 1980 and 1988 due to a projected moderation in Chinese economic growth and resistance to sustained high import penetration in some sectors.

(4) U.S.-Indian trade will maintain an annual growth rate of 8 per cent (as between 1980 and 1988) until 2010. The Indian reform process is more gradual than that of the Soviet Union or China, and there is no significant reason to anticipate a sharp increase in U.S.-Indian trade growth beyond the 1980-88 rates.

Source: Overseas Development Council projections. Data for 1980 and 1988 from U.S. Bureau of the Census, *Highlights of U.S. Export and Import Trade (FT 990)* (Washington, D.C.: U.S. Bureau of the Census), December 1980 and December 1988, respectively.

About the Overseas Development Council

The Overseas Development Council is a private, non-profit organization established in 1969 for the purpose of increasing American understanding of the economic and social problems confronting the developing countries and of how their development progress is related to U.S. interests. Toward this end, the Council functions as a center for policy research and analysis, a forum for the exchange of ideas, and a resource for public education. The Council's current program of work encompasses four major issue areas: trade and industrial policy, international finance and investment, development strategies and development cooperation, and U.S. foreign policy and the developing countries. ODC's work is used by policy makers in the Executive Branch and the Congress, journalists, and those concerned about U.S.-Third World relations in corporate and bank management, international and non-governmental organizations, universities, and educational and action groups focusing on specific development issues. ODC's program is funded by foundations, corporations, and private individuals; its policies are determined by a governing Board and Council. In selecting issues and shaping its work program, ODC is also assisted by a standing Program Advisory Committee.

Victor H. Palmieri is Chairman of the ODC, and Wayne Fredericks is Vice Chairman. The Council's President is John W. Sewell.

Overseas Development Council
1717 Massachusetts Ave., N.W.
Washington, D.C. 20036
Tel. (202) 234-8701

238

Overseas Development Council
Board of Directors*

Overseas Development Council
Program Advisory Committee

The Series Editors

Economic Reform in Three Giants: U.S. Foreign Policy and the USSR, China, and India is the fourteenth volume in the Overseas Development Council's policy book series, U.S.-Third World Policy Perspectives. The co-editors of the series—often collaborating with guest editors contributing to the series—are Richard E. Feinberg and Valeriana Kallab.

Richard E. Feinberg, Executive Vice President and Director of Studies of the Overseas Development Council, is co-editor of the Policy Perspectives series and a co-author of this volume. Before joining ODC in 1983, he served as the Latin American specialist on the Policy Planning Staff of the Department of State from 1977 to 1979, prior to which he worked as an international economist in the Treasury Department and with the House Banking Committee. He also has been an adjunct professor of international finance at the Georgetown University School of Foreign Service. Dr. Feinberg has held fellowships from the Brookings Institution, the Council on Foreign Relations, and the Woodrow Wilson International Center for Scholars of the Smithsonian Institution. He has published numerous articles and books on U.S. foreign policy, Latin American politics, and international economics in this series as well as *The Intemperate Zone: The Third World Challenge to U.S. Foreign Policy;* (as editor) *Central America: International Dimensions of the Crisis;* and *Subsidizing Success: The Export-Import Bank in the U.S. Economy.*

Valeriana Kallab is Vice President and Director of Publications of the Overseas Development Council and co-editor of the ODC's U.S.-Third World Policy Perspectives book series. She has been responsible for ODC's published output since 1972. Before joining ODC, she was a research editor and a writer on international economic issues at the Carnegie Endowment for International Peace in New York. She was co-editor (with John P. Lewis) of *Development Strategies Reconsidered* and *U.S. Foreign Policy and the Third World: Agenda 1983;* and (with Guy Erb) of *Beyond Dependency: The Third World Speaks Out.*

Guest Editors and Authors

John Echeverri-Gent—a guest editor and contributing author of this volume and a 1988–89 MacArthur Scholar in Residence at the Overseas Development Council—is an Assistant Professor in the Woodrow Wilson Department of Government and Foreign Affairs at the University of Virginia. He will also serve as Associate Director of the Center for South Asian Studies at the University of Virginia beginning in the fall of 1990. Dr. Echeverri-Gent is the author of various publications in the fields of comparative public policy and the political economy of development in India. His articles have appeared in *Asian Survey, American Journal of Sociology, The Journal of Asian Studies, Ethics,* and *Contemporary Sociology.* He is currently completing a book comparing poverty alleviation programs in India and the United States. His research interests also include science and technology policy in the developing world.

Friedemann Müller—a guest editor of this volume and a 1988–89 MacArthur Scholar in Residence at the Overseas Development Council—is head of research coordination at the Stiftung Wissenschaft und Politik (SWP) in Ebenhausen (near Munich), West Germany. SWP is the largest research institute on international affairs in Western Europe. With the exception of his year at ODC and another as Ford Foundation Fellow with the RAND Corporation in Santa Monica, California (1980–81), Dr. Müller has served at SWP continuously since 1973. His research has focused on the Soviet economic system as well as Soviet trade and cooperation with the South and the West. He has published widely on the USSR's foreign trade system, the effects of sanctions against the Soviet Union, Soviet energy production and trade, the financing system in socialist countries, and the reform process within the Soviet Union. Before joining SWP, Dr. Müller did research at Moscow State University (1970–71) as a Fellow of the Deutsche Forschungsgemeinschaft.

Rensselaer W. Lee III is President of Global Advisory Services, Inc., in Alexandria, Virginia—a consulting firm that specializes in investment risk analysis and international development issues. He is concurrently an Associate Scholar at the Foreign Policy Research Institute in Philadelphia and Professorial Lecturer at the Ellicot School of International Affairs, George Washington University. He has consulted widely for the U.S. Government and for private industry. Dr. Lee has written several articles on narcotics trafficking in Latin America and is the author of *The White Labyrinth: Cocaine and Political Power*. Recently he has provided testimony on narcotics matters to the U.S. House of Representatives (The Committee on Foreign Affairs, Subcommittee on the Western Hemisphere, The Select Committee on Narcotics Abuse and Control, and The Committee on Government Operations) and to the U.S. Senate (The Committee on the Judiciary, Caucus on International Narcotics Control). He has also appeared on the CBS Evening News, Cable News Network, ABC's "Good Morning America," and ABC's "Nightline." Dr. Lee formerly taught political science and Asian politics at the City College of New York.

Richard P. Suttmeier is Henry P. Bristol Professor of International Affairs at Hamilton College. He is the author of *Research and Revolution: Science Policy and Societal Change in China* and *Science, Technology, and China's Drive for Modernization;* a co-author of *Technology Transfer to China* (a 1987 report of the Congressional Office of Technology Assessment); and the author of numerous articles on science and technology issues in China and Japan. He is currently engaged in a study of science and technology resources in East and Southeast Asia. Dr. Suttmeier previously served as a Senior Analyst for the Office of Technology Assessment, and, in 1987, he directed the Beijing Office of National Academy of Sciences/Committee on Scholarly Communication with the People's Republic of China. He has held fellowships at the East-West Center, The Institute of Policy Science at Saitama University in Japan, and the Hoover Institution.

Elena B. Arefieva is a Leading Research Fellow at the Institute of World Economy and International Relations (IMEMO) of the USSR Academy of Sciences in Moscow. In addition to contributing to this ODC volume, she is one of a team of Soviet authors participating in an ODC-IMEMO book project comparing U.S. and Soviet experience in development assistance; the exchange project is sponsored by the International Research Exchange (IREX), and the joint book will be issued in both the United States and the USSR in 1990. Before joining IMEMO in 1986, Elena Arefieva was a head of the Section of External Economic Relations of the Asian Countries at the Institute of Oriental Studies of the USSR Academy of Sciences. She is the author of two books and numerous other publications and journal and newspaper articles focusing on Third World states' relations with the developed countries and on Soviet economic policy toward the Third World.

PULLING TOGETHER: THE INTERNATIONAL MONETARY FUND IN A MULTIPOLAR WORLD
Catherine Gwin, Richard E. Feinberg, and contributors

Side-stepped by the developed countries, entangled in unsuccessful programs in many Latin American and African nations, whipsawed by heavy but inconsistent pressure from commercial banks and creditor countries, and without effective leadership from its major shareholders, the IMF is losing its bearings. It needs a sharp course correction and a strong mandate from its member countries to adjust its policies on each of five criticial issues: global macroeconomic management, Third World debt, the resuscitation of development in the poorest countries, the integration of socialist nations into the global economy, and relations with its sister institution, the World Bank. In addition, the IMF needs to bolster its own bureaucratic, intellectual, and financial capacities.

In an economically interdependent but politically centrifugal world, a strong central institution is needed to help countries arrive at collective responses to complex global economic problems. But only if its member states are willing to delegate more authority to the IMF can it help pull together a multipolar world.

Contents:

Catherine Gwin, guest co-editor of this volume, is currently the Special Program Advisor at the Rockefeller Foundation. In recent years, she has worked as a consultant on international economic and political affairs for The Ford Foundation, The Rockefeller Foundation, The Asia Society, and the United Nations. In the late 1970s and the early 1980s, she was a Senior Fellow at the Council on Foreign Relations and at the Carnegie Endowment for International Peace, where she directed the Study Group on international financial cooperation and developing-country debt. During the Carter administration, she served on the staff of the International Development Cooperation Agency (IDCA). Dr. Gwin has taught at the School of International Affairs at Columbia University and has written frequently on international development cooperation, the World Bank, and the International Monetary Fund.

Richard E. Feinberg is Executive Vice President and Director of Studies of the Overseas Development Council. Before joining ODC in 1983, he served as the Latin American specialist on the Policy Planning Staff of the Department of State from 1977 to 1979, prior to which he worked as an international economist in the Treasury Department and with the House Banking Committee. He has published numerous articles and books on U.S. foreign policy, Latin American politics, and international economics, including *The Intemperate Zone: The Third World Challenge to U.S. Foreign Policy;* and (as editor) *Central America: International Dimensions of the Crisis* and *Subsidizing Success: The Export-Import Bank in the U.S. Economy.*

U.S.-Third World Policy Perspectives, No. 13
1989, 188 pp.

ISBN: 0-88738-313-0 (cloth) $24.95
ISBN: 0-88738-819-1 (paper) $15.95

BETWEEN TWO WORLDS:
THE WORLD BANK'S NEXT DECADE
Richard E. Feinberg and contributors

"essential reading for anybody interested in the Bank"
—*The Economist*

"well-researched analysis of some of the problems confronting the World Bank in the 1980s"
—*The Journal of Development Studies*

In the midst of the global debt and adjustment crises, the World Bank has been challenged to become the leading agency in North-South fiwhich must be comprehensively addressed by the Bank's new presinance and development. The many dimensions of this challenge are the subject of this important volume.

As mediator between international capital markets and developing countries, the World Bank will be searching for ways to renew the flow of private credit and investment to Latin America and Africa. And as the world's premier development agency, the Bank can help formulate growth strategies appropriate to the 1990s.

The Bank's ability to design and implement a comprehensive response to these global needs is threatened by competing objectives and uncertain priorities. Can the Bank design programs attractive to private investors that also serve the very poor? Can it emphasize efficiency while transferring technologies that maximize labor absorption? Can it more aggressively condition loans on policy reforms without attracting the criticism that has accompanied IMF programs?

The contributors to this volume assess the role that the World Bank can play in the period ahead. They argue for new financial and policy initiatives and for new conceptual approaches to development, as well as for a restructuring of the Bank, as it takes on new, systemic responsibilities in the next decade.

Contents:
Richard E. Feinberg—Overview: An Open Letter to the World Bank's Next President
Gerald K. Helleiner—Policy-Based Program Leading: A Look at the Bank's New Role
Joan M. Nelson—The Diplomacy of Policy-Based Lending
Sheldon Annis—The Shifting Grounds of Poverty Lending at The World Bank
Howard Pack—The Technological Impact of World Bank Operations
John F. H. Purcell and Michelle B. Miller—The World Bank and Private Capital
Charles R. Blitzer—Financing the World Bank

Richard E. Feinberg is vice president of the Overseas Development Council and co-editor of the U.S.-Third World Policy Perspectives series. From 1977 to 1979, Feinberg was Latin American specialist on the policy planning staff of the U.S. Department of State. He has also served as an international economist in the U.S. Treasury Department and with the House Banking Committee. He is currently also adjunct professor of international finance at the Georgetown University School of Foreign Service. Feinberg is the author of numerous books as well as journal and newspaper articles on U.S. foreign policy, Latin American politics, and international economics.

U.S.-Third World Policy Perspectives, No. 7
June 1986, 208 pp.
ISBN: 0-88738-123-5 (cloth) $19.95
ISBN: 0-88738-665-2 (paper) $12.95

FRAGILE COALITIONS:
THE POLITICS OF ECONOMIC ADJUSTMENT

Joan M. Nelson and contributors

The global economic crisis of the 1980s forced most developing nations into a simultaneous quest for short-run economic stabilization and longer-run structural reforms. Effective adjustment is at least as much a political as an economic challenge. But political dimensions of adjustment have been much less carefully analyzed than have the economic issues.

Governments in developing countries must balance pressures from external agencies seeking more rapid adjustment in return for financial support, and the demands of domestic political groups often opposing such reforms. How do internal pressures shape external bargaining? and conversely, how does external influence shape domestic political maneuvering? Growing emphasis on "adjustment with a human face" poses additional questions: Do increased equity and political acceptability go hand in hand? or do more pro-poor measures add to the political difficulties of adjustment? The capacity of the state itself to implement adjustment measures varies widely among nations. How can external agencies take such differences more fully into account? The hopeful trend toward democratic openings in many countries raises further, crucial issues: What special political risks and opportunities confront governments struggling simultaneously with adjustment and democratization?

The contributors to this volume explore these issues and their policy implications for the United States and for the international organizations that seek to promote adjustment efforts.

Contents:

Joan M. Nelson has been a visiting fellow at the Overseas Development Council since 1982; since mid-1986, she has directed a collegial research program on the politics of economic adjustment. She has been a consultant for the World Bank, the Agency for International Development, and for the International Monetary Fund, as well as a staff member of USAID. In the 1970s and early 1980s, she taught at the Massachusetts Institute of Technology, the Johns Hopkins University School of Advanced International Studies, and Princeton University's Woodrow Wilson School. She has published books and articles on development assistance and policy dialogue, political participation, migration and urban politics in developing nations, and the politics of economic stabilization and reform.

U.S.-Third World Policy Perspectives, No. 12   ISBN: 0-88738-283-5 (cloth) $24.95
1989, 186 pp.   ISBN: 0-88738-787-X (paper) $15.95

ENVIRONMENT AND THE POOR: DEVELOPMENT STRATEGIES FOR A COMMON AGENDA

H. Jeffrey Leonard and contributors

Few aspects of development are as complex and urgent as the need to reconcile anti-poverty and pro-environmental goals. Do both of these important goals—poverty alleviation and environmental sustainability—come in the same package? Or are there necessary trade-offs and must painful choices be made?

A basic premise of this volume is that environmental degradation and intractable poverty are often especially pronounced in particular ecological and social settings across the developing world. These twin crises of development and the environment can and must be addressed jointly. But they require differentiated strategies for the kinds of physical environments in which poor people live. This study explores these concerns in relation to irrigated areas, arid zones, moist tropical forests, hillside areas, urban centers, and unique ecological settings.

The overview chapter highlights recent efforts to advance land and natural resource management, and some of the real and perceived conflicts between alleviating poverty and protecting the environment in the design and implementation of development policy. The chapters that follow offer economic investment and natural resource management options for reducing poverty and maintaining ecological balance for six different areas of the developing world.

Contents:

H. Jeffrey Leonard, guest editor of this volume, is the vice president of the World Wildlife Fund and The Conservation Foundation and Director of the Fairfield Osborn Center for Economic Development. Dr. Leonard has been at The Foundation since 1976. He is the author of several recent books, including *Pollution and the Struggle for the World Product, Natural Resources and Economic Development in Central America,* and *Are Environmental Regulations Driving U.S. Industries Overseas?* He is also editor of *Divesting Nature's Capital: The Political Economy of Environmental Abuse in the Third World* and *Business and Environment: Toward a Common Ground.*

U.S.-Third World Policy Perspectives, No. 11
1989, 256 pp.
ISBN: 0-88738-282-7 (cloth) $24.95
ISBN: 0-88738-786-1 (paper) $15.95

DEVELOPMENT STRATEGIES RECONSIDERED

John P. Lewis and Valeriana Kallab, editors

"First-rate, comprehensive analysis—presented in a manner that makes it extremely valuable to policy makers."
—Robert R. Nathan
Robert Nathan Associates

Important differences of opinion are emerging about the national strategies best suited for advancing economic growth and equity in the difficult global adjustment climate of the late 1980s.

Proponents of the "new orthodoxy"—the perspective headquartered at the World Bank and favored by the Reagan administration as well as by a number of other bilateral donor governments—are "carrying forward with redoubled vigor the liberalizing, pro-market strains of the thinking of the 1960s and 1970s. They are very mindful of the limits of government." And they are "emphatic in advocating export-oriented growth to virtually all comers."

Other prominent experts question whether a standardized prescription of export-led growth can meet the needs of big low-income countries in the latter 1980s as well as it did those of small and medium-size middle-income countries in the 1960s and 1970s. They are concerned about the special needs of low-income Africa. And they see a great deal of unfinished business under the heading of poverty and equity.

In this volume, policy syntheses are proposed to reconcile the goals of growth, equity, and adjustment; to strike fresh balances between agricultural and industrial promotion and between capital and other inputs; and to reflect the interplay of democracy and development.

Contents:

John P. Lewis—Overview —Development Promotion: A Time for Regrouping
Irma Adelman—A Poverty-Focused Approach to Development Policy
John W. Mellor—Agriculture on the Road to Industrialization
Jagdish N. Bhagwati—Rethinking Trade Strategy
Leopoldo Solis and Aurelio Montemayor—A Mexican View of the Choice Between Inward and Outward Orientation
Colin I. Bradford, Jr.—East Asian "Models": Myths and Lessons
Alex Duncan—Aid Effectiveness in Raising Adaptive Capacity in the Low-Income Countries
Atul Kohli—Democracy and Development

John P. Lewis is Professor of Economics and International Affairs at Princeton University's Woodrow Wilson School of Public and International Affairs. He is simultaneously senior advisor to the Overseas Development Council and chairman of its Program Advisory Committee. From 1979 to 1981, Dr. Lewis was chairman of the OECD's Development Assistance Committee (DAC). From 1982 to 1985, he was chairman of the three-year World Bank/IMF Task Force on Concessional Flows. He has served as a member of the U.N. Committee for Development Planning. For many years, he has alternated between academia and government posts (as Member of the Council of Economic Advisors, 1963-64, and Director of the USAID Mission to India, 1964-69), with collateral periods of association with The Brookings Institution, The Ford Foundation, and the World Bank.

Valeriana Kallab is vice president and director of publications of the Overseas Development Council and series co-editor of the ODC's U.S.-Third World Policy Perspectives series. She has been responsible for ODC's published output since 1972. Before joining ODC, she was a research editor and writer on international economic issues at the Carnegie Endowment for International Peace in New York.

U.S.-Third World Policy Perspectives, No. 5
1986, 208 pp.

ISBN: 0-88738-044-1 (cloth) $19.95
ISBN: 0-87855-991-4 (paper) $12.95

GROWTH, EXPORTS, AND JOBS IN A CHANGING WORLD ECONOMY: AGENDA 1988

John W. Sewell, Stuart K. Tucker, and contributors

"particularly timely, as the Administration and Congress face critical decisions on the trade bill, the budget, and other issues affecting the economic future of the U.S. and countries around the globe"
—Frank C. Carlucci, Secretary of Defense

Agenda 1988, the eleventh of ODC's well-known assessments of U.S. policy toward the developing countries, contributes uniquely to the ongoing debate on U.S. jobs and trade competition with other nations.

The administration that takes office in 1989 faces a situation without precedent in the post-1945 period. Like many developing countries, the United States has to balance its trade accounts, service its foreign debts, and rebuild its industrial base. The challenge is twofold.

The immediate task is to restore the international economic position of the United States by taking the lead in devising measures to support renewed *global* growth, especially rapid growth in the developing countries.

Meanwhile, however, the world is on the threshold of a Third Industrial Revolution. Rapid technological advances are radically changing the familiar economic relationships between developed and developing countries. The kinds of policies needed to adjust to these technology-driven changes—policies on education, training, research and development—generally have longer lead times than the immediate measures needed to stimulate global growth. In the next four years, the United States must therefore proceed on *both* fronts at the same time.

John W. Sewell—Overview: The Dual Challenge: Managing the Economic Crisis and Technological Change
Manuel Castells and Laura D'Andrea Tyson—High-Technology Choices Ahead: Restructuring Interdependence
Jonathan D. Aronson—The Service Industries: Growth, Trade, and Development Prospects
Robert L. Paarlberg—U.S. Agriculture and the Developing World: Opportunities for Joint Gains
Raymond F. Mikesell—The Changing Demand for Industrial Raw Materials
Ray Marshall—Jobs: The Shifting Structure of Global Employment
Stuart K. Tucker—Statistical Annexes: U.S.-Third World Interdependence, 1988

John W. Sewell has been president of the Overseas Development Council since January, 1980. From 1977 to 1979, as the Council's executive vice president, he directed ODC's programs of research and public education. Prior to joining the Council in 1971, Mr. Sewell directed the communications program of the Brookings Institution. He also served in the Foreign Service of the United States. A contributor to past *Agenda* assessments, he is co-author of *Rich Country Interests and Third World Development* and *The Ties That Bind: U.S. Interests in Third World Development.* He is a frequent author and lecturer on U.S. relations with the developing countries.

Stuart K. Tucker is a fellow at the Overseas Development Council. Prior to joining ODC in 1984, he was a research consultant for the Inter-American Development Bank. He has written on U.S. international trade policy, including the linkage between the debt crisis and U.S. exports and jobs. He also prepared the Statistical Annexes in ODC's *Agenda 1985-86.*

U.S.-Third World Policy Perspectives, No. 9
1988, 286 pp.

ISBN: 088738-196-0 (cloth) $19.95
ISBN: 0-88738-718-7 (paper) $12.95